Issues and Controversies in Policing Today

Issues and Controversies in Policing Today

Johnny Nhan

ROWMAN & LITTLEFIELD
Lanham • Boulder • New York • London

Published by Rowman & Littlefield
An imprint of The Rowman & Littlefield Publishing Group, Inc.
4501 Forbes Boulevard, Suite 200, Lanham, Maryland 20706
www.rowman.com

6 Tinworth Street, London SE11 5AL

British Library Cataloguing in Publication Information Available

Library of Congress Cataloging-in-Publication Data

Names: Nhan, Johnny, 1977- author.
Title: Issues and controversies in policing today / Johnny Nhan.
Description: Lanham, Maryland : Rowman & Littlefield, [2019] | Includes bibliographical references
    and index.
Identifiers: LCCN 2018054397 (print) | LCCN 2018057092 (ebook) | ISBN 9781538117552 (Elec-
    tronic) | ISBN 9781538117545 (pbk. : alk. paper)
Subjects: LCSH: Police--United States. | Police administration--United States.
Classification: LCC HV8139 (ebook) | LCC HV8139 .N43 2019 (print) | DDC 363.2/30973--dc23
LC record available at https://lccn.loc.gov/2018054397

♾ ™ The paper used in this publication meets the minimum requirements of American
National Standard for Information Sciences Permanence of Paper for Printed Library
Materials, ANSI/NISO Z39.48-1992.

Printed in the United States of America

Table of Contents

Chapter One

Introduction

This chapter introduces the most visible and often controversial part of the criminal justice system: the police. Specifically, the role of American policing will be explored, focusing on the unique societal functions of the police and powers granted to them by law.

Topics explored in this chapter:

Social contract, social control and the police
The power of the police
Police and the criminal justice system

SOCIAL CONTRACT

Social contract, as written by French Enlightenment philosopher Jean-Jacques Rousseau,[1] is the tacit agreement of relational arrangement between individuals and society. In order to live in civilized society, individuals must forego some personal liberties, such as the ability to wage vigilante justice. In return, individuals are granted the benefits of civilized life, which includes safety. In other words, you give up a number of "freedoms *to* _____" in exchange for "freedom *from* _____." The state (a term used to describe government in general), takes over justice duties, such as apprehending and punishing law-breakers. Therefore, one of the freedoms under social contract is the freedom from crime and violence. Notice that in criminal cases, the state is the primary plaintiff. For example, a murder case may be labeled *State of Texas vs. Smith*, versus civil cases where individuals file suits against other individuals, such as *Wilson vs. Smith*.

The concept of social contract came about during the ***Age of Enlightenment***, or the *Age of Reason*, a period of radical change in Europe during the

1

seventeenth and eighteenth centuries. This period of time was considered a social and cultural renaissance that stressed modern concepts such as free thought, free will, and individualism. This belief in individual agency was in stark contrast to the days of the Middle Ages, a period of time that was dictated by religious dogma that oppressed creativity and intellect and that preceded the Age of Enlightenment. Instead, the Enlightenment period stressed creative arts, science, and other expressions of free will and thought. Moreover, the Age of Enlightenment was also considered the birth of west-ernized thinking that manifests in today's laws, with concepts such as *no cruel and unusual punishment, freedom of speech,* and *due process of law.*

Enlightenment-period French philosopher Jean-Jacques Rousseau, in 1762, wrote about social contract, stating that civilized man must enter social contracts with others, where all free men forfeit some personal liberties equally while taking on social responsibilities. According to Rousseau, laws cannot be divine or dictatorial in nature as previously applied, but based on reason and the collective will and applied to all equally as part of the rules of living in society. Therefore, slavery laws were not considered legitimate and states that exercised this power could not flourish. Rousseau's writings were in large part the basis of modern democracies.

Key elements to establishing the legitimacy of free democracies during the Enlightenment period were radical propositions by political philosopher John Locke. Locke proposed that a central purpose of government is to protect individual rights and freedoms while limiting itself, instead of grant-ing unlimited tyrannical power to a ruler. Specifically, Locke asserted that individuals possessed a "natural" right to *life, liberty,* and *possessions,* and it is the primary function of government to preserve these rights as part of the social contract.

Today, these principles are the basis of much of the Bill of Rights of the US Constitution. Locke's principles serve as the basis of due process as expressed in the Fifth Amendment, which states that the government cannot deprive a person of "life, liberty, or property, without due process of law." The inverse of this portion of the amendment is very powerful—it grants the government, as represented by police, the full power to *take away* life, liber-ty, and property.

THE POLICE AND SOCIAL CONTRACT/SOCIAL CONTROL

Social control is defined as efforts to ensure conformity to norms in society.[2] Norms are rules and expectations of behavior in any given society. Norms can range from not-so-serious unwritten rules of communication, such as not interrupting someone who is speaking, to more serious, major expectations of behavior, such as not killing someone. Norms that society feels are important are usually codified into law. Controlling these behaviors can mean the ability of a person to control oneself, to applying official sanctions toward rules violations. There are several types of social control, including:

Internal control: The ability of a person to control themselves through a process of internalizing society's norms, such as expressed in Michael Gottfredson and Travis Hirschi's self-control theory.[3]

External control: The ability of a third party or society to get a person or group of people who have violated social norms, rules, or laws, to reconform to these expectations of behavior.

Informal control: Efforts to get a person or group of people who have violated social norms, rules, or laws, to reconform to these expectations of behavior by nonstate actors. In other words, by people who are not officially sanctioned by the government to serve as agents of social control. These people include parents, relatives, friends, social groups, etc. Oftentimes these individuals apply non-official incentives and sanctions to get the person to recomply, ranging from praising a person to shunning or labeling them.

Formal control: Efforts to get a person or group of people who have violated social norms, rules, or laws, to reconform to these expectations of behavior by state actors. These include actors of the criminal justice system, such as police officers, court officials, and corrections administrators and officers. These individuals are given legitimate official state power through social contract to enforce law violations. Agents of formal social control can levy official sanctions, ranging from fines to arrest and incarceration in order to correct or stop certain behaviors.

Police officers are formal control agents. In fact, they are the most well-known and visible agents of formal social control. As society has become more populated and complex, informal social controls have become inadequate. For example, think of a small town and how its members deal with deviance and crime. If a neighborhood kid vandalizes a car, a neighbor spotting him will likely know him and will call his parents who will probably settle things without calling the police—perhaps make him apologize for his actions, pay for the damages, etc. However, if a car is being vandalized in an apartment complex with hundreds of units in an urban area, a witness will probably not know the owner of the car or the perpetrator, and he will call the police if he's a Good Samaritan.

The reliance on police has grown in the past few decades. The breakdown of informal social controls, coupled with the police professional movement (to be discussed later) has resulted in the police becoming **panaceas**, or "cure-alls," for societal problems. This means that police handle a lot of non–law enforcement/crime control duties. A naked person running down the street? Call the police. Neighbors playing loud music? Call the police. Cat stuck up the tree? You get the story.

POLICE POWERS GRANTED BY LAW

The decline of informal social controls has meant that society relies more heavily on formal social controls, especially police. As stated earlier, police hold a very special and unique position in society. They are officially sanctioned by the state to apprehend and arrest suspected violators of the law and have the ability to use deadly force to do so. State and local law enforcement agencies are granted powers by the Tenth Amendment[4] of the Constitution, which states:

> *The powers not delegated to the United States by the Constitution, nor prohibited by it to the states, are reserved to the states respectively, or to the people.*

This implies under state sovereignty that states reserve the right to legitimately grant police power to use physical force to uphold legal sanctions and laws. This position was further reinforced in 1996 with the passage of the *Tenth Amendment Enforcement Act*, which states:

> *To protect the rights of the states and the people from abuse by the federal government; to strengthen the partnership and the intergovernmental relationship between state and federal governments; to restrain federal agencies from exceeding their authority; to enforce the Tenth Amendment to the Constitution; and for other purposes.*

Note that the United States is a **federalist** country, meaning that the Constitution grants power to both the federal government and state governments. Due to this dual system, both federal and state law enforcement agencies sometimes have overlapping jurisdictions and functions. Regardless of jurisdiction, law enforcement agencies share the responsibility of upholding and enforcement of the law granted to them by the Constitution, which includes an element of maintaining order or peace. Police officers are often referred to as public "peace officers."

The assortment of agencies that enforce the law in the United States is no accident. According to the Bureau of Justice Statistics' Census of State and Local Law Enforcement Agencies, there are nearly 18,000 law enforcement agencies.[5] The system was purposely designed to be decentralized as post-revolutionary American colonists resisted adopting an organized, armed, and uniformed police force akin to an occupying British standing army. Moreover, this decentralized arrangement of law enforcement agencies reflected the Constitutionally defined decentralized government structure of checks and balances and separation of powers among three branches. Consequently, policing agencies can be described as a hodgepodge of overlapping jurisdictions and functions.

Despite its decentralized arrangement, law enforcement agencies serve the same primary purpose regardless of specialty of jurisdiction: To serve as the primary gatekeepers into the criminal justice system by preparing individuals suspected of crimes for court or legally deciding body. More specifically, police must "clear" a case to consider it "solved." Clearance rates are considered by nearly all police departments as the primary performance measurement for police departments. The FBI's Uniform Crime Report (UCR), which gathers quantitative data reported by nearly all law enforcement agencies of all jurisdictions in the United States on *index crimes*, publishes these data, including agency clearance rates. Since its inception in the 1930s by the FBI, International Association of Police Chiefs (IACP), and National Sheriffs' Association, UCR clearance rate data have been used and analyzed by researchers and policing agencies to guide policy and allocate resources.

To clear a case for prosecution, law enforcement agencies must complete several essential functions. First, officers must identify the suspected offender. This identification process can range from the initial encounter at the moment of the offense, such as the officer observing a traffic violation to detectives identifying a suspect using various investigative techniques. Second, police must collect and preserve evidence to justify an arrest and submit that information to a prosecuting body for preparation for a court hearing. This evidence can range from physical proof, such as fingerprints, to witness statements and confessions. Finally, to clear a case, if the crime warrants custody the officer must take the suspect into custody and confine him or her before a court appearance. This confinement is often a city or county jail, with some police departments having their own jail. If, however, officers encounter special circumstances that prohibit the agency from the previous steps, out of the control of the agency, a case can be *exceptionally cleared*. Exceptional circumstances can range from the suspect dying to inability to extradite an individual to the prosecutorial jurisdiction.

In examining the clearance process, it becomes clear that the police, while having a degree of discretion, do not directly determine legal outcomes. Instead, the police's role at the front end of the criminal justice system is to prepare cases for the legal system.

THE POLICE AND THE CRIMINAL JUSTICE SYSTEM

The police exist at the front-end of the criminal justice system. To most individuals, they are the first contact with the system and entryway into the system. As discussed earlier, police are being called more and more for social issues not associated with law enforcement, known as order maintenance and peace keeping duties. These duties, for example, can range from responding to arguments between private parties to directing traffic. Despite these expanded duties, the primary function of the police remains simply to apprehend persons suspected of crimes under standards and means prescribed by the law and prepare a case for prosecution.

Police have a lot of power by virtue at being at the front-end of the criminal justice system. But society cannot afford to have "**full enforcement**" of all crimes, as reflected by the criminal justice funnel, because we simply do not have the capacity to lock everyone up for committing crimes. Police, therefore, are granted high levels of discretionary power. For instance, an officer can choose to give a warning rather than issue a citation or make an arrest.[6] Influences on an officer's discretion can range from personal reasons, such as nearing the end of a shift to structural and systemic factors, such as the prosecutors' willingness to bring charges.[7,8]

Not surprisingly, the relationship between prosecutors and police is sometimes contentious and is itself a controversial issue. Researchers have conducted numerous socio-legal studies as far back as the 1970s; looking at the complex police/prosecutor relationships found various structural and cultural frictions between the organizations. One 1975 study that polled both prosecutors and police found problems in dealing with various crime types stemming from frequency of communications, disagreements on whether prosecutors should exert control over law enforcement practices, and variations on the frequency of police being considered during plea negotiations and other legal processes.[9] More recently, researchers have examined the police/prosecutor relationship in the context of homicides and sexual assault cases, identifying factors in cases that significantly impact the relationship.[10]

SOCIETY WITHOUT POLICE

It would not be difficult to imagine a modern society without the presence of police. Some would picture rampant chaos—where lawbreakers would have no disincentive to break the law. Police themselves perceive their primary role in society within this orientation with a popular aphorism that police represent a ***thin blue line*** that serves as the moral force standing between good and evil, order and chaos. Some popular novels and movies often depict this scenario, such as in the novel *Lord of the Flies*, in which a group of English boys were left stranded on an island without any type of authority figure.

The symbolism of the thin blue line has in recent years become a literal and highly visible symbol in society among police and police supporters who display and wear images of a single blue stripe across a black and white American flag to represent supporting police and fallen officers. Like many things policing related, this symbol and the display of this symbol has also come to signify a controversial issue that is explored later in this book. The popular symbol emerged to represent the *Blue Lives Matter* countermovement, in defense of officers and in condemnation of the killing of officers, as a response to the *Black Lives Matter* movement formed in reaction to several high-profile police shootings that sparked race-based civil unrest.

The need for some type of law and order is necessary for modern society to function properly. Order and stability are keys to a functioning capitalist marketplace. One can imagine vigilante groups emerging to fulfill the need for order. This scenario underscores the need for public law enforcement in a criminal justice system. In the United States, the police are one of the most vital components of the criminal justice system.

A BRIEF SNAPSHOT OF THE CRIMINAL JUSTICE SYSTEM

The criminal justice system in the United States is often metaphorically described as a "leaky funnel." It gets its nickname as the "**criminal justice funnel**" from the surprisingly few numbers of people who are incarcerated relative to the amount of crime committed, forming one end of a funnel shape that's large on one end and small on the other.[11] First, it is estimated that half of individuals who commit crime never even enter into the system. Criminal activities can be, simply, not realized, or, victims do not report the crime.

The Bureau of Justice Statistics' (BJS) National Crime Victimization Survey (NCVS) estimates that less than half of violent crimes are reported to police.[12] Reasons for not reporting violent crime to police include dealing with the matter in a personal way, victims feeling the crime was not important enough, the perception that police would not or could not help, and the fear of reprisal.[13,14]

Second, there is a large amount of discretion at any given point in the system that causes individuals being processed to "leak" out of the system. As indicated from figure 1.1, there is a significant drop-off from crimes reported, to an actual arrest. By design, the system is designed to accommodate discretion throughout the criminal justice process. We simply do not have the capacity for *full enforcement*, or mandating arrest and prosecution for every crime committed without any discretion.

At the front end of the criminal justice system, police have a relatively wide range of discretion in invoking the criminal process. This area has been studied extensively since the 1960s, in the wake of public scrutiny for biased arrests. Legal scholars and criminologists looked at extra-legal factors that affect arrest decisions, such as opting to seek arrest warrants; a decision not

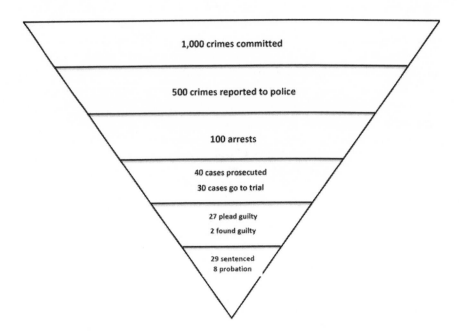

1,000 crimes committed

500 crimes reported to police

100 arrests

40 cases prosecuted

30 cases go to trial

27 plead guilty

2 found guilty

29 sentenced

8 probation

Figure 1.1. *Source: Larry J. Siegel and John L. Worrall. Introduction to Criminal Justice, 16th ed.: Boston, MA: Cengage, 2018.*

to arrest despite evidence of crime and the suspect being present; and taking a suspect into immediate custody. These extra-legal factors can range from individual officer ideologies and attitudes of suspects, to avoidance of persons deemed to have mental health issues. Moreover, arrest decisions can be influenced by structural variables, such as prosecutorial agendas, organizational structure, and limits on manpower and resources.

This power of discretion, which is a necessary function of police, tests the limits of police power as defined by the law and in practice. These limits are constantly defined and shape the worldview of the officers as well as having a profound impact on public perceptions of police.[15] Criminologists have found that police discretion raises public concerns based on factors that include prior victimization, the neighborhood context, minority civil rights, race and age of the respondent, and the general worry about crime.[16]

Likewise, prosecutors often strike plea bargains or may choose not to file, and so on and so forth. The third reason for the expulsion of individuals who enter the system is simply the cost of criminal justice. We simply do not have enough resources to operate a full-capacity system. There are an estimated 2.3 million individuals incarcerated in the United States at any given moment. When you consider that constitutes approximately 5 percent of the population that committed a crime, it becomes clear that this system exists out of necessity.

Police discretion is just another of many issues of policing that can have the potential for a profound impact on society. Like controversial issues in policing, it appears superficially to be simply a single decision for an officer to make an arrest as a prescribed mandate serving as a criminal justice gatekeeper. The culmination of such decisions among all officers, however, can have profound implications, such as bias and even racism. They highlight the fragility and contentious nature of police-citizen and reveal the boundaries of police legitimacy.

OUTLINING THE REST OF THE BOOK

This book is structured in a way that explores critical or controversial issues in policing. Before jumping into these controversies, a foundation of American policing will be presented.

Chapter 2 discusses the history and evolution of the police. This history will contextualize the behavior of modern police officers, based largely on the development of a subculture, or set of informal normative values and behavioral expectations.

Chapter 3 explores the police subculture, which serves as the foundation for understanding much of police behavior, ranging from their interactions with the public to deviance. Under the umbrella of the police subculture are shared mentalities, such as:

Group cohesion or the "blue brotherhood"

An antagonistic relationship with the public known as an "us versus them" mentality

The idea that police are the only force of order keeping society from plunging into anarchy, known as the "thin blue line"

Unwritten codes of conduct, such as not reporting other officers' misconduct, known commonly as the "blue wall of silence."

Chapter 4 examines police recruitment and training to trace the development of the police subculture. The transformation of the recruit to a street-ready police officer gives valuable insight into future deviant and non-deviant behavior.

Chapter 5 explores the police officer experience, ranging from shift work (the abnormal hours police officers work) to patrol work, and the changes to an officer throughout a career. Real and perceived dangers of the job will contextualize how officers interact while on duty.

Chapter 6 discusses issues with police perceptions in popular media, including film and television. The realities of police work will be analyzed, including published information on the effectiveness of police on crime and media depictions of police. The myths and realities of policing will be explored.

Chapter 7 looks at police brutality and use of force, ranging from well-known incidents such as the Rodney King beating, which sparked the Los Angeles riots in the 1990s. Other incidents of police brutality and corruption will be explored, including organizational responses to such incidents. Issues of race and class will be discussed in detail.

Chapter 8 takes an in-depth look at racial profiling, exploring its validity, frequency, and underlying causes. Legal issues will also be explored.

Chapter 9 analyzes the actual effectiveness of police on crime with increases in police officers. There is little doubt that running a police department is very expensive and a large portion of municipal budgets, but does adding more police officers to the street help reduce crime? Are high-speed pursuits worth the risk to the public? These questions will be explored.

Chapter 10 discusses the life-course of the police officer's career. The evolution of the rookie officer to the seasoned veteran reveals the impact of a unique and stressful occupation. The dark realities of policing and its impact on the social, psychological, and physical lives of officers will be analyzed.

Chapter 11 explores the role of women in policing. The role of women in the male-dominated masculine profession of policing reveals that only certain types of women actually thrive as police officers, and why women still constitute only a small fraction of police officers. A brief history of the first policewoman, LAPD officer Alice Wells, shows the evolution of women as officers.

Chapter 12 discusses LGBTQ police officers and their experiences on the force. Issues pertaining to the hypermasculine police world and that impact on LGBTQ officers will be explored.

Chapter 13 analyzes controversies with community policing and other strategies that try to improve police-community relations. Contemporary policing strategies, such as "broken windows policing" will be discussed in depth, along with issues of implicit bias and training.

Chapter 14 explores problematic and emerging crime issues in twenty-first-century policing that police often have difficulty addressing, such as white-collar and computer crimes.

Chapter 15 discusses the fundamental changes in police that have occurred in the Information Age. Challenges and controversies to policing in today's world are discussed.

Chapter 16 looks at police legitimacy in the age of social media. Social media use will be explored as well as some of the hazards associated with engaging with the public.

NOTES

1. Jean-Jacques Rousseau, *Du Contrat Social: Ou Principes du Droit Politique* (Amsterdam: 1762).

2. Erich Goode, *Deviant Behavior,* 6th ed. (Upper Saddle River: Prentice Hall, 2000).

3. Michael R. Gottfredson and Travis Hirschi, *A General Theory of Crime* (Stanford: Stanford University Press, 1999).

4. "S. 1629—the Tenth Amendment Enforcement Act of 1996: Hearings before the Committee on Governmental Affairs, United States Senate, One Hundred Fourth Congress, Second Session," http://archive.org/stream/s1629thetenthame00unit/s1629thetenthame00unit_djvu.txt

5. Brian A. Reaves, "Census of State and Local Law Enforcement Agencies," US Department of Justice Bureau of Justice Statistics, 2008, https://www.bjs.gov/content/pub/pdf/csllea08.pdf.

6. Andy Myhill and Kelly Johnson, "Police Discretion: The Ideal versus the Real," *Public Administration Review* 23, no. 3 (1963): 140–148, doi: 10.1177/1748895815590202.

7. Richard F. Groeneveld, *Arrest Discretion of Police Officers: The Impact of Varying Organizational Structures* (El Paso: LFB Scholarly, 2005).

8. Claudia Mendias and E. James Kehoe, "Engagement of Policing Ideals and Their Relationship to the Exercise of Discretionary Powers," *Criminal Justice & Behavior* 33, no. 1 (2006): 70–92, doi: 10.1177/0093854805282509.

9. Donald M. McIntyre, "Impediments to Effective Police-Prosecutor Relationships," *The American Criminal Law Review* 13, no. 2 (1975): 201–234.

10. Marc Riedel and John G. Boulahanis, "Homicides Exceptionally Cleared and Cleared by Arrest: An Exploratory Study of Police/Prosecutor Outcomes." *Homicide Studies* 11 no. 2 (2007): 151–164.

11. Ronald G. Burns, *Policing: A Modular Approach.* (Upper Saddle River, NJ: Pearson, 2013).

12. Lynn Langston, Marcus Berzofsky, Christopher Krebs, and Hope Smiley-McDonald, "Victimizations Not Reported to the Police, 2006–2010," *US Department of Justice Bureau of Justice Statistics*, 2012, https://www.bjs.gov/content/pub/pdf/vnrp0610.pdf.

13. Jennifer L. Truman and Rachel E. Morgan, "Criminal Victimization, 2015," *US Department of Justice Bureau of Justice Statistics*, 2016, https://www.bjs.gov/content/pub/pdf/cv15.pdf.

14. Wayne R. Lafave, *Arrest: The Decision to Take a Suspect into Custody* (Boston: Little, Brown, 1965).

15. Samuel Walker, *Taming the System: The Control of Discretion in Criminal Justice 1950–1990* (Oxford: Oxford University Press, 1993).

16. Abdulah Cihan and William Wells, "Citizens' Opinions about Police Discretion in Criminal Investigations," *Policing: An International Journal of Police Strategies and Management* 34, no. 2 (2010): 347–362, doi: 10.1108/13639511111131120.

Chapter Two

A Brief History of American Policing

Many of the issues and controversies in policing today can be contextualized with the historic evolution of American policing. This chapter discusses and expands upon criminologists George L. Kelling and Mark H. Moore's[1] classification of three distinct eras of American policing: the *political era* circa the 1840s to the early turn of the twentieth century, the *reform era*, circa the early 1900s to the 1970s, and the *community problem-solving era*, which began in the late 1970s and lasted until 2001. Kelling and Moore's three eras of policing are bookended by a period of time before organized policing, where volunteer **night watchmen** patrolled the streets, and a fourth era of policing ushered in by the September 11, 2001, terrorist attacks on the World Trade Center in New York and the Pentagon in Virginia.[2]

In essence, police evolved from a loosely organized group of untrained "night watchmen," peacekeepers who were criticized for being inept and corrupt, to bureaucratic "professional" law enforcers who were criticized for being impersonal and at times, brutal. The community era, marked by the "community policing" paradigm, sought to find a balance between the two previous eras, where police officers can enforce the law without severing relationships with the public they serve. The manifestation of a unique police mentality and subculture are the focus of this chapter's topics.

BEFORE OFFICIAL POLICING: THE NIGHT WATCHMEN

Police history in the United States is an often-incoherent account pieced together from the experiences of thousands of decentralized departments throughout the country. Despite this fragmentation, the evolution of police is often a response to societal and social-sea changes, and further shaped by responses by large departments in metropolitan areas, such as New York and

Los Angeles. Ironically, some social changes may be triggered by police themselves in the form of riots derived from real or perceived misconduct. Nevertheless, there are fundamental functional changes that are demarcated by different policing eras, starting before there was organized police.

Organized police, as we know it today, did not always exist. In fact, for a long period of time during colonial America, there was virtually no organized police force. Newly independent US citizens, wary of a standing army reminiscent of the British army, did not form a centralized police force. However, the lack of an organized police force did not mean that there was no crime or that security was not necessary. The earliest forms of police were informally known as the "night watchmen."

Night watchmen were a group of loosely organized volunteers or low-paid individuals who patrolled local communities, typically at night. Night watchmen were not trained, usually unarmed, and were appointed the position by a local authority figure, such as a town mayor. An important aspect of the night watchmen was that they were not a professional security force. That is, they had other primary occupations, such as blacksmith or carpenter. Providing nightly security was performed on a part-time basis.

The night watchman's primary function was to serve as emergency warning and to keep the peace and maintain order. Note that these **order maintenance** and peacekeeping duties are still primary functions of today's police. However, for the night watchmen, enforcement of the law was not an explicit or expected duty. Instead, these early watchmen walked on foot and simply deterred or resolved disputes based on community norms. In other words, night watchmen did not necessarily enforce activities that were illegal, but instead, enforced activities that a community deemed was right or wrong. For example, the watchmen could enforce petty theft but overlook illegal gambling or prostitution if citizens supported those activities. The night watchman would enforce community norms over the letter of the law.

There were a couple of main reasons why the night watchmen prioritized community norms over the law. First, night watchmen were first and foremost community members with shared values. The primary identity of the night watchman was a citizen with an occupation, such as a baker or blacksmith, not a law enforcer. This was how the community identified with the watchman and the watchman with the community. He may not have felt that the activities of the community, such as gambling and prostitution, were wrong. He was simply an ordinary citizen who walked around and patrolled at night.

A second reason why night watchmen seemingly ignored laws in favor of community norms can be explained by the reliance on the community. During the eighteenth and nineteenth centuries, communications technologies used by today's police did not exist. There were no two-way radios, call boxes, or even telephones. Due to these limitations in technology, the unarmed night watchman could not call for backup when problems arose—note that night watchmen often carried a lamp on a stick. He could contact other officers by tapping his stick on the ground if other officers were close enough to hear the taps. However, it was more often the case that he relied on community members for assistance. Citizens willingly offered help to who they saw as a fellow townsperson or neighbor in trouble.

Enforcing the law over community norms could be problematic for the night watchman. Upsetting the community by strictly enforcing the law meant that the officer could lose critical assistance during emergencies, where they were often outnumbered and backup may not have existed. In more extreme cases, a community could turn on the single officer for going against them. As mentioned before, this was not likely the case, as the night watchman shared community values and norms.

As the nascent country's law enforcement needs grew, however, the night watchmen model would evolve and eventually be replaced by more organized forms of policing. For example, by the early 1700s many night watchmen came under the supervision of constables, which expanded the role of the night watchmen to include functions, such as tax collection and slave patrols. By the late 1700s there was no doubt that organized policing would be necessary with the establishment of the country's first federal law enforcement agency, the US Marshals Service.

THE POLITICAL ERA OF POLICING: 1840S TO EARLY 1900S

The Need for Organization

The industrial revolution in the United States, which began circa 1880 to 1929, ushered in urbanization. New economic opportunities in newly emerged metropolitan cities, such as New York and Philadelphia, triggered mass national and international migration. The mixture of ethnicities and cultures in these areas quickly resulted in racial tension and conflict among different groups. Consequently, these urban areas became centers that attracted crime. It quickly became apparent that the night watchmen and constable model of policing was inadequate, and some form of organization for policing was necessary to maintain order.

Police organization and the development of police departments earlier in nineteenth century England served as a model for replacing the obsolete watchmen model. Police reformer Sir Robert Peel was instrumental in passing the Metropolitan Police Act in 1829, which established the London Metropolitan Police Department with its staff of full-time officers that prioritized order maintenance and police-community relations. The London department became the blueprint for modern police departments and became an ideal solution for growing policing needs during American industrialization.

Along with the growing disharmony in rapidly growing metropolitan areas, power struggles emerged among different racial and political groups vying for power and influence. An organized and more locally centralized police force became an essential tool to exert power and gain influence among political groups with competing interests. Early organized policing soon became entangled with local politics, which began the political era of policing.

The Police, Politics, and Corruption

The **political era** was aptly named in reference to the role of police being used as political tools. The municipal police system replaced the night watchman–style police system in the late 1700s and lasted to the early part of the twentieth century. In New York City, the Tammany Society, informally referred to as "Tammany Hall," was a political group that supported the Democratic Party. One of the society's main functions was supporting poor immigrants entering into the country. In return, these immigrants supported Tammany Hall's political machinery that influenced mayoral races and other local politics. The newly formed New York Police Department (NYPD), arguably the oldest police department in the United States, became the vehicle for furthering Tammany Hall's political goals in New York City, including crimes that included grafting.

The NYPD during the political era consisted largely of appointed individuals based on ethnicity and loyalty to the political machinery. One immigrant group, the Irish, came to politically dominate Tammany Hall and New York City in the latter half of the nineteenth century. In the mid-nineteenth century, more than one and a half million Irish immigrated to New York, Boston, and other US cities because of the great Irish potato famine.[3] By 1880, with the help of the Tammany political machinery, New York's first Irish Catholic mayor was elected because of a pro-Irish environment. Consequently, Irish immigrants were awarded NYPD officer positions based on their loyalty to the political party, strengthening their dominance with the department serving to further their corrupt political ends.

Tammany Hall, with its leader William M. Tweed at the helm, and NYPD muscle during the political era, began garnering a reputation for corruption. Tammany Democrats were marred by public scandals, fraud, embezzlement, and election rigging. Police drew criticism for using intimidation and violence to execute this political will in an atmosphere of sharp political and ethnic divide. Newspapers began publishing editorials and political cartoons that sharply criticized Tammany Hall and the corrupt police department.[4]

Perhaps the greatest source of police criticism came from an unexpected group: **White Anglo-Saxon Protestants** (WASPs). More specifically, Protestant women who were strongly influenced by Victorian values blamed police corruption for the prevalence of vices in the community. Victorian values were derivates of the Age of Enlightenment or Age of Reason during the seventeenth and eighteenth century Europe, where religious dogma was shed in favor of social progress through science and culture. The WASPs saw society in a state of moral crisis, with a large influx of immigration from industrialization. Women and children, who were seen under Victorian values as feeble and needing men's protection, were observed to be working and engaging in leisurely activity alone. Moreover, the proliferation of vices, such as gambling, alcohol, and prostitution during industrialization, raised grave concern.

WASP women crusaded to influence the law to reflect Victorian values for the protection of women and children and to restore moral order. Despite success changing the law to criminalize immoral behaviors, many of these activities continued to thrive in industrial urban areas. These women began to realize that the new laws were simply not enforced. Recall that police at the time enforced local and political norms over the letter of the law.

Using their political influence as the wives of the elite, WASP women began criticizing police for being corrupt and pushed for reform. Other groups began to support this reform movement, including academia.

In addition to the harsh criticism, police were motivated to reform from other groups who successfully silenced critics and benefited greatly through professionalization. Several occupational groups successfully "**professionalized**" and changed criticisms of incompetence into prestige, respect, and high pay. Physicians were perhaps the most successful group to turn their image around. Initially, doctors were seen by the public as the proverbial "snake oil salesmen" who often did more harm than good. However, through education, training, and other methods, doctors have become one of the most prestigious, respected, and highly paid professionals.[5] Concurrently, lawyers were undergoing similar changes with success.

The most influential group of professionals on ushering in police reform were scientists. During the late nineteenth and early twentieth century, the "hard sciences," such as physics, chemistry, and biology, began to gain a tremendous amount of legitimacy. Science and technology began to directly impact people's lives for the better. These tangible accomplishments gave a lot of legitimacy for the hard sciences in academics. One police reformer considered by many to be the "father of modern law enforcement," August Vollmer, took note of the increasing success of the hard sciences and used this scientific approach as a model for police reform, thus ushering in the professional era of policing.

THE REFORM ERA: EARLY 1900S TO THE 1970S

Key figures:

August Vollmer, chief of police, Berkeley, California
O. W. Wilson, police officer and chief of police, Fullerton, California
J. Edgar Hoover, director, Federal Bureau of Investigations (FBI)
Richard Sylvester, chief of police, Washington, D C, and director of the
    International Association of Chiefs of Police (IACP)

The reform era marked a radical shift for law enforcement. Several key changes occurred during this time period, including:

- Police incorporated a hierarchical bureaucratic command structure.
- Police performance became based on crime-control oriented measures of success, namely, the FBI's Uniform Crime Report (UCR).
- Uniform training and the introduction of the police academy.
- Full-time officers with salary.
- Introduction of crime-control technologies, such as the two-way radio, patrol cars, and firearms.
- Officer specialization, such as detective units.
- Reliance on other police officers instead of community members.

Ushering in Police Reform

In addition to the growing criticism of police corruption and incompetence, the loosely organized night watchman style was simply overwhelmed by changes in society. Industrialization ushered in a new urban America, where informal social controls gave way to more reliance on formal social control, or police. French sociologist Emile Durkheim explained the increased presence of crime during times of social turmoil, such as industrialization, using a term he called "**anomie**," which means being in a state of normlessness.[6] That is, industrial society with its influx of different immigrant groups bringing with them their own set of norms and values, often conflict with each other. This conflict leads to a state of temporary instability from the breakdown of informal social controls and collective efficacy, or a community's ability to self-police.

When informal social controls break down, formal social controls (i.e., police), become increasingly necessary. For example, for decades American suburban neighborhoods were designed with curvilinear and looped streets that often led to dead ends compared to traditional grids, intersections, and mixed uses. This is commonly known as the cul-de-sac, French for "bottom of the sack," which became synonymous with suburbanization in America, was designed in principle with security and **collective efficacy** in mind.[7] By eliminating through-traffic and transient populations, neighborhood experiences and bonds are shaped by close proximities of families in shared communal spaces. While the design has been criticized by many, the design has been touted by others as providing a secure environment for children to play in being naturally supervised through a **panoptic surveillance**, and drawing families together. If, for example, a parked car was being stolen or broken into, it is very likely that a neighbor would witness the event, recognize the car, know its owner, and act.

In contrast, large modern apartment complexes, many would argue, are more prone to crime. These apartments often have hundreds of residents living in close quarters in relative anonymity. These strangers have little sense of community from a transitory population and consequently little collective efficacy. It is often the case that crimes, such as auto theft, can occur that may not draw any attention at all. If conflicts among neighbors arose, such as one resident being too loud, the police will most likely be contacted instead of handling the matter informally. This problem is exacerbated if there are a mix of different individuals with different cultures and norms.

The **heterogeneity** of a transitory population full of strangers, akin to the apartment example, means that neighborhoods relied heavily on formal forms of social control to resolve disputes. Moreover, higher crime from the breakdown of informal social controls meant officers such as a night watchman was no longer adequate. Increased demands for service coupled with growing criticism of police corruption served as the impetuses for a paradigm shift in policing. One police reformer, August Vollmer, had a vision of a professional police force that was better suited for industrial society.

August Vollmer

One of the most influential police reformers during the 1920s and 1930s was Berkeley chief of police, August Vollmer. Vollmer's goal was to transform the police from incompetent and corrupt bunglers to professional crimefighters. Inspired by an era where other occupations were professionalizing, such as scientists, physicians, and attorneys, Vollmer sought the same outcome for police officers. These professional occupations achieved professionalism through lengthy training and education.

Vollmer's academic background, with the backdrop of Berkeley, California, home of the University of California, served as a natural inspiration to incorporate training and education for his vision of the professional officer. Vollmer envisioned the "scientific crime fighter" who was able to make decisions based on his expertise in crime. These professional abilities would be developed in a dedicated police academy with a rigorous physical and academic curriculum in "police science."

Vollmer's ideal officer was intelligent, an expert in crime, mentally and physically sound, and who can use his expert ability to exercise discretion in dealing with matters of crime. Vollmer sought to tie physical training and the classroom together by expecting recruits to complete a significant number of university-level courses. His proposal for an academic police academy included classes and readings that included: [8]

First Year:

> Physics
> Chemistry
> Biology, physiology, and anatomy
> Criminology, anthropology, and heredity
> Toxicology

Second Year:

> Criminological psychology
> Psychiatry
> Criminology (theoretical and applied)
> Police organization and administration
> Police methods and procedure (e.g., finger print classification, etc.)

Third Year:

> Microbiology and parasitology
> Police microanalysis
> Public health
> First aid to the injured
> Elementary and criminal law

Vollmer hoped that by aligning police officers and the profession of policing with higher education and the hard sciences, police would gain the prestige and legitimacy enjoyed by physicians. Vollmer's professional officer would be able to draw from his education and experience to make expert discretionary decisions. However, Vollmer's vision of the highly educated police officer has yet to be fully realized. Today, the majority of police officers do not hold a bachelor's degree, and the requirement for most departments remains a high school equivalent degree. However, Vollmer's vision evolved through another police reformer, his student successor, O. W. Wilson, who had a different vision of the professional police officer.

O. W. Wilson

A protégé of Vollmer, O. W. Wilson started his police career as a police officer at the Berkeley Police Department before becoming police chief in Fullerton, California, where he furthered Vollmer's vision of professionalization.[9] Before his career in law enforcement, Wilson was a World War II Army veteran and retired with the rank of colonel in the military police. Wilson incorporated elements of his military background into civilian policing. Wilson's most significant contribution to police professionalization arguably was his adoption of the paramilitary model that fit well with eradicating the image of corruption and sloppiness during the political era. This structured environment required the type of officers that were akin to soldiers.

Wilson's version of the officer differed fundamentally from Vollmer's. Wilson's key changes to policing stemmed from his vision of the "professional" police officer. Whereas Vollmer envisioned a professional officer who exercised high levels of discretion based on his expertise in police science and ability to think on his feet, Wilson's officer should exercise as little discretion as possible. Instead, officers would act algorithmically based on predefined policies and procedures that dictate the officer's actions for any given situation. Minimizing officer discretion serves several key purposes:

1. Ameliorates the primary cause of corruption: differential treatment that can be prone to or perceived as bias and favoritism. In other words, everyone is treated equally regardless of the officer or the person the officer is dealing with, eliminating the "unfairness" variable.
2. Furthers police legitimacy as professional crime fighters.
3. Severs the relationship between the police and the public, which was a source of corruption.

Police officers under Wilson's supervision acted indifferent to the general public. In order to treat everyone equally, officers were to keep a professional distance in order to not befriend citizens. Officer/citizen friendliness can be considered a slippery slope that leads to favoritism and ultimately corruption. Instead, officers would treat citizens equally and with a stoic demeanor. Wilson's officer/citizen interactions were characterized as impersonal and based strictly on the law enforcement task at hand.

Wilson's professional officer can be exemplified by Detective Sergeant Joe Friday from the fictional LAPD show *Dragnet*. Sgt. Joe Friday's stoic demeanor was famously exemplified by his response to distraught crime victims trying to explain their story, "Just the facts, ma'am." Meaning, all other information that does not pertain directly to the criminal incident or investigation is extraneous and is unimportant to the police. Sgt. Friday was also well known for methodically solving crime, a quality of the professional officer. Under Wilson's model, every officer's actions were based on predefined rules, thereby creating very uniform behavior. All officers should act and carry themselves like Joe Friday. Moreover, while it may seem that an emotionless officer under this model may seem cold or even rude, there is nothing wrong with officers having a bad attitude.

The professional officer was supervised under the **paramilitary bureaucratic command** structure adopted from Wilson's military experience. A bureaucracy is a hierarchical system of organizational governance based on rules that are external to any one individual. Power is defined and distributed based on prewritten rules, which dictates both the roles and behavior for any individual within the bureaucracy. All individuals are directly supervised by a higher authority and all individuals are interchangeable. Under the bureaucracy, all individuals are held accountable and supervised by higher level authorities whose power is based on predefined rules and laws. Just like the military, police officers are hierarchically ranked, such as sergeants who are supervised by lieutenants, who may be supervised by captains, and so on.

Also adapted from the military to civilian police was **stress training**, where uniformity and compliance to the predefined rules was emphasized in a high-stress environment. Police recruits during the reform era underwent academy stress training, where officers experience high-pressure training designed to simulate the stresses of police work and dealing with an often-times hostile public. Under the stress training model, recruits were subject to verbal stressors, such as constant yelling and degradation from training personnel, as well as physical stressors that included a lot of running and physical punishment, such as pushups, when recruits failed to meet expectations for certain tasks.

Officers who withstood verbal and physical strain at the academy, in theory, were able to keep calm and maintain a professional demeanor under all circumstances, while ensuring officers acted uniformly. Police researcher John Violanti found that successful recruits were those who were able to employ effective coping techniques such as distancing and planful problem solving versus less effective techniques, such as avoidance.[10] These skills translated to, in principle, better police officers. To ensure these results under professionalism, recruits must pass a series of **litmus tests**, or tests of elimination based on both decision making and physical performance. The conceptual result was an unbiased officer who acted professionally and uniformly under all circumstances and with all individuals.

Academy stress training under the reform era of policing served a secondary purpose of creating officer camaraderie. The constant stress of academy served to reinforce collective solidarity to ultimately indoctrinate the recruit into the police fraternity. This was especially important during the reform era of policing, where officers had to rely on each other for emergency backup and support instead of citizens of the community, as found during the days of the night watchmen.

The bureaucratic model, officer attitudes, limitations on discretion, and crime control technologies under Wilson's professional model effectively severed police/citizen relations to eradicate police corruption. Furthermore, it served to enhance the image of the police officer as a true professional akin to scientists and physicians, who were worthy of high levels respect, prestige, and pay. Many consider the Federal Bureau of Investigation (FBI) and its agents the law enforcement agency that was the pinnacle of professionalism and the professional lawman during the reform era.

J. Edgar Hoover's G-Men

In 1935, J. Edgar Hoover became the director of the FBI and transformed it to be the most successful professional law enforcement organization. [11] Hoover was instrumental during the reform era in defining the professional model of policing. His professional vision of the FBI agent was consistent with Vollmer and Wilson's concept of law enforcement as being a white-collar profession. One can argue that FBI agents today are regarded as an ideal model of professionalism, the most successful, prestigious law, and most importantly, corruption-free law enforcement agency. [12]

Hoover was able to transform his agents in several ways. In the previous administration, FBI agents were criticized for being politically appointed or a product of nepotism. Consequently, like many other law enforcement agencies at the time, agents were criticized for being corrupt and incompetent. Hoover's FBI began with him as a reformer in the 1920s who fired over 100 special agents who he considered incompetent and corrupt "political hacks." These and other actions produced an agency that was organized, professional, and effective during prohibition, a time when gangsters, corrupt politicians, and law enforcement ran local politics.

Hoover implemented several institutional changes to ameliorate corruption within the bureau. First, Hoover set higher qualifications for agents, which included extensive background checks, candidate interviews, and physical litmus tests, as well as requiring specialized legal or accounting skills. Second, Hoover instituted a more stringent, formal two-month academy training for agents. Finally, similar to Vollmer's vision, the FBI incorporated the hard sciences by becoming a federal forensics lab and implementing fingerprint identification technology that assisted other agencies.

Symbolically, Hoover changed the image of the FBI agent to associate more with that of a professional. Instead of a uniform typically worn by local and state police officers, special agents wore black suits, pressed white shirts, and ties, typical of white-collar professionals. In addition, agents carried a firearm and trained extensively in marksmanship. Agents, who were highly trained, unlikely to be susceptible to corruption, and investigated the most important of federal crimes, became informally known as "government men" or "G-Men" for short.

Functionally, Hoover's FBI incorporated many crime control duties that improved the image of the agency. For example, the FBI published a "Ten Most Wanted" fugitive list. By employing the public's assistance, the FBI was seen as dealing with the most dangerous crimes. Furthermore, the agency was seen as at the forefront of dealing with crimes that were considered the most serious threats to the nation. These threats ranged from prohibition to the communist red scare.

Perhaps the most significant contribution of Hoover's FBI in reforming the police toward professionalism was the Uniform Crime Reporting Program (UCR). Created by the International Association of Chiefs of Police (IACP) in 1929, the UCR was operationalized by the FBI in 1930, which still collects and publishes crime data for a number of "index crimes" reported by federal, local, state, and other law enforcement agencies around the country. Index crimes include, among other offenses, rape, murder, and robbery. In addition to these serious crimes, the UCR also includes data for less serious "Part II index" offenses, such as DUIs, fraud, and gambling. These statistics have become a proxy measure for police performance. Included with UCR statistics are **clearance rates**, or the ratio of crimes that have been "cleared," (arrests have been made and legal paperwork forwarded for prosecution) to total number of crimes reported.

Clearance rates and other statistical measures of success during the reform era fundamentally changed measures of police performance, which altered officer behavior. The primary function of police shifted from *peace keeping* and *order maintenance* to *crime control* and *law enforcement*. Recall that the night watchman's primary duty was keeping the peace and maintaining order. A quiet, uneventful night meant a successful shift for the watchman. In other words, a good night meant "nothing happened." Under the professional model of police based on measured crime control measures of success, a night where "nothing happened" meant failure. In other words, the officer did not adequately perform his duties.

Richard Sylvester and the International Association of Chiefs of Police (IACP)

Whereas physicians and attorneys have professional trade groups that advances their profession and advocates for its members' interests, the American Medical Association and American Bar Association respectively, police established their own trade group. The International Association of Chiefs of Police was established in 1893 as an important element in unifying and establishing professionalism among law enforcement agencies. Police chiefs met to share and advocate administrative and professional practices that focused on policy and operations.

Richard Sylvester is best known for being one of the first and most significant presidents of the IACP. The IACP's primary focus under Sylvester was to establish police professionalism and incorporate a paramilitary command structure. Sylvester advocated the "citizen-soldier" model, which stressed paramilitary organization and tactics used by civilian police. Crime control technologies, such as fingerprint identification, were stressed by the organization during the turn of the twentieth century. As mentioned, in 1929, the IACP developed the UCR, which was executed by the FBI in 1930 as a key element toward police reform and professionalization.

Sylvester implemented a number of crime control tactics under professionalism that are still in use by police departments today. For example, officers were divided into three military-like platoons that patrolled the streets in eight-hour shifts. In addition, he was the first to use a briefing system that informed officers-of-the-day of current criminal activities and lookouts. Sylvester advocated officers being placed in patrol cars in order to cover more ground and respond more quickly to reported incidents, which changed the nature of police from a proactive force as exemplified by the night watchmen to one that was, by design, reactive under the professional model.

The culmination of structural changes under the vision of Vollmer, Wilson, Hoover, and Sylvester shaped the agenda of the reform era of policing to reach the goal of professionalization. These reformers fundamentally altered the means by which professional officers functioned and measured their success, which ultimately changed how police officers viewed themselves and how the public viewed the police.

THE PROFESSIONAL

Under the professional model, some of the performance measures and tactics stressed include:

Law enforcement and crime control
Fast response times to calls of service
Clearance rates
Random patrols
Special weapons and tactics
Specialized detective divisions

Under the professionalization, the development of the 9-1-1 call system arguably epitomized the notion that police were the experts in crime control. The system, meant to allow citizens quick and easy access to emergency police services, represented the complete shift from order maintenance and peace keeping to crime control functions for police. The police represented the true crime control experts, where the only role for citizens was limited to reporting crime. Citizens then handed all enforcement duties to the real experts, the police. This passive role for the public is still found with today's police/citizen relationship. For example, when a request for assistance in finding a suspect is broadcast, citizens are warned to only call the police and not actively engage the suspect or help in the investigation. Well-intentioned sleuths or vigilantes can cause more harm to a case. The separation between the police and the public, which was by design to eradicate corruption, was not completely without flaws.

SOME ATTITUDES THAT DEVELOPED: FORESHADOWING OF THE POLICE SUBCULTURE

Major structural changes to policing that fundamentally altered officers' functions from proactive peace keepers to reactive law enforcers resulted in changes in how officers viewed and interacted with the public. As police became more insulated from the public, officers knew very little of the community they served. Inversely, the community viewed police as nameless, faceless, uniformed men in their patrol cars.

Consequently, without frequent and positive interactions with the public in non-crime related circumstances, officers became insulated from and insensitive to the changing dynamics of their work environment.

Impoverished ethnic enclaves emerged from increasingly dense cities with shifting populations from the 1960s to 1980s. These inner-city populations became wrapped in turmoil and mistrust in government amidst harsh crime control policies and a slew of government misconduct. Police/citizen relations became severely strained as the police force found themselves at odds with an unrelatable growing inner-city population that did not reflect their values of law and order. Furthermore, the police force were being increasingly criticized by communities for functioning as the enforcement arm of a hostile government and corporate culture.

Police, reactive by nature and unable to actively reduce tensions as in the past under the night watchman model, responded to the public in the only way they knew how: powerfully and brutally. The ensuing decades after the 1950s were marked by turmoil and social upheaval. At the center of the action was the police—one riot after another. For example, in the 1960s police responded heavily to civil rights activists, resulting in the Watts Riots in Los Angeles that were sparked by a California Highway Patrolman beating a black man during a DUI stop. In the 1960s and 1970s, once again, police were sent to restore order against Vietnam War protests. In 1991, the infamous Rodney King beating caught on camera sparked another major riot in Los Angeles.

The next chapter explores the manifestation of a strained relationship between police and certain communities and the emergence of a **police subculture** that further insulated officers from the public.

NOTES

1. George L. Kelling and Mark H. Moore, "The Evolving Strategy of Policing," in *Policing: Key Readings* (Portland, OR: Willan Publishing, 2005).

2. Willard M. Oliver, "The Fourth Era of Policing: Homeland Security," *International Review of Law, Computers and Technology* 20 no. 1 (2006): 49–62.

3. Joseph R. O'Neill, *The Irish Potato Famine* (Edina: ABDO Publishing, 2009).

4. Charles Mahan and Larry Bush, "Art of the Poison Pens: A Century of American Political Cartoons," USF Tampa Libraries, 2012, http://exhibits.lib.usf.edu/exhibits/show/poison-pens/new-century/nast.

5. S.E.D. Shortt, "Physicians, Science, and Status: Issues in the Professionalization of Anglo-American Medicine in the Nineteenth Century," *Medical History* 27 (1983): 51–68.

6. Emile Durkheim, *On Suicide: A Study in Sociology* (New York: The Free Press, 1979). (Original work published 1897.)

7. Thomas R. Hochschild Jr., "Cul-de-sac Kids," *Childhood* 20, no. 2 (2012): 229–243. doi: 10.1177/0907568212458128.

8. August Vollmer and Albert Schneider, "The School for Police as Planned at Berkeley," *Journal of the American Institute of Criminal Law and Criminology* 7, no. 6 (1917): 877–898.

9. Orlando W. Wilson, *Police Administration.* 2nd ed. (New York: McGraw-Hill, 1963).

10. John M. Violanti, "Coping Strategies among Police Recruits in a High-Stress Training Environment," *The Journal of Social Psychology 132*, no. 6 (1992): 717–729. doi: 10.1080/00224545.1992.9712102.

11. Rhodri Jeffreys-Jones, *The FBI: A History* (Binghamton, NY: Vail-Ballou, 2007).

12. Joseph W. Koletar, *The FBI Career Guide: Inside Information on Getting Chosen for and Succeeding in one of the Toughest, Most Prestigious Jobs in the World* (New York: AMACOM, 2006).

Chapter Three

The Police Subculture

This chapter explores the *police subculture*, which often explains and serves as the basis for many of the controversial issues covered in this text. Every group has its own culture, but the reason why it is often referred to as a "subculture" is because a particular group culture often conflicts with societal norms. For instance, street gangs often have a code of conduct and a set of mentalities that coincide with their behaviors. These activities, however, often conflict with the socially accepted expectations of behavior and are therefore deemed deviant, such as fighting to resolve disputes. Sometimes these activities cross the line into what society defines as illegal behavior, such as tagging or drive-by shootings. Policing can be the same way, where **police misconduct** can range from deviance to breaking the law.

This chapter is broken into several themes that answer the following questions:

1. What is a subculture?
2. What is the police subculture?
3. How does the subculture contribute to police misconduct?
4. How did it develop?
5. What can be done to change it?

WHAT IS A SUBCULTURE?

A **subculture** is a set of normative values and beliefs held by a subset of the population that shapes the group's worldview and subsequent behavior based on those values and beliefs.[1] A subculture can include behavior that is conforming to societal norms as well as deviant behavior. Collectively, all these conforming and deviant behaviors are considered normal to a group.

Subcultures exist in virtually all groups, ranging from more law-abiding groups, such as among office workers and church groups, to more deviant groups, such as the set of values held by street gangs. The key point is that the behavior, whether law-abiding or law-breaking, is viewed as normal and expected by the group. In essence, a group's subculture consists of behaviors and mentalities that are considered normal to the group. Deviations from these behavioral expectations are usually considered violations of the group norms.

One example of a subculture that conflicts with societal values is street gangs, and the often derided "gang culture." From an outsider's perspective, gang violence, particularly when rival gang members attack each other and even police officers for no apparent reason, does not make sense. For example, in Oakland in the 1990s, rival gangs attacked each other once they sighted each other. When sociologist Victor Rios examined these motivations, he found this violent behavior as rational to the gangs because the gangs live by the "code of the streets," where violence was necessary to maintain respect among members and more importantly, was a deterrent for future violence.[2] The gang culture valued toughness and machismo over conforming to the law, even with the possibility of jail time. The subcultural norms trumped the norms of society, including in police departments.[3]

Subcultures exist in virtually all social groups, including different occupations. Occupational groups often share mentalities that are formed through interactions with each other and with the work environment. In certain occupations, employees often develop similar mindsets and attitudes toward outsiders who are not part of the group. These attitudes can manifest in many ways, including shared negative attitudes and stereotypes of those who are not part of the group.

One example of an occupation group that shares these characteristics is restaurant workers. Servers often develop positive and negative attitudes toward certain groups based on shared experiences. For instance, which groups tend to tip more than others. These group stereotypes can include age, race, physical appearance, and other characteristics.[4] Based on these stereotypes, certain groups may receive differential treatment. These stereotypes have been documented by both scholars and published restaurant workers, including Chefs such as the late Anthony Bourdain.[5]

A second manifestation of the restaurant subculture is group solidarity that is formed by a variety of factors. Using our restaurant example: workers often develop idiosyncrasies with language and even deviant behavior, including illicit drug use. Bonds among workers are reinforced through shared experiences with a stressful environment that only other employees in the field can truly understand.

Most activities and mentalities fit within the bounds of the law and social norms. However, in almost all work places, there are some behaviors that may be considered deviant, abnormal, or even illegal. With most occupations, deviant activities are often acceptable with no member of the group reporting illegal activities. These illegal activities may include, as mentioned, dealing or using drugs within the company, which is tacitly accepted by and not reported by other employees.

With some occupational subcultures, deviant or illegal activities are not only overlooked, but expected. Some businesses underreport taxable income for cash transactions and many work places have acceptable practices that are illegal and considered part of the job, or in some cases, entire industries. White-collar crime scholars, for instance, have examined employees rarely reporting illegal activities such as illegal toxic dumping.[6] **"Sludge running,"** for example, was an illegal practice of opening a spigot on a waste disposal truck and letting toxic waste drain while driving through different neighborhoods.

Even well-respected professions, such as medicine, have deviant subcultures. It was found that doctors and hospital administrators routinely bilked Medicaid during its early years, which was considered common practice in the industry.[7] For police, the subculture is particularly strong and has been the subject of much research, and moreover, has been blamed for controversial issues ranging from misconduct to brutality.

THE POLICE SUBCULTURE

The police have a notably strong subculture that stems from the unique aspects of the job. That is, they have a particular **"worldview,"** or shared group perspective, that is unique to law enforcement.[8] This worldview serves several purposes, which includes helping officers cope with stress, both internal (administrative stress) and external (dealing with the public). The greatest contributor of the police subculture is the real and perceived dangers of the profession. Unlike other police professions, police must constantly negotiate the meanings and expectations of their job, which is often contradictory in nature; police must serve others while enforcing the law.

The contradictory role of the police officer is summed up nicely by the late radio broadcaster Paul Harvey, who described the "policeman" in his narration in 1970:

> A Policeman is a composite of what all men are, mingling of a saint and sinner, dust and deity.
>
> Gulled statistics wave the fan over the stinkers; underscore instances of dishonesty and brutality because they are "new." What they really mean is that they are exceptional, unusual, and not commonplace.

Buried under the frost is the fact: Less than one-half of one percent of policemen misfit the uniform. That's a better average than you'd find among clergy!

What is a policeman made of? He, of all men, is once the most needed and the most unwanted. He's a strangely nameless creature who is "sir" to his face and "fuzz" to his back.

He must be such a diplomat that he can settle differences between individuals so that each will think he won.

But . . . If the policeman is neat, he's conceited; if he's careless, he's a bum. If he's pleasant, he's flirting; if not, he's a grouch.

He must make an instant decision which would require months for a lawyer to make.

But . . . If he hurries, he's careless; if he's deliberate, he's lazy. He must be first to an accident and infallible with his diagnosis. He must be able to start breathing, stop bleeding, tie splints and, above all, be sure the victim goes home without a limp. Or expect to be sued.

The police officer must know every gun, draw on the run, and hit where it doesn't hurt. He must be able to whip two men twice his size and half his age without damaging his uniform and without being "brutal." If you hit him, he's a coward. If he hits you, he's a bully.

A policeman must know everything-and not tell. He must know where all the sin is and not partake.

A policeman must, from a single strand of hair, be able to describe the crime, the weapon and the criminal—and tell you where the criminal is hiding.

But . . . If he catches the criminal, he's lucky; if he doesn't, he's a dunce. If he gets promoted, he has political pull; if he doesn't, he's a dullard. The policeman must chase a bum lead to a dead-end, stake out ten nights to tag one witness who saw it happen—but refused to remember.

The policeman must be a minister, a social worker, a diplomat, a tough guy and a gentleman.

And, of course, he'd have to be genius. . . . For he will have to feed a family on a policeman's salary.

These pressures as described by Paul Harvey highlight the uniquely stressful environment officers must navigate. The stress is derived from the various roles and expectations of the officer as well as the work environment. Specifically, a large part of the subculture and officer identity is shaped by collectively facing real and perceived dangers of the job in which they can be purposefully injured or killed.

The uniqueness of policing stems from its potentially hazardous duties and mandates being substantively different than other professions. Police are given the legal and legitimate permission to use physical force, including deadly force, to apprehend and detain suspects. They must do so within the narrow bounds of the law. If the use of force is inappropriate, the officer can be criminally liable and charged with a crime as well as face civil litigation. In many regards, an officer's power is greater than even that of the president. An officer can directly take a person's life using lethal force.

The shared dangers of the job and pressures of the profession manifest in group introversion and cynical attitudes toward individuals and groups who are not law enforcement.[9] Since police solely rely on each other during emergency situations, strong bonds form among officers. They must trust each other with their lives against an unknown public that they do not know, and could harm them. Perhaps the phrase that best describes the police subcultural worldview is "**us versus them**," a belief that describes the relationship between the police and a public who is constantly out to criticize and attack them.

The police subculture can be characterized by the following perspective as outlined by criminologist Peter Manning who describes it as a "siege mentality":[10]

- People can't be trusted
- Experience is better than rules
- You must make people respect you
- Everyone hates cops
- Legal system is untrustworthy
- People who are not controlled will break laws
- Policemen can most accurately ID crime and criminals
- Major jobs are to prevent crime and enforce laws
- Stronger punishment will deter criminals

Police officers, by default, only trust one another while distrusting non–law enforcement. The strong bonds that form among officers is often described as being part of a family and described as a "**blue brotherhood**." Consequently, police have developed social norms to protect one another, even when it comes to misconduct.

The subcultural norm for police is not to report misconduct on fellow officers and be a whistleblower, commonly known as the "**blue wall of silence**." To ensure absolute trust among them, which is vital during emergencies, police officers must never violate this trust. Therefore, any misconduct must not be reported. Officers who violate this unwritten code are often ostracized by the group and even subjected to danger and violence. In the case of NYPD in the 1960s and 1970s, whistleblower Officer Frank Serpico (whose story was depicted by Al Pacino in the movie titled *Serpico*) reported widespread departmental corruption. Consequently, during a drug bust, Serpico was shot in the face when fellow officers refused to inform dispatch of the officer being shot and request medical assistance. Ultimately, a neighbor reported Serpico's shooting and requested assistance.

Another shared mentality amongst officers that reinforces group solidarity under the police subculture is the idea that police are the only force that's keeping civil society from falling into chaos. Deemed the "thin blue line," police officers feel their role in society is of utmost importance and they are disrespected by the public who does not acknowledge and appreciate the gravity and importance of their role. Ironically, police themselves have developed negative and cynical attitudes toward the public.

To further illustrate the cynical mentality as part of the subculture developed under professionalism, consider John Van Maanen's 1978 article, "The Asshole," about how police officers typically perceive and approach non-police on traffic stops.[11]

"THE ASSHOLE"

The "asshole" is a derogatory term used to describe people who make a police officer's job more difficult. Assholes are individuals who do not accept and respect an officer's authority, control, and definition in a situation. Note that police officers under the professional model must maintain control of a situation at all times since they are the experts in crime control. Moreover, it is a way for officers who are insulated to the public by design, to minimize danger. A person who is an affront to this command is considered an asshole, which can be described as:

- Creep
- Bigmouth
- Bastard
- Animal
- Mope
- Rough
- Jerkoff
- Clown
- Scumbag
- Wise guy
- Phony
- Idiot
- Shithead
- Bum
- Fool

Every person the officer encounters is a potential asshole. Once a person is deemed an asshole by the officer, he or she can be subjected to "**street justice**." Street justice is a means to force respect toward the officer using unjustified and often illegal use of force.[12] In the 1960s and 1970s, at the time of Van Maanen's article, this often meant beatings meted by police.

Note that street justice is an unintended consequence or manifestation of the police subculture and the reform era of policing. Police professionalism was intended to eradicate police brutality from the late-nineteenth-century practice of "clubbing," or using clubs and blackjacks to beat citizens, and from the 1920s, when police investigators commonly performed violent interrogation tactics known as the **"third degree"** on suspects and organized criminals linked to the Prohibition. However, the practice of street justice became commonplace among police during the 1960s, when officers used physical force to suppress social upheavals and mass demonstrations.

Determining whether a person is an asshole is a multistaged process where a person's perceived level of threat by the officer can change. Van Maanen classifies individuals who come into contact with police into three categories or ideal types:

1. *Know nothings*—these are typical of almost everyone. Officers do not know enough information about these individuals to make a judgment . . . just yet.
2. *Suspicious persons*—individuals that police believe committed a serious crime, but have yet to be revealed to the police.
3. *Assholes*—individuals who do not accept the police definition of a given situation.

Upon encountering police, such as in a traffic stop, individuals navigate and negotiate their status in all three categories. During the initial contact, all individuals are considered either know-nothings or suspicious persons based on preconceived notions and past experiences of the officer. Know nothings can escalate to suspicious persons and ultimately assholes in any given situation. The escalation process typically begins with:

Stage 1: An affront, or challenge to the officer's authority, control, and definition of the situation.

Stage 2: A secondary stage where the suspect is given an opportunity to explain himself or accept the officer's authority and command of the situation. Questions that the officer may ask himself are: Could this person have acted differently given the circumstance? If so, was the person aware of the consequences of acting like this?

Stage 3: If the answer to the aforementioned questions were yes, implying the willful challenge of the officer's authority, there is a possibility or likelihood of "street justice."

A person can deescalate the situation at the second stage in which a suspicious person can make a correction by accepting the officer's control of the situation. For example, an apology or acceptable explanation of the initial affront toward the officer can change the status of the person from suspicious person and potential asshole that is subject to street justice, back to suspicious person.

Other options available to the officer, depending on the ability of the suspect to act differently and having knowledge of what he's doing include *ignoring* the situation, *isolating* the individual, or *teaching* the individual on how to act.

MORE MANIFESTATIONS OF THE POLICE SUBCULTURE

The police subculture can explain a lot of officer behavior not related to police misconduct. Paramount to the police subculture is extremely strong group solidarity leading to group introversion. The interdependence among officers in a perceived dangerous occupation creates a strong bond, which is necessary to ensure trust that help will arrive quickly during emergencies. This leads to police officers primarily associating with only other officers. Oftentimes, new officers soon realize that the majority of their friends are composed almost entirely of other officers. Consequently, officers often find themselves isolated from the rest of the population, including their old friends and acquaintances. Conversely, these old friends can find themselves uncomfortable with spending time or even associating with the officer. Ask yourself this: If you are not an officer, would you invite a police officer friend to a party?

In addition, **shift work** further isolates the officer from the public. Shift work is defined as work that is associated with providing continual service for twenty-four hours per day, seven days per week. Examples of shift workers range from firefighters to hospital emergency room nurses. Rookie officers often find themselves without seniority in picking shifts that coincide with typical work hours and days, such as 9 a.m.–5 p.m. from Monday to Friday. Instead, they are often given less desirable shifts and days off, such as working night shifts without weekends off. Consequently, they find it difficult to partake in social activities with non-police friends. A culmination of these and other factors contribute to the "us versus them" mentality.

At worst, police isolation from the public coupled with the siege mentality can have profound social impacts. Unlike the night watchman who was intimately familiar with the local population, professional officers find themselves dealing with strangers who they must assume are dangerous. This worldview requires officers to treat every situation as potentially dangerous and respond with excessive force which can spark social upheaval. This aggressive response in turn creates tension with the community, especially in poorer ethnic enclaves. In the past, this has resulted in urban riots—from the 1960s Watts Riots to the 1992 Rodney King riots, and more recently, protests and riots in Ferguson, Missouri.

The LAPD, specifically, was the focus of many incidents involving the police and citizens that have led to large-scale urban riots. Several incidents of abuse sparked public outrage spanning several decades during the professional era, including:

1951 Bloody Christmas: LAPD officers under Chief William H. Parker, a champion of police professionalism, beat seven men (five of whom were Hispanic) on Christmas day. LAPD officers responded to a report of underage drinking. Upon their initial investigation, IDs were presented showing they were of drinking age. When they refused to vacate the area, a fight ensued and the men were severely beaten.

Watts Riots: The infamous 1965 riots pitted LAPD officers against many of the citizens of the city during six days of violence that resulted in thirty-four deaths, over a thousand injured, and over 3,400 arrests. Amid growing racial tension from the racial desegregation, tension between African American Los Angeles residents and officers grew. The tension erupted when a California Highway Patrol officer pulled over a Black motorist for a suspected DUI, which then escalated in the neighborhood as residents jumped the officers. As LAPD backup arrived, they became entangled with a hostile crowd which escalated to the riots.

39th and Dalton: In 1988, LAPD Chief Daryl F. Gates declared a war on crime with "operation hammer" amidst escalating gang violence stemming from the crack cocaine market in Los Angeles. The operation called for strong-arm tactics by specialized LAPD gang units. One unit in particular, the notorious C.R.A.S.H. (Community Resources Against Street Hoodlums) consisted of LAPD SWAT team members who were instructed to aggressively tackle four apartment complexes in the neighborhood at 39th and Dalton, which had become infested with gang and drug activities. CRASH officers sent a strong message by a widespread abuse of power—including assaulting individuals, vandalizing the properties by kicking holes, using an axe, tagging walls, etc. Innocent victims were swept up in the police activity, which was a massive violation of civil rights.

Rodney King Riots: Suspected DUI suspect Rodney King was pulled over by a group of LAPD officers who were videotaped beating King while he was on the ground. The tape quickly spread amongst news channels as the trial for King resulted in the acquittal of the officers involved. This verdict outraged the African American community in South Los Angeles, where six days of riots resulted in uncontrolled violence, looting, arson, and murder. Order was finally restored when thousands of California National Guardsmen were deployed.

THE DEVELOPMENT AND CHANGE OF THE
POLICE SUBCULTURE

Several aspects have led to the development of the police worldview and subsequent subculture. As discussed last chapter, police sought to insulate themselves from the public in order to ameliorate and eradicate corruption. To this end, they initially succeeded. However, the radical shift toward professionalism has strained relationships between the police and the public. Many poor urban areas populated by ethnic minorities, specifically, have become wary and fearful of a perceived hostile police force. They distrust the police, and with good reason—police have historically, on occasion, abused their power.

With a growing number of incidents sparked by police, reform was sought after by policymakers and federal authorities in order to prevent further incidents of social upheavals. Investigators found that the problem in the department was not just the proverbial "bad apple" problem officers, but the police organization itself, or the "rotten barrel." Specifically, a strong LAPD subculture was largely attributed to incidents that resulted in urban riots.

The investigation of the Rodney King beating by the independent commission on the Los Angeles Police Department, commonly referred to as the Christopher Commission, found department-wide attitudes directly related to the police subculture.[13] They found that despite the LAPD's insistence during the 1990s that it was a community policing department, officers were evaluated on crime control criteria and rewarded for being "hardnosed," which created a siege mentality that alienated officers from the community. The Christopher Commission found LAPD officers commonly viewed citizens in minority areas with resentment and hostility, resulting in many cases of police brutality which was tacitly accepted department-wide. A large number of Mobile Digital Terminal (MDT) computers that officers use to communicate with dispatch showed not only acceptance of brutality, but many officers laughed and made jokes about beating suspects.

A follow-up investigation and report five years after the Rodney King incident by a special council still found systematic issues at the department. The council found "no meaningful, institutionalized effort by the [LAPD] to do work history reviews for officers generating an unusually high number of uses of force or force-related complaints." These findings are consistent with the subcultural "blue wall of silence" where officers tacitly accepted bad behavior from peers and subordinates in order to maintain trust.

Taking the recommendations of the Christopher Commission Report into account, many police reformers have sought to weaken the police subculture through policy and personnel changes, with somewhat limited success.[14] Perhaps the most popular method of weakening the impact of the police subculture and restoring community relations among minority enclaves is to create a police force that better reflects the demographics of the community, namely hiring more women and minority officers.[15] Despite the intent to reduce the impact of the police subculture, changing the institution of policing is extremely difficult.

STRUCTURAL AND CULTURAL LIMITATIONS TO CHANGE

Police reformers have sought to change the police subculture through several means. First, many departments have sought reform through policy changes, such as establishing or updating rules that govern the use of force, high speed chases, etc. Second, politicians have replaced police chiefs. At the LAPD, for example, Chief Daryl F. Gates resigned after the Rodney King beating and ensuing riots. He was replaced by Chief Willie Williams, an African American and the first LAPD chief who was a department outsider. Despite the change at the top, Chief Williams was unable to have a lasting impact on the LAPD culture. Finally, as previously discussed, women and minority officers are often hired to better reflect the demographics of the community. Unfortunately, these women and minority hires have not been found to have a significant impact on the relationship between the police and community, or on softening the police subculture.

The question remains: Why do such logical changes have such little impact on the police subculture? The answers relate to the momentum of the existing culture and structure that makes change very slow and difficult. Three main reasons explain why the police subculture is so difficult to change.

Those Attracted to the Job

The first reason why changing the police subculture is so difficult is its focus on law enforcement and crime control over order maintenance and peace keeping duties. This emphasis on crime control is shared by individuals interested in policing.[16] In other words, those who are attracted to the occupation of policing are mainly interested in "catching bad guys," making arrests, etc., over directing traffic, resolving issues, and other peacekeeping duties. While most recruits cite more altruistic reasons for wanting to become officers, such as a desire to "give back" to their communities, surveys of academy recruits find that they value crime control aspects of the job: physical training, self-defense, and marksmanship. Moreover, most officers in large cities, such as Los Angeles, tend to reside outside of their work city or area.

There is little variation among women and minorities in wanting to become a police officer. Most applicants and recruits cite the opportunity to help others, job benefits, and job security as primary reasons for joining the police force. However, the proverbial "catching bad guys" associated with justice and crime control still remains one of the key reasons for considering a career in law enforcement.

Police Advertising

Police departments frequently produce recruitment videos in order to attract applicants. One just needs to watch a few videos on YouTube under the search phrase "police recruitment video" to notice a pattern. Police videos focus on the crime control and action-oriented aspects of the job instead of the order maintenance realities of police work. The LAPD, for example, has a three-part Hollywood-style video featuring a number of women and minority officers in high-speed chases, helicopters, guns drawn . . . you get the picture. Even suburban departments with extremely low violent crime rates produce videos of a similar nature. The Lubbock, Texas, County Sheriff's Office's slick recruitment video features officers making felony stops, SWAT teams, police dogs, high-tech equipment, explosions, and other law enforcement/crime control activities. Both videos of course prominently showcase women and minority officers in those roles.

The reality of routine police work, however, is not accurately depicted by recruitment videos. According to police researcher David Bayley, the majority of a police officer's day has very little to do with crime.[17] According to the Uniform Crime Report (UCR), only 13 percent of all reported crime is serious, such as homicide, assault, and robbery. The role officers are most likely to engage in does not involve crime control and arrests, but merely "sorting out" conflicts with no clear offenders or victims. The majority of an officer's time is spent on peacekeeping duties, such as on patrol responding to calls of service and to a lesser extent, traffic enforcement. According to Bayley, patrol officers on average make only nineteen arrests per year—far from the action-packed shifts portrayed on television and in the movies. Political scientist William K. Muir Jr. described police work as rather boring with very little "proactive" work.[18]

Ultimately, attracting individuals to the profession who can potentially change the police subculture, such as good communicators and those more interested in service activities, is challenging. Prospective recruits who may want to join policing for aspects of the job other than crime control are not sent the message that police place much importance on anything other than law enforcement.

Police Academy and Field Training

Police academies and field training further "weed out" recruits that do not fit in with the culture of the department. Recruits who do not fit what a department values are eliminated from becoming officers through a series of inter-views and physical and psychological litmus tests. Litmus tests are tests that determine whether a recruit proceeds with the training process. In other words, a recruit must pass the test to move on, or fail the test which ends the hiring process. For example, many female recruits have difficulty in parts of the physical agility test, particularly scaling a six-foot wall.

In addition, recruits must "fit in" with the existing culture and personnel. Rookie officers, informally known as **"boots,"** must not only pass a variety of physical litmus tests ranging from pull-ups to driving at the academy but must also pass a probationary field-training period. Boots ride with veteran **field training officers** (FTOs) and must perform to the FTO's standards. Rookies who do not fit in with the culture are typically not given much leeway.

Cultural transmission occurs frequently at police academies, which serve to reproduce and reinforce the culture of the department. Recruits are often told "war stories" by veteran and training officers that highlight the dangers of the job. Much less emphasis is placed on cultural sensitivity training and other non-crime control related activities and instruction. These war stories and activities designed to foster group solidarity serve to reinforce the exist-ing subculture.

Recall that police recruits undergo stress training, wherein recruits are subjected to constant yelling in a high-stress environment designed to simu-late and prepare them for the difficulties of the job. Recruits who cannot handle the constant stress drop out of the academy.

The culmination of police recruitment, interviews, training, and other activities collectively produce a very homogenous group of individuals that think and act very similarly. These individuals share similar values and worldviews, regardless of gender and race. This means that individuals who could potentially change or soften the police subculture were never interested in the job or have been eliminated, thereby reinforcing the existing culture and structure.

SUMMARY

This chapter discussed the police subculture, a set of normative values unique to police officers that shape their worldview and guide their behavior in their working environment. This subculture is characterized by strong group introversion and cynicism toward outside individuals and groups, as captured in the saying, "us versus them."

While there is nothing wrong with having a subculture, for police it can manifest in many negative forms with real consequences. Most notably, these can range from negative attitudes to excessive use of force which can ultimately lead to urban riots. More importantly, it appears as the tacit consent by other police in the organization who turn a blind eye to misconduct, referred to as the "blue wall of silence."

The strong subculture was derived from the evolution of police, where their relationship with the public eroded and was largely severed by professionalization under the reform era. Without many personal positive contacts with the public by a police force now judged on crime control criteria, mutual mistrust developed, particularly with poor minority communities. Rebuilding this trust remains difficult due to the strong subculture that replicates itself through hiring and training.

The next chapter examines police selection and police training, looking at the controversies of academy training as well as field training, where new recruits are introduced into the world of the police officer, often described among police circles as a "front row seat to the greatest show on earth."

NOTES

1. Johnny Nhan, "Police Culture," in *The Encyclopedia of Criminology and Criminal Justice,* (Hoboken: Blackwell, 2014), doi: 10.1002/9781118517383.

2. Victor M. Rios, *Punished: Policing the Lives of Black and Latino Boys* (New York: NYU Press, 2011).

3. Randall Sullivan, *LAbyrinth: A Detective Investigates the Murders of Tupac Shakur and Notorious B.I.G., the Implications of Death Row Records' Suge Knight, and the Origins of the Los Angeles Police Scandal* (New York: The Grove Press, 2002).

4. Gary A. Fine, *Kitchens: The Culture of Restaurant Work* (Berkeley: University of California Press, 2009).

5. Anthony Bourdain, *Kitchen Confidential: Adventures in the Culinary Underbelly* (New York: Bloomsbury, 2007).

6. Stephen M. Rosoff, Henry N. Pontell, and Robert Tillman, *Profit without Honor: White Collar Crime and the Looting of America,* 6th ed. (New York: Pearson, 2014).

7. Paul Jesilow, Henry N. Pontell, and Gilbert Geis, *Prescription for Profit: How Doctors Defraud Medicaid* (Berkeley: University of California Press, 1993).

8. John Van Maanen, "Police Socialization: A Longitudinal Examination of Job Attitudes in an Urban Police Department," *Administrative Science Quarterly* 20, no. 2 (1975): 207–228.

9. Joan C. Barker, *Danger, Duty, and Disillusion: The Worldview of Los Angeles Police Officers* (Prospect Heights, IL: Waveland Press, 1999).

10. Peter K. Manning, "The Police: Mandate, Strategies, and Appearances," in *Policing: Key Readings* (Portland, OR: Willan, 2005), 191–214.

11. John Van Maanen, "The Asshole," in *Policing: A View from the Street* (Santa Monica, CA: Good Year Publishing, 1978).

12. Marilynn S. Johnson, *Street Justice: A History of Violence in New York City* (Boston: Beacon Press, 2003).

13. Report of the Independent Commission on the Los Angeles Police Department (1991) https://archive.org/details/ChristopherCommissionLAPD.

14. Edwin Chemerinsky, "An Independent Analysis of the Los Angeles Police Department's Board of Inquiry Report on the Rampart Scandal," *Loyola of Los Angeles Law Review* 34, no. 2 (2001): 547–656.

15. Anthony J. Raganella and Michael D. White, "Race, Gender, and Motivation for Becoming a Police Officer: Implications for Building a Representative Police Department," *Journal of Criminal Justice* 32, no. 6 (2004): 501–513.

16. Michael D. White, Jonathan A. Cooper, Jessica Saunders, and Anthony J. Raganella, "Motivations for becoming a Police Officer: Re-assessing Officer Attitudes and Job Satisfaction after Six Years on the Street," *Journal of Criminal Justice* 38, no. 4 (2010): 520–530.

17. David H. Bayley, "What Do the Police Do?" in *Policing: Key Readings* (Portland, OR: Willan, 2005), 141–149.

18. William K. Muir Jr., *Police: Streetcorner Politicians* (Chicago: University of Chicago Press, 1979).

Chapter Four

Officer Selection and Training

One of the biggest and most complex challenges that every law enforcement agency faces is hiring and preparing the right people for the profession. Each new hire represents a multimillion-dollar investment by an agency over the course of the officer's career. Hiring the wrong person or ill-preparing him or her may cause friction and problems within a department. More importantly, given the awesome power and responsibility of police, a bad hire can be a potential legal liability and can mean unnecessary injuries and even death.

This chapter examines controversial issues in both the hiring and training processes, paying particular attention to academy and field training, the two formative and perhaps most critical stages in shaping an officer's worldview and identity.

CRITICAL ISSUE: OFFICER SELECTION

Becoming a police officer is a lengthy and multistaged process. It often takes over one year from the time someone submits their application to the time he or she starts their first day on patrol. The process is even lengthier if one includes field training[1] and the probation period for a new officer. A fully trained officer has often spent over two years getting to that point. Generally, the application process in larger departments can take up to several months before departments can process an application. Next, the hiring process itself can take several more months before the applicant enters academy training.

Before entering the academy, applicants must undergo a lengthy selection process containing parts that are considered controversial. Prospective members are typically given psychological testing, intense face-to-face interviews, job analysis, extensive background checks, physical tests, drug tests, and a polygraph examination, in no particular order. Psychological tests administered to applicants are one of the areas of controversy.

PSYCHOLOGICAL PRESCREENING

Recall that police reformer August Vollmer envisioned a professional officer who was physically and mentally sound. Mental soundness became a national issue in 1967, when President Lyndon Johnson's Commission on Law Enforcement and Administration of Justice released a report that specifically made recommendations for psychological screening of new police recruits part of their objective in improving police personnel.[2] This report was released during a time of a sharp increase in crime and turmoil in a country that was confronted with racial tension and public conflict over the Vietnam War. This conflict was frequently broadcasted on television with images of seemingly overly aggressive officers trying to control groups of protestors.

Today, most police applicants are screened for psychological problems as part of the hiring process. One of the main purposes of performing psychological screening for applicants is to ensure emotional and mental stability in a profession that can be highly stressful. Certain traits are considered undesirable by police departments. For example, police typically do not want individuals who may have short tempers and act too aggressively.

Military candidates may be suffering from psychological trauma that could be considered a risk to the general public. While police departments cannot reject all candidates, such as military veterans with **post-traumatic stress disorder** (PTSD), because of the American with Disabilities Act, many departments evaluate a candidate's mental health in becoming a police officer. Candidates that have or have previously had PTSD can affect their performance as an officer by becoming a liability when a department is being sued, and the condition can be used to attack their credibility when they are called to testify.[3] Consequently, psychological testing of candidates is often a standard requirement for public service employees in relation to public safety, which is critical when you recall that police officers are uniquely granted by the State the legitimate power to arrest someone and use deadly force.

THE MINNESOTA MULTIPHASIC
PERSONALITY INVENTORY (MMPI)

MMPI is the most common psychological test administered to applicants. The most current version, the MMPI-2 and its multiple variations, uses different clinical subscales to measure and assess psychopathology and personality, ranging from depression and paranoia to aggression and levels of constraint. These psychological tests are increasingly important as part of a department's overall assessment of a candidate, often including informal assessments such as observations and unstructured interviews. Despite its seemingly objective scientific nature, many consider psychological tests like the MMPI an imperfect science.

Perhaps the main controversy with psychological tests is potential bias. The MMPI-2 has been criticized by some academics as having a racial bias against African Americans. Some psychologists have found statistically significant differences in scores between Caucasian and African American chemical dependency inpatients. For example, one study using self-reported instruments and structured interviews found that African American male veterans seeking substance abuse treatment had higher MMPI-2 scores.[4] However, other studies have refuted claims of racial bias. For example, one meta-analysis of twenty-five studies showed that overall results did not unfairly portray African Americans and Latinos as pathological.[5]

There is a possibility that psychological testing may be completely irrelevant. There is research to suggest that these psychological tests do not serve as good predictors of job performance. Many scholars found no linkages between MMPI scores and job performance. One study, for instance, looked at the "big five" measures of personality factors (neuroticism, extraversion, openness, agreeableness, and conscientiousness) in the MMPI and the Inwald Personality Inventory (IPI) and found that personality measures are unrelated to measures of cognitive ability.[6]

Despite its controversies, psychological tests remain one of the tools police departments use in their repertoire of candidate assessment in hopes of predicting the future behavior of officers.[7] While psychological tests are not the sole determinant of an applicant's hiring, it can serve to eliminate candidates that raise concern. The goal of a hiring committee is minimizing risk in an increasingly consequential profession. Another area of risk is assessing the trustworthiness of a candidate.

CRITICAL ISSUE: POLYGRAPH EXAMINATION

Perhaps the most important concern for departments hiring a potentially new police officer is determining the candidate's trustworthiness. Ask virtually any background investigator and they will give the adage, "honesty is the best policy." In other words, it is better for applicants to openly report to past misdeeds than to have the hiring department discover it and assume the candidate was concealing that information. Past activities may be explained and overlooked, but any breach of trust is often the automatic disqualifier.

Lengthy background checks are intended to find activities that may help background investigators gauge a candidate's honesty and integrity. After all, trust is paramount in a profession where everyone must trust each other with their lives. Candidates, therefore, are often subjected to a polygraph exam, popularly referred to as the "lie detector" test. Unlike what its nickname implies, the test does not directly test whether a person is lying but tests a body's autonomic response systems that may trigger responses. These responses are often tied to background information already obtained by the background investigators to gauge trustworthiness.

The **polygraph examination** measures the body's physiological changes when asked questions. The exam consists of a series of tests where participants are asked a variety of questions. Test questions include "baseline" innocuous calibration control questions that measures a person's emotional and physical state and actual measured questions. Physiological anomalies in answering these questions compared with baseline questions indicate nervousness and other signs of a "probable lie." In other words, a person's response to baseline questions, which are answered truthfully, will produce a consistent measurement. When deception occurs, (in theory) physiological measurements will differ significantly from the responses to baseline questions that are answered.

While the polygraph examination is not considered perfect and many people have boasted of "beating" or "gaming" the test using various techniques,[8] polygraph examiners often counter with the argument that the test measures body functions that are impossible to control. The polygraph examination measures the body's *autonomic nervous system,* which cannot be consciously controlled. Autonomic body functions include heart rate, perspiration, respiratory rate, pupil dilation, and blood pressure.

The actual test lasts approximately one to three hours. As mentioned, the entire polygraph examination consists of a series of exams and not a single test. Collectively, the test, at least in principle, is supposed to measure a candidate's trustworthiness. Recall that trustworthiness is considered the most important factor in police hiring and is most often the disqualifier even for candidates who excel physically or during tests. Federal hiring for law enforcement positions typically consist of:

- A pretest interview administered by examiners allows the hiring agency to inquire about medical conditions and other factors that may affect the outcome and validity of the test. In addition, the initial interview gives the agency a chance to explain the procedures of the test and underscore the seriousness of the test. This explanation discourages applicants from trying to "game" the system to influence the validity of the test results. In addition, applicants are given consent procedure information.
- During the test, electrodes and a blood pressure monitor (sphygmomanometer), and a pneumograph, which measures respiration rates, are attached to the test subject. A series of questions are asked in ten to fifteen second intervals. These questions include a combination of control ques-

tions and relevant questions. In theory, deceptive answers will trigger a measured response while baseline control questions and truthful answers will be constant.

- A post-test interview is given to the subject after the exam is administered. Subjects are sometimes given opportunities to explain answers that were deemed deceptive or even elicit admission of wrongdoings that were not previously disclosed during the application process.
- For more details of the type of tests and procedures, see http://www.fas.org/sgp/othergov/polygraph/ota/varieties.html

The polygraph examination is just one tool in a variety of methods used to assess the trustworthiness of a candidate. Specifically, departments often use the polygraph examination for eliciting negative information that was not previously disclosed by the applicant. In other words, the hiring department is interested in determining whether a candidate is using deception by concealing some element of the applicant's past. A polygraph inconsistency can give a skilled investigator a prompt to further inquire about certain elements of a person's past.

Despite its usefulness, the polygraph is one of the most controversial devices that departments and agencies employ. Notice that it is used primarily during hiring but never used to determine the innocence or guilt of a person. In fact, if the lie detector test was that effective, there would be no need to conduct investigations. Investigators would simply apply the test to everyone. The primary source of controversy is revealed in its nickname, the "lie detector" test, implying that it can tell whether a person is lying. However, the machine simply measures physiological responses to stimuli, in this case, questions being asked by an examiner. It cannot tell if a person is lying or not, since that is a psychological response. However, since it is a type of scientific instrument, it is often considered by lay people to be a legitimate scientific procedure.

The power of tying scientific inquiry to something abstract, such as telling the truth, gives the impression of objectivity. Legal scholar Samuel Highleyman explained in 1958, that the lie detector was initially "heralded as a scientific instrument immune from a 'lawyers oratory,' and endowed with the ability to protect the innocent, expose the guilty, expedite justice, reduce court costs and discourage false claims."[9] Any device that can accurately decipher truth from lies can virtually eliminate lawyers whose function is to convince a lay juror of guilt or innocent. This is especially useful in eliminating the imperfect human factor in legal inquiry, which has produced hundreds of wrongful convictions in the past. For instance, the Innocence Project, a group of legal volunteers have exonerated hundreds of innocent individuals convicted of crimes. Therefore, according to Highleyman, the polygraph when first conceived was considered an infallible scientific instrument that was a "panacea for the ills that perennially beset the administration of justice."

Today, however, lie detection is considered a pseudoscience and polygraph results are not admissible as valid scientific evidence in a courtroom. In fact, the issue has been debated in academic and legal communities, where it is viewed with skepticism. [10] The admissibility of scientific evidence in the courtroom stems primarily from several legal standards deriving precedence from previous cases:

First, the *Frye Standard* (Frye v. United States, 1923), states that scientific evidence must be "generally accepted by the scientific community" in order to be considered admissible to the courts. This standard has been superseded by the **Daubert Standard,** in 1993. [11]

Second, the courts rely on the *Daubert Standard* where the admissibility of evidence is determined by a judge who considers whether the evidence is derived from the scientific method. That is, it must be based on empirical testing, falsifiable, and peer reviewed in a publication. The original case dealt with expert testimony, but the idea behind the standard is that the scientific evidence must pass the rigors of the scientific community.

The scientific community has pointed to many flaws with the polygraph examination as being an apparatus to detect lies. First, the scientific validity of the test is highly questioned by the scientific community. The National Research Council's blue-ribbon panel, in 2003, conducted a study of the examination and found no evidence of polygraph validity (see http://www.nas.edu/nrc/). The American Psychological Association (APA) agreed with the panel's finding, citing the inherent nature of deception in the test that cannot be disentangled from the objective measurements, which makes it impossible to validate the test.

Second, experts question the reliability of the test. For example, researchers found that the commonly used Control Question Test (CQT), which compares responses to relevant questions to control questions, detects deception better than chance but has unacceptably high error rates. The test has high rates of *false positives* (wrongly identifying truthful subjects as lying) and *false negatives* (failing to detect deceptive individuals).

Finally, there is evidence that the polygraph exams can be beaten. According to the APA, physical movements, psychological interventions, and pharmacological agents can affect the test results. In addition, researchers have found the use of benefits and penalties by testers influenced the results of the test. For instance, threats to a subject as well as psychopathy can skew test results. This is especially relevant for police applicants since polygraph examinations are administered under high stress to applicants who have substantial employment consequences for failing the exam.

POLYGRAPHS AND THE COURTS

Due to the lack of general acceptance by the scientific community based on the Daubert Standard and subsequent legal rulings and standards, as well as other issues with the polygraph examination, the courts have generally ruled that polygraph examination evidence is not admissible in court. The inadmissibility of polygraphs as scientific evidence was cemented in 1998 by the US Supreme Court, who ruled in US v. Scheffer that polygraph results were inadmissible in court-martial decisions.

Newer forms of lie detection tests are also controversial. The latest version is Functional Magnetic Resonance Imaging (FMRI) technology, which uses neuroimaging in the form of MRI scans in order to detect changes in brain activity during questioning. The scans detect changes in blood and oxygen levels in the brain in response to some sort of stimulus. The jury is still out (pardon the pun) on the admissibility and validity of fMRI as a more accurate form of lie detection. Despite these scientific advances in brain imagery technology, the art of lie detecting remains a controversial part of policing.

THE POLICE ACADEMY

Once a recruit passes the interview process, which includes a baseline physical test, psychological tests, and lengthy background investigation, he or she enters the police academy. The advent of the police academy was a key part of the reform era of police professionalization. Recall that police were criticized for being corrupt and incompetent. The police academy was designed to be a training school for police recruits as based on standardization, physical training, and legal and technical knowledge.

The police academy consists of classroom and practical instruction which lasts between twelve weeks and one year. Recruits often take a variety of courses, such as state law, criminal investigations, patrol procedures, computer skills, and even cultural sensitivity training. In addition, practical courses are taken that involve practical knowledge, such as self-defense, first aid, firearms training, and traffic control.

Police academies are often run by a law enforcement agency. Larger departments oftentimes run their own academies, such as with the Los Angeles Sheriff's Department. Police academies can also be run by local community colleges that can serve as regional training centers. Some individuals pay for their own academy training before applying for employment in a law enforcement agency.

Once recruits complete academy training, they must pass a state licensing exam. In Texas, recruits are required to take the Texas Commission on Law

Enforcement Officer Standards and Education (TCLEOSE) Basic Peace Officer Licensing Exam. In Michigan, the equivalent test is the Michigan Commission on Law Enforcement Standards (MCOLES). There are also national versions of these tests that some departments accept. These licensing exams are written tests on a variety of questions that include reading comprehension, writing, math, and logic.

CONTROVERSY: POLICE ACADEMY STRESS TRAINING

In principle, the police academy is designed to prepare officers with the knowledge and skills to perform police work. However, the method of instruction, *stress training*, has a greater purpose. **Stress training** is a type of training that is based on creating a high-stress environment for recruits. This stress level is created by instructors who constantly barrage recruits with intense exercises, yelling, insults, etc. Academy stress is designed to mimic the highly stressful environment police officers face daily on the job. In other words, if a recruit cannot handle the stress in an academy setting, such as being yelled at, how can he or she handle it while on patrol?

Stress training was adopted from the military during police professionalization in the reform era in order to create a more uniform police department where officers limited the use of discretion. O. W. Wilson, who was a World War II veteran and retired US Army colonel, with other leading police reformers, adopted many military policies, procedures, and command structures. Reformers felt that stress training used in boot camp with its rigorous regimen was very effective in mentally and physically preparing soldiers for combat. Trainees must follow exact instructions and never question authority within a chain of command. In principle, the end result of stress training is the disciplined officer who follows policies and procedures and will not act on emotional reactions, and more importantly, will not show favoritism or bias, which was the source of corruption.

Despite fitting well with police professionalism, academy stress training is not without controversy. Stress training does not adequately train officers how to effectively communicate.[12] It can be argued that despite its intended purpose of teaching officers how to stay calm when being yelled at and belittled, one must question how often members of the public get to yell at a police officer. One would argue that that generally does not happen. The police, however, in learning in the academy to assert a command presence (a type of forced respect and control that officers demand in any given situation), often do the yelling. Is this the best way to handle volatile situations?

Researchers have criticized police academies, especially during professionalism, for not keeping up with the demands of today's policing. The trend in policing for the past few decades has been toward the direction of community policing, a policing philosophy that emphasizes the interconnectivity between the police and communities through active partnerships. Recruits are often evaluated on completing tasks but spend little time developing problem-solving, interpersonal, and decision-making abilities. One of the most important skills of an officer today is the ability to effectively communicate. However, many individuals who may be good communicators can be eliminated during training if they do not fit into the existing culture.

CONTROVERSY: POLICE ACADEMY— WEEDING OUT INDIVIDUALS

Stress training systematically "weed-outs" certain recruits who do not fit into the existing convention of the police officer. The elimination process is done in two ways: (1) Individuals who cannot pass physical litmus tests and (2) those who cannot successfully adapt to the culture. [13]

Litmus tests are single-factor tests that are given to recruits to gauge future success or failure. Cadets are presented with a series of these single-factor pass/fail tests throughout academy training. For example, if a recruit cannot complete an obstacle course within a certain time, they are kicked out of the academy. These litmus tests, in theory, are important in establishing a minimum level of competency that ensures all officers meet physical and mental standards.

Litmus tests are not controversial and are found in virtually every professional occupation, from physicians to attorneys. However, controversy arises when we take a closer look at *who* gets screened out by these tests in policing. The answer, historically, has been women and minority groups. Note that women and minorities are the two primary demographics that police departments are heavily recruiting today to better reflect the community as part of community policing. Women, specifically, who generally have weaker upper body strength compared to men, have historically had difficulties with certain physical activities and tests. For instance, when the US Marine Corps tried to integrate more women into combat roles in 2014, they found systematic barriers that limited their participation. The Marines found that more than half (55 percent) of female Marines in boot camp could not complete the minimum three pull-ups. [14]

Similarly, one litmus test in policing that has eliminated the largest number of female cadets is scaling a six-foot wall. The LAPD, for example, requires applicants to scale "the wall," at the LAPD police academy as a pass/fail requirement. It is one of the biggest reasons why women are eliminated from the department, with nearly one third of women who take the test failing to pull themselves over, compared to only 5 percent of men. [15] In 1994, that controversy drew public attention with the murder of female rookie LAPD officer Christy Lynne Hamilton, who was a recruit who struggled to scale the wall.

TWO SIDES OF "THE WALL"

1. Supporters of keeping the wall in place point to Officer Hamilton's story—she was shot to death. Critics argue that her marginally passing the wall after building a replica wall in her back yard to practice means she was not the best candidate for the job. Note that the LAPD allows one retake of the physical abilities test and offers special training to help struggling recruits. Critics further point to the lowering of standards in policing in general, which began with lowering, then eliminating minimum height requirements for officers (from 6' to 5'10" to 5'8" to 5'0" and some departments with no requirement).

2. Critics of the wall argue that it represents an obsolete barrier that eliminates many women who would make effective officers. The LAPD during 1994 sought to boost the number of women officers from 15 percent to 43 percent. Moreover, women, it is argued, are better communicators and fit well with community policing, where communications skills are paramount in establishing bonds with the community. Policing, it is argued, is no longer a profession that requires brute strength that favors the ex-military strongman type. Instead, it is one that requires close contact with neighborhoods and strong communication skills.

CONTROVERSY: POLICE ACADEMY CULTURAL TRANSMISSION, MASCULINITY

Recall that the police culture and its strong worldview were blamed for the growing police-community tensions and ultimately social upheavals in large urban cities, such as New York and Los Angeles. A major part of police reform after such events, as indicated by ad-hoc committee reports (Knapp Commission, Christopher Commission, etc.) was to lessen the impact of the police subculture. However, lessening the influence of this culture is very difficult, in large part, due to academy training.

The police academy not only serves as an environment for instruction, but also an important means of socialization. Police academy instructors are typically veteran officers, who in addition to passing along instruction, also pass along wisdom and knowledge gained from experience on the job. Specifically, **storytelling** is a major component of the academy. These stories, as presented, glorify the crime-control aspects of the job while underscoring the dangers associated with police work. This emphasis on the real and perceived dangers and risks of the job reinforces the priority of being a police officer: law enforcement and crime control over "soft" mandates, such as service and order maintenance (which are the majority of police work).

Individuals who do not share in the belief system typically do not pass the academy. Recall that the police subculture stresses loyalty to other officers ("blue wall of silence" of not reporting misconduct) and the importance of crime control ("thin blue line" as police are the only force standing between orderly society and chaos). Note that those recruits who are receptive to the storytelling and socialization can sometimes suffer from "blue flame syndrome," where enthusiastic rookies get teased by their veteran peers for excessive bravado and standing out while off-duty by broadcasting their police identity instead of blending in.

To get recruits to internalize the belief system, one of the main purposes of training is social conditioning to create group solidarity through desocialization/resocialization. Akin to military boot camp, police academies attempt to replace the individual's beliefs and behaviors with that of the group. In the military, the idea is to break down and eradicate the civilian personality traits and replace them with the group loyalty. This is done, perhaps, through push-ups as a form of punishment, humiliation, etc. that results in the individual internalization of the group identity. The result is a fiercely loyal and selfless individual who perceives the group, in this case other police officers, as a surrogate family. Group solidarity is important for building trust. The paramount concern of all police officers: you must be able to trust other officers with your life because during emergency situations, they are the only ones who you can rely on for assistance.

Academy training, however, can be very hostile to those individuals who do not "fit in." The academy creates a "bubble" that is often criticized as hypermasculine, sexist, and sometimes racist. Some police researchers have argued that there is a hidden curriculum in the police academy that encourages masculinity amongst recruits, with both male and female recruits. Masculinity, it is argued, is essential to police work. Consequently, a hostile environment is created for women and less-masculine male cadets. Cadets watch and learn from instructors and from each other, which results in perceived exaggerated differences between men and women, excluding women students in social activities, and belittling women in general, often referring to them as "bitches."[16] The hostile academy environment translates into a hostile work environment, which can explain the historically low percentage of women police officers.

QUITTING POLICE WORK: IT'S NOT FOR EVERYONE

Becoming a police officer is not for everyone. Successful candidates usually have similar qualities and beliefs, which means that the police profession is a very homogenous group (everyone acts and thinks very similarly). Individuals who have priorities and beliefs that differ from the group often find themselves isolated and eventually drop out of the academy.

Recruits typically value the following:

1. **Physical training**—along with instructors who emphasize the real and perceived dangers of the profession, police recruits typically feel the physical training is of the utmost importance. The job is dangerous and they must be physically prepared for any altercation at any given moment. Physical training is part of making the recruit fit for the job. Candidates who do not value this aspect of the job are in the minority.
2. **Self-defense**—Similar to physical training, recruits view self-defense as something that can save their lives. Stories and videos are shared with recruits of seemingly routine traffic stops that turn deadly instantly. The only thing that can save their lives is their self-defense training.
3. **Marksmanship** – Recruits must pass firearms proficiency tests in the academy. Shooting is considered very important to both recruits and instructors and similar to physical training and self-defense, can save a recruit's life. However, in reality, the vast majority of police officers never fire their service weapon during their entire career. In other words, it is a relatively rare occurrence. According to the 2011 NYPD Annual Firearms Discharge Report (see http://www.nyc.gov/html/ nypd/downloads/pdf/analysis_and_planning/nypd_annual_firearms_ discharge_report_2011.pdf) ninety-two incidents of police shootings were recorded. The report states, "In context, the rarity is even more apparent: in a city of 8.2 million people, from a Department of nearly 35,000 uniformed members who interacted with citizens in approximately 23 million instances, 62 officers were involved in 36 incidents of intentional firearms discharges during an adversarial conflict, with 19 subjects injured and nine killed."

As mentioned, recruits and instructors in police academies value crime-control oriented activities and training. They deemphasize "other" instructional activities, such as the classroom lessons. For example, recruits often view cultural sensitivity training as something that is considered not "real" police work and is put in place due to political correctness. In other words, anything that is not crime control oriented is not considered *real* police work.

The problem is—if police reformers are trying to change the police sub-culture, how can they do so at the police academy that filters out recruits that may change the culture? These individuals may have different perspectives on what is important and what is not. In other words, many individuals who deemphasize the crime control aspects of police work may be in a better position to change the police culture.

WHY IS THIS IMPORTANT?

The vast majority of police work is not crime-control and law enforcement oriented; instead, it is mostly order maintenance and peace keeping. So what do the police actually do?

According to criminologist David Bayley, only 13 percent of crime in the United States reported is classified as a serious crime. Moreover, patrol offi-cers on average make only nineteen arrests per year.[17] Nearly two-thirds of police work consists of patrol and responding to calls, with the rest split evenly between crime investigation, traffic, and administrative duties. In other words, police work is mostly order maintenance.

Police academies, by design, create a homogenous group—important for creating group solidarity in a dangerous occupation. They do this by weeding out individuals who do not fit with the group and by desocialization/resocial-ization. This process creates an officer with the following traits:

1. Authoritative and conservative—they are very law-and-order types
2. Loyalty and trust are paramount
3. Having an "us versus them" mentality

FIELD TRAINING

One of the most influential periods in a new officer's career is during field training. **Field training** is a training period immediately after the academy when a new officer is assigned a field training officer (FTO) whose primary role is to further educate the new officer while evaluating officer perfor-mance and competency. Some agencies employ field training programs that are divided into different phases, each phase is designed to expose the officer to different functions of police work, each with different levels of respon-sibility for the rookie officer. Field training can last from several months to a year in most departments. At the end of the field training period, the rookie officer who performs satisfactorily will pass his or her probationary period and become a full-status officer. In many departments, the new officer can work alone in a patrol car.

Field training was designed to fill the gap between classroom training and the "real world" of police work. The inception of formalized field training was influenced by the recommendations of three national commissions and the first law enforcement accreditation body: the 1931 Wickersham Commission; 1967 President's Commission on Law Enforcement and Administration; 1973 National Advisory Commission on Criminal Justice Standards and Goals, and the Commission on Accreditation for Law Enforcement Agencies (CALEA). The CALEA recommended the incorporation of formalized field training into training to create uniform standards for professionalization.

The first formalized field training program was conceived in 1972 in San Jose, California. According to the **San Jose field training model**, specially selected and trained FTOs provided rookie officers with tangible street training to ensure the new officer was not only familiar with department policies but could effectively handle responsibilities before doing patrol work alone. FTOs also serve a critical evaluative role during field training, when a rookie officer can still be weeded out of the department based on the evaluation of the FTOs, but oftentimes remedial additional training can be recommended.

One of the controversies with police field training administered in the past few decades under the San Jose model of training has been the cultivation or cultural transmission of a **"warrior" mentality**. Many elements of academy training that stress officer awareness in critical areas, such as racial sensitivity training, can be undermined by field training officers with a variation of the proverbial first day advice for rookies, "forget everything they taught you in the academy . . . your real training starts now." This warrior mind-set refers to the mental toughness that officers need to maintain in an intensely dangerous and hostile working environment, no matter what the difficulties are. Hypervigilance is communicated to rookie officers in order to uphold the most important objective or "first rule" in law enforcement, which is to survive and go home at the end of the shift. Having a warrior mentality means the officer is mentally prepared to "react violently" to any given situation.

The hyperaggressive mentality can develop negative ramifications for the relationship between police and citizens. According to the *Harvard Law Review*, warrior officers tend to aggravate situations that increase the risk of violence to the officer, as well as future citizen-officer encounters.[18] Furthermore, the warrior mentality encourages tactics that needlessly create use-of-force situations and hostile rhetoric that further strains community relationships and undermines public trust.

Efforts to ameliorate this aggressive stance in relation to training have been the introduction of an entirely different paradigm in police field training: the **Police Training Officer (PTO) model**. Developed by the Reno Police Department in Reno, California, and the US Department of Justice's Community Oriented Policing Services (COPS), the PTO model of field training stresses independent problem-based learning that encourages critical thinking in complex situations. The trainee is encouraged to utilize community resources and members under more realistic conditions in the community context. Performance evaluations are not based on a checklist of actions the rookie officer must take, but instead based on holistic solutions and critical problem-solving skills that were developed entirely by the trainee. Several core competencies are stressed instead of phases based on location or other more rigid criteria.

Officers trained under the PTO model tend to fall under the "guardian" metaphor for officers. The **guardian mindset** gives priority to service as part of community policing, over strictly crime fighting that was emphasized under the more traditional FTO-based San Jose model of field training. According to the Harvard Law Review, the guardian mindset stresses communication over commands, cooperation rather than compliance, and legitimacy of police power instead of authority. This is achieved through incorporating "nonenforcement" training blocks where rookie officers spend time in meaningful communications with community members where elements of law enforcement are entirely removed. Ideally, officers' contact with citizens should not ask for identification, not run background checks, not issue tickets, and not make arrests.

Whether this model works is debatable, but it does challenge the current paradigm of training.

CHAPTER SUMMARY

Police selection and training serves to reinforce the perpetuate the police subculture. While many agencies today desire to soften the culture, which has been previously found to be a primary cause of police-citizen friction leading to urban riots, selection and training undermine efforts to attract and retain individuals who can change the organization.

Individuals who significantly differ from existing officers are eliminated during the selection and training process. These individuals who can potentially change the organizational culture must pass a series of litmus tests and "fit in" with the existing group. Most these candidates are eliminated, resulting in those who are left to add to the homogeniety of the organization.

Individuals who successfully navigate the training are socialized with the emphasis on crime control and law enforcement in the academy. Recruits are frequently warned of the dangers of the job through academy training, field training, and storytelling by veteran officers. The underemphasis of service and order maintenance activities, which are the majority of police work, can leave officers ill-prepared for community policing duties.

To address the issues of today, police training has been evolving the past few decades. For instance, some departments are replacing traditional field training under the San Jose FTO model which emphasized adherence to policy and procedures, to the Reno PTO model, which stresses problem solving and smart discretion.

NOTES

1. Michael S. Mc Campbell, "Field Training for Police Officers: The State of the Art," *National Institute of Justice* (1987), https://www.ncjrs.gov/pdffiles1/nij/105574.pdf.

2. Nicholas Katzenbach et al., *The Challenge of Crime in a Free Society: A Report by the President's Commission on Law Enforcement and Administration of Justice* (Washington, DC: United States Printing Office, 1967), https://www.ncjrs.gov/pdffiles1/nij/42.pdf.

3. Simone Weichselbaum and Beth Schwartzapfel, "When Veterans Become Cops, Some Bring War Home," *USA Today*, March 30, 2017.

4. Matthew J. Monnot, Stuart W. Quirk, Michael Hoerger, and Linda Brewer, "Racial Bias in Personality Assessment: Using the MMPI-2 to Predict Psychiatric Diagnoses of African American and Caucasian Chemical Dependency Inpatients," *Psychological Assessment* 21, no. 2 (2009): 137–151. doi: 10.1037/a0015316.

5. Gordon C. Hall, Nagayama Bansal, and Irene Lopez, "Ethnicity and Psychopathology: A Meta-Analytic Review of 31 Years of Comparative MMPI/MMPI-2 Research," *Psychological Assessment* 11, no. 2 (1999): 186–197.

6. Jose M. Cortina, Mary L. Doherty, Neal Schmitt, Gary Kaufman, and Richard G. Smith, "The 'Big Five' Personality Factors in the IPI and MMPI: Predictors of Police Performance," *Personnel Psychology* 45 (1992): 119–140. doi: 10.1111/j.1744-6570.1992.tb00847.x.

7. James N. Butcher, "Use of the MMPI in Personnel Selection," In *New Developments in the Use of the MMPI* (Minneapolis: University of Minnesota Press, 1979), 165–201.

8. Christopher J. Patrick and William G. Iacono, "Psychopathy, Threat, and Polygraph Test Accuracy," *Journal of Applied Psychology* 74, no. 2 (1989): 347–355.

9. Samuel L. Highleyman, "The Deceptive Certainty of the Lie Detector," *Hastings Law Journal* 10 (1958): 47–64.

10. Rachel Adelson, "The Polygraph in Doubt," *Monitor on Psychology* 35, no. 7 (2004): 71.

11. Daubert v. Merrell Dow Pharmaceuticals, 1993.

12. David Bradford and Joan E. Pynes, "Police Academy Training: Why Hasn't It Kept up with Practice?" *Police Quarterly* 2, no. 3 (1999): 283–301. doi: 10.1177/109861119900200302.

13. Bruce L. Berg, "First Day at the Police Academy: Stress-Reaction-Training as a Screening-Out Technique," *Journal of Contemporary Criminal Justice* 6, no. 2 (1990): 89–105.

14. Brad Knickerbocker, "Just Three Pull-Ups: Too Many for Women in the Marine Corps?" *The Christian Science Monitor*, January 4, 2014.

15. Marc Lacey, "LAPD's 'Wall' May Topple as Part of Entrance Exam: Police: Scaling the Six-Foot Barrier is a Key Obstacle for Applicants, Particularly Women. Critics say It's Obsolete," *Los Angeles Times,* April 1,1994, http://articles.latimes.com/1994-04-01/news/mn-41017_1_police-academy.

16. Anastasia Prokos and Irene Padavic, "'There Oughtta Be a Law against Bitches': Masculinity Lessons in Police Academy Training," *Work and Organization* 9 (2002): 439–459. doi: 10.1111/1468-0432.00168.

17. David H. Bayley, *Police for the Future* (New York: Oxford University Press, 1994).

18. Seth Stoughton, "Law Enforcement's 'Warrior' Problem," *Harvard Law Review* 128, no. 255 (2015).

Chapter Five

The Police Officer Experience and Changes to an Individual

The previous chapter discussed the hiring and training process when a person becomes a police officer and some of the changes to the individual have already started to occur. This chapter further examines the transformation to police officer as one's primary identity. In most professions, one's identity is not often predominantly defined by an occupation. However, for others, the powerful socialization process mentioned in chapter 2 coupled with a strong public response furthers police officer as one's primary identity. For instance, an off-duty officer in a social setting, meeting people for the first time who find out his or her occupation, may elicit a variety of reactions based solely on his or her work identity, ranging from appreciation and inquisition to discomfort and perhaps hostility. Either way, there is usually a strong response that results in the officer experiencing very little separation between work life and social life.

Rookie officers quickly see drastic changes in their lives, from how they view themselves to how others perceive and treat them. In addition, they are shaped by academy and field training, where the individual is socialized into the culture of police work and strong, sometimes life-long bonds have already developed with their academy classmates. This process is further strengthened as the officer immerses him- or herself into the culture, worldview, and ultimate identity through the following topics that are covered in this chapter:

The effects of shift work
The effects of patrol work
The uniform, gun, and badge

If there is doubt that the police identity is intense and present early in an officer's career, consider the following story.

THE BLUE BROTHERHOOD: OFFICER ASHLEY GUINDON

On February 27, 2016, newly minted 28-year-old rookie officer Ashley Guindon started her first shift at Prince William County Police Department in Virginia. She was sworn in two days earlier. As she responded to her first domestic call that early Saturday evening, the suspect, Ronald Williams Hamilton, opened fire on Officer Guindon and her partners as they approached the door, killing her and wounding her partners on her first day on the job.

The following week, thousands of police officers from throughout the country descended on West Springfield, Massachusetts, where the rookie officer was buried. Her procession of hundreds of police and other emergency vehicles stretched for miles as their red and blue lights lit the evening darkness of a winding highway. Thousands of mourning police officers from around the country wept for the new officer they had never met. In fact, very few officers within her own department knew her well. However, to a police officer, Guindon's death was equivalent to the death of a family member.

In what other profession would the death of a colleague in the same field elicit such a strong emotional response that colleagues would be willing to travel the country to attend the funeral?

A BRIEF HISTORIC CONTEXT

Recall that during the reform era of policing, policing sought to professionalize in order to shed the image of the corrupt, brutal, and incompetent officer of the political era. By design, officers became insulated from the public. Active walking beats were replaced by reactive vehicle patrol where they could cover more ground and respond more quickly to emergencies, which was a performance metric under professional standards, namely the UCR.

The negative ramification of being insulated in a vehicle was police becoming isolated from the public. Officers became nameless, faceless entities that strictly enforced the law without bias and prejudice. Whereas the night watchman was a member of the community with a day job and only patrolled at night, the modern day police officer is not considered a full member of the community and works in isolation. Again, this was by design to prevent the slippery slope of corruption.

Today, policing has evolved into a profession with many inherent contradictions as a manifestation of professionalization. One may say police are victims of their own success. On the one hand, police salaries, education, and expertise have gone up considerably. While Vollmer's vision of the college-educated, highly specialized, scientific crime fighter has not come to fruition, there are many elements of police that are professional. Police have positioned themselves to be the universally acknowledged experts in crime control. By incorporating crime control technologies, such as two-way radios, patrol vehicles, and 9-1-1 dispatch systems, they have been able to improve on crime control metrics, such as the UCR.

On the other hand, police professionalization has raised expectations for responding to all acts of deviance, whether they are criminal in nature or not. Police have essentially become a panacea, or "cure-all," for all social ills. They are asked to respond to non-crime related matters that many officers feel are frivolous, ranging from noise complaints to snakes found in houses. Calling 9-1-1 has become so popular that in many large cities early systems were inundated with non-emergency calls that made it difficult for callers with real emergencies to get through. This social expectation for the police to "do something," has affected the police officer experience, even while off duty.

WHAT IS IT LIKE TO BE A POLICE OFFICER?

The moment a new officer dons the police uniform and badge, he or she dons the full history and reputation of the profession, including the misdeeds of the past, or "sins of the father." The new officer is subject to the same treatments and biases for and against them, by strangers. Famed police novelist Joseph Wambaugh's wrote about this phenomenon in his 1975 novel, *The Choirboys*, where fictional LAPD officer Francis Tanaguchi was taken aback when complete strangers shot at him and his partner, not knowing who he was as a person, but just treating him badly and shooting at him simply because he was a person in a blue uniform. [1] For most new officers, similar experiences of being treated with a police-stereotyping lens slowly transforms the person's master status as police officer.

For most new officers, police work is a 24/7 job where he or she is always a police officer. The new officer, through training and hearing stories of the dangers of the job, becomes hypervigilant on and off duty. The officer becomes increasingly socially isolated from non-police individuals and groups. They tend to increasingly reject their friends who were friends prior to becoming a police officer, and their friends increasingly reject them being a police officer. Over a short period of time, the police identity becomes the dominant identity of the officer. [2]

Contributing to this police identity and social isolation is shift work, which is a work schedule that takes place outside of the normal 9 a.m. to 5 p.m. hours. When combined with the inherent dangers of the profession, shift

work contributes to group introversion and the police subculture while affecting the mental and physical health of the officer.

SHIFT WORK

Shift work describes a profession that provides around-the-clock, twenty-
four-hour service, seven days per week, for the entire year, including holi-
days. Work is divided into fixed "shifts," which includes atypical evening
and nightshifts, in order to provide gapless service. Shift work is usually
found in emergency services, such as firefighting and hospitals, where service must be uninterrupted.

Police officers typically work in shifts. The length of their shifts varies
depending on the police department. Some departments require officers to
work in eight-hour shifts for five days a week, while other departments may
require ten or twelve hour shifts with fewer days worked per week, often
called "flextime." Shift work in general has some positive and negative consequences.

Officers typically like working flextime schedules, which means more
days off. When the LAPD switched most of its shifts to a 3/12 schedule
(three-day and four-day, twelve-hour workday), officers responded positively. When the *Los Angeles Times* interviewed one LAPD officer, Stephen
Knight, he stated positively, "I love it. I love that I get to spend more days
with my family. . . . I can be there when my sons get home from school and
help them with homework. I'm recharged when I get back to work."[3]

In addition to the days off work, many officers enjoy working atypical
hours that are not the common 9:00 a.m. to 5:00 p.m. typical workday. Many
officers enjoy working evening and night shifts (a.k.a. "graveyard shifts"),
typically from around 9:00 p.m. to 7:00 a.m. Some officers prefer the different environment the night shift offers, where the crimes are escalated at
night. There is less traffic and hustle and bustle of daytime business at night,
for officers to deal with. The officers who prefer nightshifts like the fact that
at night, it is the proverbial "just us and the bad guys."

There is often less administrative supervision and oversight during a night
shift. Police administrators and high-level officers typically work normal
hours, which means less scrutiny during night shifts. Most departments operate with a shift supervisor, who is typically a sergeant in charge. This allows
officers more autonomy. An interview by the *Sacramento Press* with Sacramento, California, police Sergeant Patrick Kohles shows the affinity of some
officers for night shifts. He expressed, "I think it [nightshift] is the best work
in the department if you have to work patrol. The work is fun. I also think the
teams are a lot closer with one another because we don't have access to many
of the other resources that are available on other watches. The officers and

supervisors develop a stronger bond with one another, which often carries over into their personal lives."[4]

For many officers with children, working nightshifts allows them to see their children off to school, pick them up from school, be there for dinner, and leave for work around bedtime. Despite these benefits, working at night has significant drawbacks that may adversely affect the officer mentally and physically.

THE HAZARDS OF SHIFT WORK

The most obvious effects on officers that work the night shift are significant health ramifications. A 2012 study found that police officers are more prone to heart disease, obesity, and being overweight from the stress and fatigue from shift work. The researchers compared day shift officers with non-day shift officers and found that those who did not work during day shifts got significantly less sleep (less than 6 hours per day) and poorer quality sleep.[5] The researchers also noted an alarming trend where 83 percent of officers said that occasionally they would wake up early for work the day after working a night or evening shift. This meant the officer was working with virtually no sleep.[6]

While we may view officers as generally young and healthy, sleep deprivation has some serious consequences for officers and the public. A Harvard study published in the *Journal of the American Medical Association* looked at nearly 5,000 officers and found that those with sleep disorders (nearly 40 percent):[7]

Had a 25 percent higher risk of expressing uncontrolled anger towards a suspect or citizen, with a 35 percent chance of having a citizen complaint against them.

Had 51 percent higher chance of falling asleep while driving on duty.

Had a 43 percent higher chance of making a serious administrative mistake.

Had an eight-time higher rate of sleep apnea (waking up repeatedly due to intermittent breathing). This is nearly 33 percent of officers.

According to the study, nearly 25 percent of officers fell asleep at the wheel one or two times per month. This "drowsy driving" has contributed to motor vehicle crashes as being the most common cause of death among police officers.

Another study found that overall, police officers suffered from sleep disorders, with the problem significantly exacerbated by shift work. The Buffalo Cardio-Metabolic Occupation Police Stress study monitored the sleep patterns of 363 officers over a fifteen-year period and found that 54 percent of officers suffered from poor sleep quality, breaking down to 44 percent of day-shift officers, 60 percent for afternoon swing shifts, and 70 percent for officers working the night shift. [8]

Criminologist Bryan Vila, who directs the Sleep and Performance Research Center at Washington State University, runs computer simulation experiments on officers with various levels of fatigue and sleep deprivation, gauging critical functions of officers. The simulation research showed that officers at the end of their work week were significantly more fatigued which resulted in poorer police/citizens outcomes. Moreover, night shift officers at their end of their work week were significantly less able to effectively de-escalate encounters and find cooperative outcomes.

Sacramento police officer Chris Taylor explains a typical scenario, stating, "I'd work out really hard after my shift. I'd then drive home and fall into bed." The problem of sleep deprivation was so bad that the Los Angeles County Sheriff's Department (LASD) dropped its 3/12 work schedule due to concerns of public safety, in 2006. A *Los Angeles Times* interview with LASD captain Buddy Goldman explained that the schedule made it hard for deputies to attend mandatory training and appear in court after a twelve-hour shift.

The day and times of the shifts can have ramifications on service. Meaning, whether departments have a 5/8 (days per week/hours per day), 4/10, or 3/12 shift may affect police performance. Note that many of the effects of shift work often affect sleep patterns. Many officers working 3/12 work night schedules often switch back and forth between sleeping during the daytime during the work week and sleeping at night during their off-work days, to be in sync with sleep patterns of "normal" schedules of friends and family.

The *Los Angeles Times* also noted that moving to a modified shift schedule, such as a 3/12 affects police service and performance. The LAPD conducted a study on the effects of moving to a 3/12 from a 5/8 schedule and found the following:

- Median emergency response times went up from 5.5 minutes to 6.4 minutes.
- Median non-emergency response times went up from 33 minutes to 44.2 minutes.
- Traffic citations declined by 10.5 percent
- Time spent on enforcement activities to reduce crime declined by 13.5 percent
- Overall arrests dropped by 10.3 percent
- Arrests for serious crimes dropped by 14.5 percent
- Sick-time hours increased by 7.1 percent

- The number of times officers had to back up units from other service areas more than doubled, indicating that some areas do not have adequate staffing.

Shift work can also contribute to the police subculture by changing the nature of social interactions amongst officers and reinforcing group solidarity. Recall that one of the major contributors of police violence and misconduct, including not whistleblowing ("the blue wall of silence"), is the police subculture—set of beliefs and values held by officers described as "us versus them."

First, shift work changes the way officers socialize with non-police friends. Newer officers with little seniority often find themselves with non-normal shifts (evening and night shifts). Oftentimes their "weekends" or days off are not the usual Saturdays and Sundays. So, when their friends are having parties, dinners, social gatherings, etc., the officer finds him- or herself working. These officers often have opposite schedules, where they may have their "weekend" days off during the middle of the week, when their friends are at work. Socially, if the officer works night shifts and has Tuesday and Wednesday nights off, the officer cannot attend most, if not all, social events, assuming he or she is invited.

Over time, the officer finds himself being invited less, called less often, etc. and isolated from friends. Adding the fact that many friends may now feel uncomfortable with him around due to his occupation, he soon finds himself isolated by his friends. The officer himself may feel uncomfortable with his old friends. The officer may be faced with moral dilemmas with activities that may not be completely legal during parties, such as the presence of illicit drug use, for example.

Consequently, officers often retreat to their police colleagues. They do this for a couple of main reasons:

- *Shared experiences in a perceived hazardous work environment draw groups together.* According to sociologist Emile Durkheim, group solidarity is reinforced when fighting a common danger. Officers behave similarly, often sharing stories with each in social gatherings. The cohesiveness is especially strong amongst police officers, who consider themselves as family.
- *Shift work makes it convenient for officers to socialize exclusively with each other.* Abnormal work hours are shared with other officers on the same shift make socializing convenient and oftentimes, the only option for many officers. After work drinking is often a favorite activity amongst shift officers. This is where social bonding and storytelling take place and officers destress.

Social activities, such as after work drinking, coupled with shift work, serves to reinforce the "us versus them" mentality held amongst officers. By the nature of their work, this makes changing the police subculture and re-establishing police/citizen ties (a goal under *community policing*) extremely difficult. Contributing to the changes of the officer is patrol work, which exposes officers to a variety of dangers and unknowns.

THE EFFECTS OF PATROL WORK

The cumulative effects of patrol work further change the officer's primary identity from civilian to police.

Recall that a rookie officer's first experience outside of the academy is through a *field training officer* (FTO). The FTO has several important functions for the development of the rookie officer. While FTO is responsible for training and evaluating the rookie to make sure he or she completes the required duties, the FTO also serves as a mentor to integrate the rookie officer culturally and socially. Part of the evaluation of new recruits is how well they "fit" into the culture. FTOs act as role models on how to interact with citizens as well as other officers.

FTOs often help new officers navigate the culture and politics within a department, such as the many unwritten rules, which further engrains the "us versus them" mentality. The most recognized unwritten rule that FTOs often emphasize is the "blue wall of silence" of not reporting fellow officers' minor misconduct. Of course, it is relatively rare that police officers cover up major felonies committed by other officers, as portrayed in many movies. However, there are many instances where police engage in "gray area" activities that may not be completely legal or acceptable for officers. For example, the new officer may be introduced to the concept of "**professional courtesy**," where officers do not issue fellow officers citations for traffic infractions, such as for speeding.

Another example of a gray area—accepting discounts and free food and items at local businesses—is considered a "slippery slope" because officers and rookie officers are usually not permitted to accept these.

Imagine this scenario:

Mr. Sherman who owns a twenty-four-hour local diner often gives free meals to the local police officers. He considers their presence a welcome sight for security reasons, especially at night, and enjoys their company. One day a young officer right out of probation, during a routine traffic stop, pulls over Mr. Sherman who seemed to be swerving a little bit. He recognizes Mr. Sherman, who is slightly above the blood alcohol limit. Instead of giving him a ride home, as was given to him in the past by other officers, the young officer arrests Mr. Sherman for DWI. Consequently, the free meals stop.

Instead of getting praise for a DWI arrest, his fellow officers give the young officer a hard time.

Other unwritten rules are prevalent amongst police officers. In a police forum (see http://forums.officer.com/t10673/) officers share with each other "what not to do," in a thread titled, "Unwritten rules every rookie should know . . ." written by Dukeboy01. The rules include:

1. *Out here, everybody lies.*

    Out on the street, every non-police person you come in contact with will lie to you. The criminals will lie to you because they have to. The victims will lie to you out of embarrassment, to hide their own criminal activity, and to hide all the stupid things they did that led to their being victimized in the first place. Witnesses and other citizens will lie to you just for fun. Always know and just accept that you are never, ever being told the whole story.

2. *They lied to you during training.*

    Most of what you learned in during training will need to be forgotten. Most of what you learned in traing (sic) doesn't work. For example, unlike during training with your classmates, the bad guys on the street will not hold still long enough for you to scream, "Stop, stop, stop!", step back, and deliver a perfect knee strike to the bad guy's common peroneal (sic).

3. *Never take the word of a drunk person over that of a sober person.*

    I cannot count the number of times I have watched a rookie agonize over who to believe in a dispute between a drunk and a sober person. Simplify your life. The drunk is always wrong. The drunk is drunk and therefore, can't remember what happened anyway. Referring back to rule #1, his drunken lies will be stupid and insulting, while the sober person's lies will probably be better thought out and plausible. If you know somebody in the disorder needs to go to jail, and you can't decide which one, take the drunk.

4. *Civilian ride-alongs are not your friends.*

    My department tends to assign civilian riders to new officers, presumably because they will be more eager to get into stuff, and also because the old heads won't take them. Treat the civilian rider, especially one you didn't bring with you but was approved through the chief's office as a spy. Do not tell them war stories about how you and several other officers beat some thug down. Do not show the ride-along all the cool places where you and you partners go to hide when you don't have a call and want to slack off. Assume that everything you say to them will make it's (sic) way back to the chief because it will. Your ride-along may not personally care about the guy you and your buddies had to beat down, but if it's a good story, they'll tell a friend, who'll tell a friend. Remember that "Kevin Bacon" game. Everyone in your city is only six relationships away from your chief and probably quite less.

There are many other examples of unwritten rules and they are all over policing forums, but these were just a few.

A pattern soon emerges from examining these and countless other words of advice to rookie officers: cynicism. **Group cynicism**, which reciprocates with group introversion, produces a group of individuals who do not comfortably associate with untrustworthy "outsiders." Recall Peter K. Manning's "siege mentality" that warned against civilians as reflective of the police subculture.[9]

Criminologist Elizabeth Reuss-Ianni discusses the police subculture, and cynicism goes one step further by asserting that line-officers should not fully trust their supervisors, stating:[10]

- Don't trust a new guy until you have checked him out.
- Don't give the police administration too much activity.
- Keep out of the way of any boss from outside your precinct.
- Don't do the bosses' work for him.
- Don't trust bosses to look out for your interests.
- Don't talk too much or too little.
- Protect your ass.

The increasingly cynical worldview of the officer through training, storytelling, and personal experiences in patrol work as reflective of the police subculture creates a substantial social barrier between the police with the public. This insulation is furthered by the nature of interactions with the public, and symbolically by the police uniform and other symbols of authority.

FURTHER SEPARATION: NEGATIVE INTERACTIONS, UNIFORM, GUN, AND BADGE

The nature of police professional interactions with the public serves to further isolate officers from citizens. Recall that police, in their effort to professionalize during the reform era, minimized their interactions with the public, keeping the nature of the interactions strictly business. While police in recent decades have worked to improve community relations under the community policing model, their primary metric of performance is still based on quantitative crime control measures, such as response times. Consequently, this reactive nature means police respond from call-to-call quickly and efficiently, with little time for positive interactions and building a rapport with community members.

One of the most common ways citizens interact with police is during traffic stops. These stops give police a high level of discretion to give citations, give warnings, etc. Most police stops, especially amongst motorcycle and traffic officers, involve issuing citations. The stop itself is an act of police discretion and is steeped in controversy that ranges from class and racial profiling[11] to police personal experience. Consequently, the nature of police interactions means citizens do not perceive police as "professionals," such as doctors who are perceived as helping people, but instead, view them largely as a punitive organization staffed with biased officers.

THE POLICE UNIFORM

The police uniform was initially rejected during the time of the night watchman. A population wary of a standing army rejected the idea of uniformed officers. However, this attitude changed during professionalism (*Reform Era*), where the goal was for police to gain authority and legitimacy. Police reformers, especially those with military backgrounds, such as O. W. Wilson, felt the uniform conveyed professionalism that demanded respect. Looking sloppy was not accepted for the professional officer under any circumstance. Since the relationship with the community had been severed, officers relied on **command presence**, which is a verbal and nonverbal conveyance of authority, as a deterrent for violence.

The uniform was a key part of this presence, and has been used historically in the military, which served as a model for civilian law enforcement. The police uniform assisted in achieving this presence. A controlled experiment given to female college students who were shown pictures of officers wearing uniforms compared to officers in plain clothes, or just their faces, resulted in uniformed officers being perceived as competent, reliable, intelligent, and helpful.[12] Moreover, researchers found that the police uniform conveyed power, authority, capability, and status, which subconsciously altered the behavior of the person wearing the uniform as well as the response to it.[13]

The color of the uniform and style of the uniform can influence how citizens perceive and interact with police.[14] Studies have shown that darker uniforms, such as all black or dark blue, were viewed negatively compared with lighter uniforms, such as blue shirt and navy-blue pants, which were viewed significantly more positively.[15] Despite the push towards community policing in recent decades and the desire of many departments to have officers be more approachable, most law enforcement agencies still prefer darker uniforms. Ironically, police are increasingly adopting tactical gear and dress styles that undermine police/citizen closeness.

THE SERVICE WEAPON

Like the police uniform, firearms were not adopted in policing until police professionalism during the *Reform Era* for similar reasons. An armed standing army in uniform patrolling the streets brought back too many memories of the British Redcoats during Colonial America. However, police professionalism heavily emphasized marksmanship, which was seen as an essential part of policing. The service weapon became increasingly important since community relations were severed and officers relied solely on other officers for emergency assistance (i.e., a more dangerous occupational environment).

Police officers visibly carried their firearms for practical (easy accessibility) and symbolic reasons (authority). This visible display of authority, like uniforms, achieves a level of forced respect, but at the cost of strained relations with the community. While we take for granted that police officers carrying a service weapon at his or her side is necessary and expected, there is some psychological research that shows the mere visible presence of a weapon increases aggression.

The phenomenon known to psychologists as the "weapons effect," was discovered in 1967 by Leonard Berkowitz and Anthony LePage who conducted an experiment wherein research participants were seated at two different tables covered with items they were told to ignore, one with a shotgun and revolver and the other with badminton equipment. The experiment also included a planted person who purposely angered the participants.[16] The angered participants would later decide how much electrical shock to deliver to the planted person. The result was more shock given to the planted experiment person by the participant who visibly saw the guns.

The same effect was replicated outside of the lab environment in numerous real-world observations and experiments. For instance, another field experiment that simulated a broken-down vehicle with a visible gun in a rack was honked at more aggressively than the same truck with no gun.[17] Researchers have also found drivers who carried a concealed weapon in their cars were significantly more likely to drive aggressively, such as tailgating, and make obscene gestures.[18] In other words, more likely to "road rage."

THE POLICE BADGE

Perhaps the most famous and visible symbol of authority under professionalism is the badge. The police badge, when coupled with the uniform, is the epitome of police professionalism—under O. W. Wilson's vision, it represented a nameless, faceless officer upholding the law fairly and without bias. Unfortunately for today's officers, the badge works against their efforts at establishing community trust through close relations. Rookie officers who first don the badge often feel its immediate impact, sometimes referred to as the "weight of the badge": treatment by citizens based on past experiences they have had with police which are mostly negative. Picture a scenario where a rookie officer on his first day on the beat is already being disrespected and called pig without having personally done anything to that person.

SUMMARY

Being a police officer is a nuanced experience where officers must negotiate images and appearances with different audiences. Police are victims of their own success under professionalism—their designed isolation became the cause of police brutality by the group, causing introversion and cynicism as captured by the police subculture. The rookie officer cannot help but be drawn into a world that changes their worldview through training, storytelling, and work experience.

Changing this attitude requires the professional police to undo many of the advances under professionalism, but they cannot go back to the days of the night watchman. However, the reactive nature of their work, coupled with shift work and symbolic insulators, such as the police uniform, gun, and badge, make reestablishing community/police relations very difficult.

NOTES

1. Joseph Wambaugh, *The Choirboys* (New York: Bantam Dell, 1975).

2. John Van Maanen, "Police Socialization: A Longitudinal Examination of Job Attitudes in an Urban Police Department," *Administrative Science Quarterly* 20, no. 2 (1975): 207–228.

3. Patrick McGreevy, "LAPD's Flextime Dilemma," *Los Angeles Times,* 2006, http://articles.latimes.com/2006/oct/23/local/me-flextime23.

4. Michelle Lazark, "A Day in the Life of a Graveyard Shift Officer," *Sacramento Press,* June 14, 2009, http://sacramentopress.com/2009/06/14/a-day-in-the-life-of-a-graveyard-shift-officer/.

5. Lois James, Stephen James, and Bryan Vila, "The Impact of Work Shift and Fatigue on Police Officer Response in Simulated Interactions with Citizens," *Journal of Experimental Criminology* 14, no. 1 (2018): 111–120. doi: 10.1007/s11292-017-9294-2.

6. Sandra L. Ramey et al., "The Effect of Work Shift and Sleep Duration on Various Aspects of Police Officers' Health," *Workplace Health and Safety* 60, no. 5 (2012): 215–222.

7. Shantha M.W. Rajaratnam et al., "Sleep Disorders, Health, and Safety in Police Officers," *The Journal of the American Medical Association* 306, no. 23 (2011): 2567–2578. doi: 10.1001/jama.2011.1851.

8. Desta B. Fekedulegn et al., "Shift Work and Sleep Quality among Urban Police Officers," *Journal of Occupational and Environmental Medicine* 58, no. 3 (2016): 66–71. doi: 10.1097/JOM.0000000000000620.

9. Peter K. Manning, "The Police: Mandate, Strategies, and Appearances," in *Policing: Key Readings* (Portland: Willan, 2005), 191–214.

10. Elizabeth Reuss-Ianni, "Street Cops and Management Cops: The Two Cultures of Policing," in *Control in the Police Organization* (Cambridge, MA: MIT Press, 1983), 251–274.

11. Ronald Weitzer and Steven A. Tuch, "Perceptions of Racial Profiling: Race, Class, and Personal Experience," *Criminology* 40, no. 2 (2006): 435–456. doi: 10.1111/j.1745-9125.2002.tb00962.x.

12. Richard R. Johnson, "Psychological Influence of the Police Uniform," *FBI Law Enforcement Bulletin* 70, no. 3 (2001): 27–32.

13. Daniel J. Bell, "Police Uniforms, Attitudes, and Citizens," *Journal of Criminal Justice* 10, no. 1 (1982): 45–55.

14. Ming S. Singer and Alan E. Singer, "The Effect of Police Uniform on Interpersonal Perception," *The Journal of Psychology: Interdisciplinary and Applied* 119, no. 2 (1985): 157–161. doi: 10.1080/00223980.1985.10542882.

15. Richard R. Johnson, "Police Uniform Color and Citizen Impression Formation," *Journal of Police and Criminal Psychology* 20, no. 2 (2005): 58–66.

16. Leonard Berkowitz and Anthony LePage, "Weapons as Aggression-Eliciting Stimuli," *Journal of Personality and Social Psychology* 7 (1967): 202–207.

17. Brad J. Bushman, "The 'Weapons Effect': Research Shows the Mere Presence of Weapons Increases Aggression," *Psychology Today* (2013), https://www.psychologytoday.com/us/blog/get-psyched/201301/the-weapons-effect.

18. Charles W. Turner, John F. Layton, and Lynn S. Simons, "Naturalistic Studies of Aggressive Behavior: Aggressive Stimuli, Victim Visibility, and Horn Honking," *Journal of Personality and Social Psychology* 31 (1975): 1098–1107.

Chapter Six

Police and the Media

The Myths and Realities of Police Work

This chapter critically explores how the police are portrayed in popular media versus the realities of police work. The public has long been fascinated with the profession of policing and law enforcement. Film and television have reflected this interest since the early days of entertainment media. The lawman is often the protagonist and quintessential "good guy," such as in John Wayne westerns. The portrayal of officers, however, is not one-dimensional. Other depictions are quite negative, such as the infamous bungling Keystone Cops. This dichotomy has continued to this day, which one can argue is a reflection of the conflicted police identity.

In more recent times, police dramas and reality television have tried to give more "realistic" portrayals of police. In fact, the groundbreaking reality television show *COPS*, in which a camera crew rides along with officers on duty, has been on the air since 1989 and is still running at the time of this writing! However, despite even a camera crew capturing "real" footage of police work, one does not have to be a police officer or mass media scholar to conclude that there is a big gap between the portrayals and the realities of police work.[1] Entertainment media's portrayals of police can affect public perceptions of police which can ultimately have real impacts on officers' working environments.

Further distorting the realities of police work is police depictions by the news media. While the topic is covered in depth in a later chapter, media coverage of police often mirrors the image dichotomy, oscillating between the police as hero or villain and expert professional or incompetent.

This chapter is broken into several themes that answer the following questions:

1. How are police portrayed in popular media?
2. How does media coverage differ from the realities of police work?
3. What is the reality of police work?
4. How does this disjuncture/separation affect police and the public?
5. Where did these stereotypes come from?
6. What is the "*CSI* effect?"
7. How does news media portrayal of police reflect the dichotomy of police as hero or villain, expert or incompetent?
8. What can we do to change these perceptions?

THE POLICE ON TELEVISION: COP SHOWS

The public has been captivated by television shows that feature the police. Police shows have captivated the TV viewing audience for decades, perhaps due to the nature of policing itself which lends nicely to the very popular theme of justice: The good guys (police) versus the bad guys (criminals). A quick glance at a list of police dramas, which includes both US and foreign shows, reveals there are hundreds of shows. As of the time of this writing, Neilsen's top-rated show with over 7 million viewers is *NCIS*, a drama based on the Naval Criminal Investigative Service. *NCIS* is so popular the it has several spin-off shows, such as *NCIS: Los Angeles* and *NCIS: New Orleans*. Another top 10 show at the time of this writing is *FBI*, a show that was developed by the creators of the mega-franchise "Law & Order."

The American audience cannot seem to get enough police-themed shows. The top twenty-five most watched shows in 2018 include the remake of *Hawaii Five-O*, *S.W.A.T.*, and *Blue Bloods*, a CBS drama about an NYPD police family that has been airing since 2010. As these shows have ended, more police-themed shows have taken their place.

One of the most popular crime/police dramas of all time is the original *CSI: Las Vegas*. The show began airing in 2000 and became an instant hit, with over 20 million viewers. It maintained its top ratings for fifteen seasons before ending. The show was so popular that CBS developed two highly rated spin-off shows, *CSI: Miami* and *CSI: New York*.

Dramas are not the only way police and law enforcement agents are portrayed on television. Police comedies are a very popular genre. While there are fewer shows in this genre, they remain very popular. Perhaps the most popular recent show, which aired from 2003 to 2009, was *Reno 911!*, which featured a group of fictional Reno, Nevada, police officers that were fighting crime in the most incompetent manner imaginable. The show was shot in a style that was a parody of the reality show, *COPS*.

THE POLICE IN CINEMA: COP MOVIES

Movies that feature police and law enforcement have mirrored that of television shows: They are immensely popular and have several themes. First, crime and police dramatic movies are numerous. A quick look at IMDB's 2018 list of movies features numerous police-related titles. Some of these selections include coincidentally, *Cops*, a movie loosely based on the series where an officer is celebrated by fellow officers and harshly criticized by the public after shooting a man during an operation; *Ride Along 3*, the third installment of a police comedy; and *The Commuter*, a story of an ex–police profiler.

Historically, popular police dramatic films include movies ranging from the *Die Hard* series to *Robocop,* feature a virtually invincible protagonist with the physical ability to single-handedly stop bad guys and have the moral character to justify any means necessary. These larger-than-life portrayals of police add to the mystique of the fearless hero that faces up to most extreme challenges. While these movies portray obvious extreme versions of police work, these themes permeate the public consciousness that impacts perceptions of police work and police officers.

Similar to police television shows, police comedies are a constant in movies. Recent hits include the comedy remake of the 1980s television series, *21 Jump Street*, featuring two undercover police officers who go back to high school, with a sequel on the way. Other popular police comedies include *The Naked Gun* series, *Hot Fuzz, Super Troopers*, the *Police Academy* series, *Rush Hour* series, *Beverly Hills Cop* series, and many, many, more. Even the hit television series *Reno 911!* was given the film adaptation in the 2007 police comedy *Reno 911!: Miami*.

TWO STEREOTYPES OF POLICE

As one can see from the variety of police movies, the portrayal of police work on television and in the movies reveals a fundamental dichotomy in the portrayal of police work and the police: (1) they are incompetent fools, or (2) they are action heroes. Neither of these stereotypes are realistic or accurate depictions of police. These media and entertainment industry portrayals of police in these contrasting types endure largely as a reflection of police history.

The first stereotype of police, that they are incompetent fools, is derived from the political era of policing. Recall that police were by design politically tied, unarmed, poorly trained (if at all), poorly paid, and considered simply community members who walked the streets at night (hence, the night watchman). Police were heavily criticized for being incompetent and corrupt, which led to many portrayals of them as such in film. The most famous portrayal of police of that period was, *The Keystone Cops* during the silent film era. Keystone officers were often portrayed as bumbling idiots stumbling out of clown-like overstuffed police cars, unable to catch crooks, and creating more harm rather than helping society.

Despite efforts to professionalize, this stereotype of the officer has endured. Police comedies such as *Rush Hour*, *Police Academy*, *The Naked Gun*, *Hot Fuzz*, *Dragnet*, *Beverly Hills Cop*, and so on, have perpetuated this reputation of the inept cop.

MORE "REALISTIC" PORTRAYALS OF POLICE

A third category of police depictions in television and theater are attempts at more "realistic" portrayals of police work. Arguably the most realistic television series during police professionalism during the 1960s and 1970s was *Adam-12*, an LAPD drama that featured the dynamics of a rookie officer (Jim Reed) and his FTO (Pete Malloy). The reason why it was considered more realistic was because it featured a lot of the service and order maintenance components of police work. LAPD Officers Malloy and Reed would handle domestic calls, random disturbances, and other services where arrests were not always made. It also featured a variety of police technologies and the introduction of women into policing during that time.

A more recent police drama, *Southland*, which aired from 2009 to 2013, portrayed the LAPD officers as part of a collection of specialists and divisions that interacted symbiotically. Like *Adam-12*, *Southland* featured the dynamics between diverse personalities and roles of different officers, such as the relationship between a rookie "boot" and a veteran FTO. In addition, the show gave a more holistic view of a police department as a collection of specialized parts, such as patrol officers, detectives, management, and other specializations. The interaction of these differing roles in the context of crimes and police work highlighted the different issues police face, ranging from media coverage of police brutality to alcoholism and drug abuse by officers. Another highly popular gritty police drama based on realism is *NYPD Blue*, which aired from the 1990s to the mid-2000s.

One of the most critically acclaimed television police dramas is *The Wire* on HBO, which featured Baltimore police dealing with drugs and crime in the inner city. The show featured police undercover detective work and the dynamics amongst police officers and supervisors, as well as with the criminal element. More uniquely, the show broadened the context of police to include the dynamics of local politics, schools, federal agencies, and the pressures of performance based on crime control statistics.

Three notable LAPD-based movies have won critical acclaim by featuring critical themes and issues in police work. The 1988 drama *Colors* featured the friction between a rookie officer and his partner, and racial profiling in the violent, gang-ridden streets of east Los Angeles. The 2001 LAPD drama *Training Day* featured themes such as police corruption and the "blue wall of silence" by a rogue group of corrupt officers within the department. Finally, the 2012 film *End of Watch* highlighted the bond and friendship between officers on and off duty, as well as officer mortality. Despite these more realistic visions of police work, they are still distortions based on stereotypes for entertainment. However, even reality-based shows that capture video of actual police work are not a true depiction of policing.

THE DISTORTED TRUTH OF COPS
AND "REALITY" TELEVISION

Perhaps the most popular of all police shows is the ubiquitous police reality show: *COPS*, which began airing in 1989 and still airs at the time of this writing. The reality series, which featured camera crews filming with real-life police officers and deputies throughout the country, is the longest running show on the Fox network, with over 1,000 episodes in over thirty seasons.

COPS is one of the most polemical and controversial shows on policing. When the show first aired, it was revolutionary, and essentially created a new paradigm of genre in television. It demystified the world of policing, one the public had long sought to view and had an insatiable appetite for. It gave insight into the mind-set of the officer, the criminal justice system, and the issues and people the police dealt with daily.

Supporters of the show claim it humanized officers, gave a better understanding of their profession, and helped create more empathy for police as normal people (in the sense that they had emotions and were not robots) working a dangerous profession. Viewers essentially went on virtual ride-alongs from their living rooms and were captivated by high-speed pursuits, prostitutes, and drug busts. The show complemented another hit show, *America's Most Wanted*, in which viewers were asked to participate directly in the justice process. More recently, there have been a variety of reality police shows, including *Live PD*, which airs live encounters of police on duty and is lauded as being unfiltered and unpredictable.

Despite their popularity, there are some published criticisms on *COPS* and other reality-based police shows. Criminologists argue that *COPS* does not accurately and realistically depict the day-to-day activities of police work.[2] In order to make the show interesting to viewers, it is heavily edited to only include exciting aspects of police work, such as felony arrests, fights, and high-speed pursuits. These are generally infrequent and do not reflect the realities of police work, despite being a reality show.[3] The reality of police work in most areas is not that exciting and action-packed. Moreover, participating law enforcement have the right to veto footage they find objectionable, creating a further distortion of police work.

This distorted and edited version of reality can have several unintended consequences. By emphasizing the excitement of the crime control aspect of police work, the public understands the profession as mostly "ass-kicking," with little emphasis on the service and order maintenance component of the job. This undermines public understandings of policing efforts in community policing and influences certain personality types that are attracted to police work.

The most criticized unintended consequence of *COPS* is the creation of a public perception of crime and the criminal. Many criminologists who have written on the show have concerns that the show and others like it over represent minority groups, such as African Americans, being arrested. An analysis of the show revealed the show typically featured violent crimes committed by non-Whites on victims that were White. These distortions can further stereotypical portrayals of racial minorities while simultaneously reinforcing perceptions of African Americans as a dangerous class. Moreover, it can serve as an impetus for **moral panics** of these dangerous classes that trigger public demand for legislation based on these distorted perceptions.

Violent crimes are another factor that is overrepresented in *COPS* that furthers a distorted reality of crime. One analysis of the show asserts that violent crime, such as murder, rape, aggravated assault, and robbery were represented in the show 43 percent of the time, compared to the reality that those crimes accounted for approximately 12 percent of the crimes reported to the UCR.[4]

POLICE IN THE NEWS

One of the biggest controversies among police officers is how they are depicted in the news media. Over time, this has produced a conflicted relationship between news outlets and police agencies. Many officers criticize the media for creating narratives that may not reflect the true intentions of officers and agencies. The result of real or perceived misreporting can create conflict between certain communities and the police. However, biases in news reporting may be reflective of news, police, and societal predispositions. Moreover, bias may be inherently unavoidable.

Many sociologists, such as **symbolic interactionist** Irving Goffman, assert that reality is a social construction.[5] Meaning, reality is viewed and constructed through human lenses and subject to bias and interpretation. For example, a group of people can witness a single event and describe it completely differently. The news, despite its claimed objectivity, is no exception. Police and police activity are the subject in the news daily. A quick scan of US national news at the time of this writing shows the proverbial good, bad, and ugly and everything in between. Here is a sample of the news stories on any given day:

Good: On June 17, 2018, a Douglas County Sheriff Deputy rescued a seventy-six-year-old woman who drove off a bridge in Lake Latoka, Minnesota. The deputy tied a rope around his waist before jumping into the water to pull the woman out of the submerged vehicle.

Bad: On June 15, 2018, two Kansas sheriffs, Theresa King and Patrick Roher, were killed while transporting inmates when an inmate overpowered them outside of a courthouse. Despite the inmates being cuffed and shackled and deputies following protocol, the deputies were overpowered and shot with their own service weapons.

Ugly: On June 16, 2018, a ten-year Bexar County veteran, located in San Antonio, Texas, sheriff detention deputy Jose Nunez, was arrested for sexually assaulting a four-year-old girl over a period of months and threatened the girl's mother with deportation when she confronted him.

News coverage of police is not always accurate and is often skewed. First, routine police activities are not presented to the public. Only more sensational crimes and activities, such as high-speed pursuits and dangerous felony arrests, are usually deemed newsworthy. The ramifications of portraying the police in this crime control role includes affecting potential recruits who do not share the same crime control orientation (as discussed in previous chapters) and gives the public a skewed view of police functions and capabilities. Police are often shown in tactical gear, drawing their weapons, in high speed chases, etc.

Second, positive news coverage is often overlooked. The newsworthiness of an incident skewed towards negative events is captured in the proverbial phrase, "if it bleeds, it leads." This means news media outlets prioritize bad news events over positive news. For instance, psychologists have found that news outlets use fear-based content as teasers to grab viewers' attention and use dramatic anecdotal evidence in place of scientific research. [6] The formula of skewing news stories that promote isolated negative and dangerous events as trends has resulted in widespread fatalistic mentalities, over optimism.

Consequently, media viewers begin feeling elevated and unreasonable levels of fear. Despite a well-documented general decline in crime, including violent crime in the United States since the 1990s, it has been found that Americans who are exposed more to news media tend to believe:

1. Their neighborhoods and communities are unsafe
2. Crime rates are rising
3. Their odds of victimization are high
4. The world is an overall dangerous place

Third, police misconduct is often exaggerated and overstated. Police officers often make the claim that news coverage of accused police misconduct, such as brutality, is frequently sensational, biased, and taken out of context. This is a growing concern for officers who are increasingly recorded by the ubiquity of video recording devices, such as smartphones, as well as by their own body cameras. Any police officer will state that the use of force *never* looks good or acceptable when captured on video, even when following proper protocol.

Video captured footage does not equate to the reality of a situation. Video, despite its seemingly objective nature, does not contextualize the situation. Take for example, the infamous Rodney King beating video recorded by George Holliday from the balcony of his apartment building. The video footage shows King being beaten by officers, but does not show the prior police chase, audio during the beating, and other factors that may put in context what really happened. Furthermore, videos only capture what is in frame, but do not capture the environment that further contextualizes the event.

News coverage of controversial police cases has been criticized for editing videos to fit their narrative. Footage of before and after police brutality cases is rarely presented. Moreover, today's editorialized news broadcasts in "news shows" hosted by "personalities" present a skewed presentation of the truth. These shows tend to promote narratives that often draw public attention, such as "White officer shoots and kills an unarmed Black man." Not coincidentally, these are amongst the highest rated shows on their respective news networks. According to a PBS study, larger networks and their local affiliates simply cater to advertising dollars, which is based entirely on ratings. Journalistic integrity is becoming a larger problem as we move forward.

The effects of media on high-profile brutality cases can influence public perceptions of the events. Note that public perceptions of police are very important in our legal system given that juries are drawn from this population. A 2006 Michigan State University study found that news coverage of high-profile cases of police brutality affected citizen evaluation of guilt of the officers. The more citizens were exposed to the case through media, the more likely that citizen thought the officer was guilty.[7]

The use of technology has placed police under greater scrutiny. In-car videos today are commonplace in police patrol vehicles but remain a contentious issue. The video camera systems were put in place to restore public confidence in police to show the nature of police stops, justification in using force, deterring false allegations, etc. Despite the goals of limiting liability and more transparency (videos can be used by both prosecutors and the defense), police officers can turn video recordings on and off, making the recording system controversial.[8] Some veteran officers remain reluctant to use these cameras.

Despite the resistance, recording technology is here to stay. The growing trend among police departments is the use of embedded cameras on officers, commonly known as "body cams." According to a 2015 Department of Homeland Security–sponsored survey, approximately 95 percent of large metropolitan police departments have made significant investments or committed to integrating police body camera systems, sparked by the 2014 Michael Brown shooting in Ferguson, Missouri.[9] Despite the growing presence of body cameras, they are not immune to controversies such as officers' control of when cameras are recording.

REALITIES OF POLICE WORK

Despite efforts to depict police work in a realistic fashion, the realities of police work are still skewed and are not reflected in media, the movies, or on television. First, these shows still primarily focus on the crime control/law enforcement aspects of police work—often featuring arrests, use of handguns, chasing, wrestling uncooperative suspects, etc. The reality of the nature of police work is much different:

- *Police do not frequently make arrests.* Criminologist David Bayley found that patrol officers only make nineteen arrests per year on average.[10] Put into context, that is just a little over one arrest per month, contrary to the prolific arrests in virtually every episode of *COPS*.
- *Police work is not action-packed.* The best description of police work is from the proverbial quote, "Hours of boredom punctuated by moments of sheer terror." The first part of the quote implies that police work is generally boring. Most officers, especially in smaller towns and cities, do not have a whole lot of activities during a typical shift. Many officers find themselves driving endlessly, responding to service calls that are not considered by them to be "real" police work, or parking and chatting with other officers.
- *Police work involves a lot of paperwork.* Police are the entry way into the criminal justice system. Their primary function in the system is apprehending accused individuals for the purpose of preparing them for court. Keep in mind due process, which means the accused is innocent until proven guilty. Therefore police must document everything in a proper fashion for prosecution. Anecdotally, most officers will tell you that they

take this enormous amount of paperwork into account when using discretion to enforce the law, taking into consideration the likelihood of prosecution, time during the shift (officers tend to avoid activities that require a lot of paperwork towards the end of their shifts).

- *Real patrol work is routinely boring.* Answering calls for service and traffic stops becomes relatively perfunctory over time for most officers. Much of patrol activities involve order maintenance and service calls that officers do not consider "real" police work (crime-control activities that involve catching bad guys). For example, responding to noise complaints, domestic dispute calls the officer feels should not involve the police, and false residential burglary alarms. The problem of false alarms is so prevalent that some cities even levy fines for multiple false alarm calls.

Officers look forward to the occasional adrenaline-inducing "hot" or "heavy" call or activity. For example, high-speed chases, officer needs assistance requests, or robbery in progress. Note that officers do not want these endlessly, but occasionally to break up the boredom. After such calls, the event can become enshrined in police folklore to pass down to future officers, which reinforces the crime control aspect of police work. A quote from famed police fiction novelist and former LAPD officer Joseph Wambaugh describes this perfectly in his 1972 book, *The Blue Knight*: "In a job like this, sitting on your ass for long periods of time and then moving in bursts of heart-cracking action, you can expect heart attacks."[11]

- *Police often perceive themselves as distrusted and underappreciated.* Unlike the movies and shows, where officers are heralded as heroes and save the day, most police officers do not feel effective and appreciated by the public. Day-to-day police work involves many perceived negative interactions with the public, such as writing citations. Cumulatively, these interactions from both police and the public become based on biases and preconceived stereotypes. Consequently, the public insult officers based on these biases, with phrases such as, "Don't you have some *real* crime to deal with?" and "I pay your salary." Police, with their authority challenged (recall Van Maanen's "The Asshole") respond with enforcing petty laws that end up in arrest. The person challenging the officer was found guilty of being "in contempt of cop" (see Wambaugh, 1972).
- *Most of police work is order maintenance and peace keeping.* As previously discussed, the majority of police work is not crime control and law enforcement oriented. Instead, police officers often describe their work as "wearing many hats." Meaning, they must navigate a variety of roles in dealing with the public—oftentimes they feel like counselors and psychologists more than police officers. Police must also handle populations that they do not have any clear direction on how to deal with. The homeless

population, for example, is a growing concern for police. Crime in skid row is very high, due mainly to the disorderly environment. Researcher John Kleinig describes the ethical dilemma in policing the homeless: Police should use a peace-keeping role, but their narrow scope of function (primarily law enforcement) and resources make them ill-equipped to deal with the population.[12] He suggests police form alliances with other social service organizations.

- *Police cannot and do not solve most crimes.* Perhaps the greatest impact of the entertainment industry's impact on policing is raising the public's expectations of police abilities. Police dramas, for example, often begin with an unsolved crime and ends with the arrest of the perpetrator(s) in a conclusive, neat fashion. In reality, police detectives do not solve, or even pursue most cases. According to the FBI, in 2011, only 47.7 percent of violent crimes and 18.6 percent of property crimes were cleared by arrest (arrested the person, charged with the commission of the crime, and turned over to the courts for prosecution) or by exceptional means (identified the offender, gathered enough information to make an arrest, charged, and turned over the file to the prosecutor, but encountered a circumstance that prohibited the agency from arresting the person, charging, and prosecution) (see *2011 FBI Uniform Crime Report*).

UNREALISTIC EXPECTATIONS: THE CSI EFFECT

The "**CSI Effect**" is a term used to describe exaggerated abilities by crime scene investigators and forensic scientists to solve crimes accurately and quickly, as typically portrayed in the hit television series *CSI: Crime Scene Investigation*. In the show, investigators, using sophisticated forensic equipment, which includes powerful lasers and computers, can quickly and accurately identify suspects and reconstruct the crime with just the smallest traces of evidence. Many popular shows and movies also show detectives enhancing very grainy surveillance video into a sharp picture, which is then quickly matched in a large police database, producing the name and details of the suspect.

Shows such as *CSI: Crime Scene Investigation*, *NCIS*, and *Bones*, depict crimes that are solved quickly and accurately within the one-hour span of the show, skewing the true nature of police forensic investigations. Researchers have found that police departments do not even own sophisticated equipment such as lasers for doing forensic work.[13] They describe true police work as relatively "low-tech."

The reality of police investigative work is far different from what is depicted in *CSI* and other television shows:

- Forensic work is very slow and expensive. Due to the time and cost of a full forensics investigation, it is used very sparingly by police departments. Most police departments do not have crime labs and the work conducted by investigators is not nearly as sophisticated as what is depicted on television.
- Detective work primarily consists of the social over the physical. Meaning, physical evidence is less emphasized than interviews with witnesses, interrogations, and other forms of human investigations.
- Physical evidence alone is often not enough to solve cases. In Nhan and Huey's 2013 article, we find that even cybercrime, a seemingly high-tech crime committed by, essentially, computer nerds, still requires old fashioned detective work to find out exactly who was at the keyboard at the time the crime was committed.

There are many ramifications of the *CSI* effect on how the police function. Unrealistic expectations are becoming a burden for officers, who are often requested to perform full forensic investigations for petty crimes. One police officer, in a published journal article by police researcher Laura Huey, stated, "I've actually had people get angry at me because I wouldn't powder something . . . so now we just powder it in a sense of appeasing what their curiosity is going to be, and obviously we don't find anything."[14] The elevated expectations of officers and investigators have led to disappointments and dissatisfaction in the abilities of police—the image they were trying to ameliorate during professionalization. This has resulted in a lot of frustration amongst officers and moreover, produced strain in police-community relations.

The *CSI* effect also affects juror perceptions and ultimately case outcomes. *CSI* and similar shows have had two major consequences on jurors. First, these shows exaggerate and glorify forensic science, which places greater burdens on prosecutors to present more forensic evidence than exists. Second, these unrealistic expectations and exaltation of forensic evidence creates exaggerated faith in the capabilities and reliability of forensic science. Studies of the *CSI* effect have been relatively mixed. A 2007 experimental study found that *CSI* viewers were less likely to convict a person based on forensic evidence, having a more critical and skeptical view of the evidence.[15] However, lawyers and judges see evidence that the *CSI* effect is real, finding that more jurors are placing greater weight on forensics and making prosecutors' jobs more difficult to convict.

USA Today reported several instances of the *CSI* effect, showing the real and growing phenomenon:[16]

- In Phoenix [July 2004], jurors in a murder trial noticed that a bloody coat introduced as evidence had not been tested for DNA. They alerted the judge. The tests hadn't been needed because the defendant had acknowledged being at the murder scene. The judge decided that TV had taught jurors about DNA tests, but not enough about when to use them.

- Richmond, Virginia, jurors in a murder trial asked the judge whether a cigarette butt found during the investigation could be tested for links to the defendant. Defense attorneys had ordered DNA tests but had not yet introduced them into evidence. The jury's hunch was correct—the tests exonerated the defendant, and the jury acquitted him.
- In Arizona, Illinois, and California, prosecutors now use "negative evidence witnesses" to try to assure jurors that it is not unusual for real crime-scene investigators to fail to find DNA, fingerprints, and other evidence at crime scenes.
- In Massachusetts, prosecutors have begun to ask judges for permission to question prospective jurors about their TV-watching habits. Several states already allow that.
- In Wilmington, Delaware, federal researchers studying how juries evaluate scientific evidence staged dozens of simulated trials. At one point, a juror struggling with especially complicated DNA evidence lamented that such problems never come up "on *CSI.*"

SUMMARY

The media and entertainment industry have a real impact on what we believe the police do and their abilities to control crime. Consequently, there is a growing divide between public perceptions of policing and the reality of police work and police officers. This has a major consequence that reinforces a central controversial theme of perceptions of police work as action-packed and crime-control oriented serving to attract like-minded recruits to the job while dissuading potential candidates who do not share these values. This produces a homogenous group with strong cultural momentum, as reflected in the police subculture that is extremely difficult to change. Furthermore, police frustration with the public for unrealistic expectations further reinforces the "us versus them" siege mentality that is representative of the police subculture.

NOTES

1. Radley Balko, "Are Reality Cop Shows Altering Reality?" *The Washington Post*, January 14, 2014, https://www.washingtonpost.com/news/opinions/wp/2014/01/14/are-reality-cop-shows-altering-reality/?noredirect=on&utm_term=.d54d5a2db893.

2. Paul G. Kooistra, John S. Mahoney Jr., and Saundra D. Westervelt, "The World of Crime According to '*COPS*,'" in *Television Reality Programs* (Hawthorne, NY: Aldine De Gruyter, 1998), 141–158.

3. Aaron Doyle, "*Cops*': Television Policing as Policing Reality," in *Television Reality Programs* (Hawthorne, NY: Aldine De Gruyter, 1998), 95–116.

4. "Crime in the United States, 2011," Uniform Crime Report, 2011, http://www.fbi.gov/about-us/cjis/ucr/crime-in-the-u.s/2011/crime-in-the-u.s.-2011/clearances.

5. Edwin Goffman. *The Presentation of Self in Everyday Life* (New York: Doubleday, 1959).

6. Deborah Serani, "If it Bleeds, it Leads: Understanding Fear-Based Media," *Psychology Today,* 2011, https://www.psychologytoday.com/us/blog/two-takes-depression/201106/if-it-bleeds-it-leads-understanding-fear-based-media.

7. Steven Chermak, Edmund McGarrell, and Jeff Gruenewald, "Media coverage of police misconduct and attitudes toward police," *Policing: An International Journal of Police Strategies and Management* 29, no. 2 (2006): 261–281.

8. Jess Maghan, Gregory W. O'Reilly, and Phillip Chong Ho Shon, "Technology, Policing, and Implications of In-Car Videos," *Police Quarterly* 5, no. 1 (2002): 25–42. doi: 10.1177/109861102129198002.

9. "Major Cities Chiefs and Major County Sheriffs Survey on Technology Needs: Body Worn Cameras," Lafayette Group, December 2015, https://assets.bwbx.io/documents/users/iqjWHBFdfxIU/rvnT.EAJQwK4/v0.

10. David H. Bayley, "What Do the Police Do?" in *Policing: Key Readings* (Portland, OR: Willan, 2005), 141–149.

11. Joseph Wambaugh, *The Blue Knight* (London: Quercus, 1972).

12. John Kleinig, "Policing the Homeless: An Ethical Dilemma," *Journal of Social Distress and the Homeless* 2, no. 4 (1993): 289–303.

13. Johnny Nhan and Laura Huey, "'We Don't Have These Laser Beams and Stuff Like That': Police Investigations as Low-Tech Work in a High-Tech World," in *Technocrime: Police and Surveillance* (New York: Routledge, 2013), 79–90.

14. Laura Huey, "'I've Seen This on *CSI*': Criminal Investigators' Perceptions about the Management of Public Expectations in the Field," *Crime, Media, Culture: An International Journal* 6, no. 1 (2010): 49–68. doi: 10.1177/1741659010363045.

15. Nicholas J. Schweitzer and Michael J. Saks, "The *CSI* Effect: Popular Fiction about Forensic Science and the Public's Expectations about Real Forensic Science," *Jurimetrics 47* (2007): 357–364.

16. Richard Willing, "'CSI Effect' Has Juries Wanting More Evidence," *USA Today*, August 5, 2004, http://usatoday30.usatoday.com/news/nation/2004-08-05-csi-effect_x.htm.

Chapter Seven

Police Brutality and Use of Force

This chapter explores arguably the most controversial issue of policing: the use of excessive force and police brutality. Instances of real or perceived police brutality have been blamed for sparking several major urban riots in the past. The solution to the problem of excessive use of force is often not quite as simple as a change in policy or additional training. The use of force by police in general is often complex and has implications of the police subculture and real and perceived dangers of the job. Officer decisions to use force are often an escalating process that starts with officer cynicism and tests of an officer's control of the situation. Disrespecting an officer can result in the use of force.

The frequent use of force by police in poor minority areas, which has sparked social upheaval in the past, is often symptomatic of larger issues between the police and those communities. The use of excessive force may be a sign of a breakdown of trust and respect between police and poor minority communities. Antagonistic relationship tension between the police and certain communities can erupt into larger social upheavals. Urban riots may not be completely attributable to simply real or perceived instances of police brutality, but they may be a result of larger societal issues of poverty, lack of opportunities, and perhaps a criminal justice industrial complex and deep-rooted racism. However, the police are the most visible part of the government and gatekeepers to the criminal justice system, and therefore get the most blame.

Several themes and topics, some recurring from previous chapters, will be used to analyze police use of force and brutality. These themes include:

1. The legitimate use of force
2. Historic context and the growing need to use force

3. Urban riots
4. Explaining the use of force
5. Community trust

POLICE LEGITIMATE USE OF FORCE

Part of our **social contract** with society, as written by Age of Enlightenment thinkers such as John Locke, Thomas Hobbes, and Jean-Jacques Rousseau, is the tacit agreement that living in an orderly society requires us to surrender certain liberties and obey collective rules, as defined by social norms, customs, and laws. One of these surrendered liberties is the unrestricted right to use force, especially deadly force, for justice, against others. In other words, we have given up certain freedoms, such as the freedom to mete out vigilante justice. Instead, as part of this social contract, we have given the State (government) the power to enforce the rules on the public's behalf.

Enforcing the law is the designated role of police and other law enforcement agencies. These agencies have been legally and socially sanctioned to apprehend persons suspected of breaking certain laws and to use force if necessary, including deadly force, to carry out this function. In the United States, this includes using weapons, both nonlethal and lethal, against suspects. However, the use of force is narrowly defined by the law in order to avoid the abuse of this power. When one considers the amount of power given to police officers—the power to legally and directly take away life, liberty, and property, it is in many ways more powerful than even the president. Therefore, setting limitations on the use of force is an important aspect of the law.

The United States and many Westernized countries are considered rule-of-law countries. In principle, we believe in **supremacy of the law**. Law is external to the person (impersonal) and any power is derived from the law itself, which defines the power. In the 1940s, German sociologist Max Weber wrote about bureaucracies as an apparatus based on the **rule of law**. **Bureaucracies** are administrative systems that organize human activity and maintain order using a hierarchical structure that distributes power.[1] In a bureaucracy, power is not derived from the individual, such as in the case of a dictator, but predefined by the rules of the bureaucracy. American society can be viewed as one large bureaucratic organization that is based on rules, hierarchy, and distributed power.

Police officers must also follow predefined rules according to the law and the bureaucratic organization of the governing agency. While there is a degree of discretion, the use of force is strictly governed in law enforcement. The use of force guidelines are purposely worded ambiguously by the law and in individual agency policies and procedures to allow for some degree of individual judgment. It is impossible to predefine every use of force scenario, therefore officers are repeatedly trained to assess the appropriateness of when and how much force to use.

Use of force is broadly classified into three levels of escalation according to the National Institute of Justice (NIJ):

1. Basic verbal and physical constraint
2. Less-lethal force (technologies such as beanbags, Tasers, pepper spray, batons, etc.).
3. Lethal force

There is currently no universal standard for when and how much force should be used in any given situation. The degree to which force can be used is generally determined by the policy of the officer's department and it is ultimately up to the officer's discretion on when and how much force to use, accordingly. However, there are general guidelines recommended by the International Association of Chiefs of Police (IACP), which state that the appropriate degree of force is the "amount of effort required by police to compel compliance by an unwilling subject."[2] The NIJ states, "Police officers should use only the amount of force necessary to control an incident, affect an arrest, or protect themselves or others from harm or death."[3]

It is impossible to have strict and exacting guidelines on the use of force. If this was the case, police departments would have to predefine every conceivable situation an officer may encounter with a prescription of the exact use of force. For example, the vague phrase "amount of force necessary to control an incident" may depend on many variables, including the physical capabilities of the individual officer and suspect(s), circumstance, environment, and countless other contextual factors.

The NIJ outlines more variables that may affect the allowable degree of the use of force, which may include larger structural factors such as:

- The police department's experience
- Federal and state mandates
- Available law enforcement technologies
- The complex relationships that may exist between the police and citizens in a given jurisdiction

The vague nature of the use of force allowed by officers, as by necessity, has created problems and complications. The levels of allowable use of force is not necessarily guided by law and departmental policies per se, but historically has been guided by many larger societal factors, such as the era of policing, community tolerance for force, and the relationship between police and communities. A historic look at the context of the use of force shows the fluctuation in levels of force by police.

HISTORIC LOOK: THE NECESSITY OF THE USE OF FORCE

The use of force was not always a necessary and integral function of police. During the time when the *night watchmen* patrolled the streets, the use of force was a relatively infrequent event. Recall that the night watchman was unarmed and did not have the technological tools found with today's officers. He did not have a two-way radio, squad car, helicopters, and other modern crime fighting tools. In fact, he did not undergo police academy training, which did not exist at the time, nor did he even consider policing his occupation.

Recall also that the night watchman was a community member and often just volunteered his time at night to watch over the neighborhood. His primary function was not to enforce the law, but mainly keep the peace. His main occupation was some other occupation, such as blacksmith or carpenter. He was a true member of the community. This was an important aspect during that time. Since he was a member of the community, he relied on the community for assistance. This is especially important since there was no real way of calling for backup from another officer other than tapping his stick loudly on the ground.

The community, who considered the night watchman one of their own (just like a neighbor), was close and did not hesitate to assist him in times of need. With peacekeeping in mind, community disputes under the watchmen models often just needed informal intervention. However, in cases where there was an outsider, the community would respond to the foreign threat. In most cases, the night watchman was in no real danger.

As society industrialized and drew in foreign and domestic immigrants to city industrial centers during the political era of policing, anomic conflicts required more force by police. Politicians in large cities at the time often used police in brutal fashion to make their political point and assert their will.

During of the reform era, when police were professionalizing, the nature of the use of force changed. To ameliorate the image of brutality and corruption during the political era, police reformers such as O. W. Wilson pushed for policies that insulated the police from the public, including attitudes, demeanor, and the use of the police car. Consequently, this reform changed the fundamental structure of police from the days of the night watchman, from one that relied on community assistance to one that relied solely on other officers during emergencies.

The shift from community help to reliance on other officers can be understood as a fundamental change in society that changed how police dealt with the public and the use of force.

INFORMAL TO FORMAL SOCIAL CONTROL

Theoretically, the use of force by police, which is a form of **formal social control** is inversely related to the level of a community's ability to resolve their own problems, or **informal social control**. The breakdown of *informal social controls* means that a community relies more on formal social control in the form of police services. Informal social control is the collective effort to resolve conflict and defend against crime, also known as *collective efficacy*, by members of the community, groups, and organizations, such as family, friends, teachers, social clubs, and churches. High levels of informal social control ensure conformity to accepted norms and laws. For example, family members and close friends might confront an individual for hanging out with the local gang and participating in petty crime. However, if that informal intervention is ineffective, concerned individuals may introduce formal social control by calling the police.

During industrialization, there was a major change that created a societal shift from informal social controls to formal social controls. As factories in need of labor drew in more migrant workers, dense urban areas emerged. Consequently, greater population density meant that everyone lived mostly amongst strangers with different and conflicting norms and customs. Little collective efficacy and few ways to resolve disputes informally among the heterogeneous population meant greater reliance on agents of formal social control, or the police.

Inversely, think about situations of high levels of collective efficacy and informal social control. In the 1990s, urban designers fostered a sense of community and collective efficacy through neighborhood design in sprawling suburban communities, with branching streets that end in dead-ends, or cul-de-sacs. In these communities where neighbors are well acquainted, disputes are often settled informally, with everyone keeping an eye out for potential crime. However, large urban areas rely heavily on police.

Since professionalism during the reform era, police have virtually relied solely on each other instead of the community. In large urban densely population cities, such as New York, Chicago, and Los Angeles, many neighborhoods have little informal social controls and rely heavily on police. There are millions of residents living in these metropolitan cities with the police numbering only in the thousands. Currently, there are approximately 34,500 uniformed NYPD officers for a city of approximately 8.5 million residents (which excludes travelers), making the ratio approximately 246:1 resident to officer. In the city of Los Angeles, the second largest city in the United States, there are approximately 4 million residents with a police force of only approximately 9,000 sworn officers, making the ratio of 440:1 resident to officer.

High citizen to police ratios have a substantive effect on how officers respond to crime and interact with citizens. Historically, when officers are severely outnumbered, use of force, and sometimes excessive force, is often used as a deterrent for anyone who would challenge police authority. This forced respect was a tactic used heavily throughout the 1980s and 1990s with LAPD's infamous specialized unit that dealt with inner-city crime.

LAPD CRASH

The relatively low number of LAPD officers given the densely populated city of Los Angeles that has led to excessive force in the past. During the 1980s, crime in the city of Los Angeles was skyrocketing. The very lucrative crack cocaine market escalated gang violence as gangs jockeyed for territory. The LAPD was tasked with reducing the city's crime rate—no small task considering the relative small force. To compensate for the limited number of officers, the LAPD's tactic was to strike very aggressively in high crime areas, such as South Central Los Angeles, an area with a very high concentration of drug activity, gangs, and violence. The department formed a special tactical task force called Community Resources Against Street Hoodlums (CRASH).

LAPD CRASH units began operations that used strong-arm tactics to intimidate and bully suspects in order to establish dominance and deter criminal activity. In 1988, CRASH led Operation Hammer, a large-scale crackdown involving 1,000 police officers that descended on South Central L.A., resulting in over 1,400 arrests over a single weekend. However, this seemingly successful operation resulted in harsh accusations of racism and police brutality. An investigation revealed widespread use of excessive force by CRASH officers.

CRASH's undoing was the 39th and Dalton incident, an infamous case of police abuse of power. In 1988, LAPD CRASH members raided four apartments on the corner of 39th and Dalton Avenue, a highly concentrated gang neighborhood. Officers were directed to "kick ass," which resulted in over 100 acts of vandalism to the apartments by LAPD officers, ranging from destruction of walls to graffiti. In addition, some residents were brutalized by officers, including beating a suspect in the face with a flashlight, stomping another repeatedly in the crotch, beating a suspect with a weighted knuckle sap, and choking a suspect with a wire.

EXCESSIVE USE OF FORCE CONSEQUENCES: RIOTS, LAWSUITS, REFORM, AND FEDERAL OVERSIGHT

The use of force by police officers, due primarily to the severance between police-community relations, has sparked major social upheavals. In areas of high community tensions, incidences of police brutality have sparked large urban riots. In 1965, a White California Highway Patrol motor officer pulled over twenty-one-year-old Marquette Frye, a Black man, for drunk driving. The situation escalated quickly when Frye's brother and mother intervened with arrest. Backup officers arrived at the scene to subdue Frye's mom in front of a growing crowd, which began throwing objects at the officers. The situation escalated to one of the largest urban riots and lootings in Los Angeles spanning the course of six days, with nearly 1,000 burned, damaged, and destroyed building structures. The police finally restored order with the help of the National Guard, nearly 1,000 LAPD officers, and 700 Los Angeles County Sheriff's deputies.

In 1992, a similar incident occurred with the infamous beating of Rodney King. Racial tensions between the LAPD and ethnic minority Los Angeles residents reached its peak when four Los Angeles police officers accused of police brutality were acquitted of using excessive force against King despite video footage shot by Los Angeles resident George Holliday. The video, showing a group of officers beating King repeatedly with batons, and kicking him while on the ground, went viral after Holliday turned in the tape to a local news station.

The riot that ensued after the officers' acquittal resulted in fifty-three people killed and over 2,000 injured. Four thousand National Guardsmen were called in to restore order from widespread arson, looting, and violence. Over 3,000 fires were set to over 1,000 building structures in a six day span. In addition to turning their rage against the police, racial tensions erupted in violence between Blacks, Hispanics, and Korean Americans.

In the wake of such racially charged riots that were sparked by police use of force incidents, external independent commissions and other reformers pointed to the growing schism between the public and police as a primary reason for the eruption in violence. Specifically, the police subculture played a large part in poor community relations, as officers viewed non-police as outsiders, reflective of the "us versus them" mentality.

EXPLAINING THE USE OF EXCESSIVE FORCE

The Independent Commission on the Los Angeles Police Department, commonly known as the Christopher Commission, identified several causes of LAPD's excessive use of force in the aftermath of the Rodney King Riots.[4]

First, the Commission found that within the LAPD, there was a culture of racial, ethnic, and sexual orientation bias which manifested how LAPD officers treated minority groups in the community. Officers were prone to mistreat minorities through disrespectful and abusive language, intrusive practices such as making suspects prone-out, and disproportionate use of canines. This was evident when external investigators reviewed internal LAPD communications among LAPD officers and found that they were riddled with derogatory racial and sexual-orientation slurs.

Second, high-level supervisors condoned violent activities. Police management failed to identify and discipline officers for misconduct and use of excessive force. This is reflective of the "blue wall of silence," where officers consider each other family and do not report misconduct or blow the whistle on each other. Investigations were discovered to be lax and officers were found to be lying to Internal Affairs. Citizen complaints were largely ignored or dismissed.

Third, external oversight was virtually nonexistent at the LAPD. As part of police professionalism, police as an organization was granted autonomy, or the ability to act independently from direct external oversight. This included hiring and firing their own personnel, setting policies, agendas, etc. Consequently, group introversion developed over time and officers became insulated from and distrustful of outsiders, rejecting citizen and other external oversights. Instead, complaints of abuse were handled internally, which likely resulted in no punitive action being taken against officers, even years later.[5]

Criminologists have explored the use of force and developed theoretical explanations for police brutality. Two notable criminologists, Carl Klockars and John Van Maanen, discussed the dynamics of police interactions that can lead to the use of force.

KLOCKARS' "THE DIRTY HARRY PROBLEM"

There are many explanations for officer misconduct, ranging from it being a product of the police subculture within a department, such as the case with LAPD's CRASH unit, to a "bad apple" rogue officer who has a propensity to use excessive force and violence. Criminologist Carl Klockars explained the likelihood of excessive force used by officers using a typology scheme.

Klockars classifies officers into four typologies using *means* (the ways in which officers seek justice) and *ends* (the end goal or result) of justice. The means and ends can either be morally good or morally dirty.[6]

The first category is *morally good means*, which simply means that an officer takes a lawful approach in apprehending a suspect.

Morally dirty means denotes that an officer is using a morally questionable approach to apprehend a suspect, which can be illegal by nature.

Morally good ends means an officer's end goal is a lawful arrest of the suspect, in accordance to his lawful duty.

Morally dirty ends indicates an officer has a motive other than a lawful arrest of a suspect. Instead, the officer has defined his goal as an alternative form of justice.

Police officers can be categorized into one of the four categories. Most officers fall into the first category of morally good means with morally good ends. This is your prototypical police officer who follows the rules in apprehending suspects for the purpose of prosecution. However, the **Dirty Harry Problem** occurs when morally good ends are achieved with morally dirty means.

The Dirty Harry Problem is derived from the movie *Dirty Harry*, in which Clint Eastwood's character, a cop named Harry Callahan, must save a kidnapped girl. With little time to spare, Harry takes it into his own hands to illegally torture a suspect to find the location of the girl, who ends up already being dead. Harry's actions were considered highly illegal and inadmissible in any court, but illustrate an ends-justifies-the-means attitude that some officers hold in dealing with crime and justice. In less extreme cases, officers may mete out their own version of "street justice" when they feel the legal system will be ineffective in dealing with suspects.

The use of dirty means has some conditions that are dependent upon the officer's circumstances. First, it assumes that the officer has run out of legal morally good means to achieve justice. The officer has no choice but to resort to dirty means, a sort of exigent circumstance that can save a life. For example, if perhaps the officer can find the location of a kidnapped person or the officer can save a future victim by not letting the suspect go free.

Klockars specifies several additional conditions:

1. The operative assumption of guilt
2. The worst of all possible guilt
3. The great guilty place assumption
4. The not guilty (this time) assumption

These mentalities are used to justify alternative (dirty) means to mete out justice, which primarily involves the excessive use of force.

VAN MAANEN'S "THE ASSHOLE"

Another explanation of the use of force can be found in Van Maanen's categorization of "the asshole" by police officers.[7]

Recall that an "asshole" is a derogatory term used to describe people who make a police officer's job more difficult. These are individuals who do not respect an officer's authority, control, and definition over a situation. The asshole can be described as a person who does not accept and cooperate with the officer's command of a situation or encounter. Officers must maintain control of a situation at all times. Any person who does not accept their subservient role and the officer's power can be deemed an asshole and subjected to **street justice**.

Even persons who have not violated the law in any major way can still be subject to forms of punishment or street justice by the officer for simply being an asshole. This, in police jargon, is known as being "in contempt of cop" or "P.O.P" ("Piss Off the Police"). This can be the law school student or even the criminology student who knows enough about the law to question or challenge an officer's legal authority of a given situation.

One type of individual that has seemed to get under officers' skin is in police circles known as the "**sovereign citizen**." These individuals are part of a larger movement that believes the US government is illegitimate, and therefore reject police legal authority and openly challenge officers. These individuals risk street justice in the form of a slew of minor citations, to being arrested and taken to the local jail for identification purposes, where that person can be subjected to booking procedures, including a strip search.

The extreme form of street justice to an individual deemed an asshole is police brutality. The justification, for the officer, can be considered protecting other officers and the sanctity of the policing profession. If respect is eroded by allowing increasingly disrespectful behavior, officers can face increasing cases of citizens challenging police authority which ultimately increases the dangerousness of the job. This in turn erodes the police "**command presence**," where the mere presence of a police officer communicates supreme authority and demands respect. The effective use of the command presence can diffuse situations where violence may occur, such as a suspect at a bar dropping a broken bottle and cooperating with an arrest instead of fighting with the officer. Perhaps most importantly, officers cannot back down to any challenges to authority.

Command presence in essence, is a form of "forced respect" given to officers. In LAPD Officer William Dunn's 2008 biographical book about his rookie year on the force, Dunn shares his experience with forced respect given to officers.[8] He writes:

> *As we reach the crowd, the gangsters grudgingly make room for us. Off to one side is a cluster of older guys, in their thirties and forties, shoulders buffed by prison iron. They dully look at me with arms crossed. Many of the younger ones try and stare me down, but I don't pay them any attention. They tell you that no matter how much you want to act tough and stare back, eyes can't kill.*

Waistbands holding handguns are more of concern, as are hands moving to hiding places. And even if I did want to stare someone down, where do I begin; must be ten, twenty guys trying to get my attention for a staring contest.

Even though we are outnumbered, the Crips give us a wide berth. Six LAPD officers command a fair amount of respect, even from two hundred Crips. Not that we could handle them as we are. We have no illusion. But we can request help, and within a short time have a force to resolve any situation. One young hothead might, for a moment, get an upper hand, but there would be no long term win. And there would be a response afterward-though not what one might think. When gang members attack officers, the bad guy's homies also suffer. There will be increased enforcement in the gang area, an action that not only puts allot (sic) of homies in jail but also costs the homies money by way of traffic fines, impound fees and loss of criminal enterprise such as revenues from heavy enforcement at their dope corners.

ETHNIC MINORITIES AND MINORITY AREAS

There are conflicting studies of police bias when it comes to force toward certain racial minorities. Some studies show a pattern of a disproportionate use of force on African Americans. A 2016 study that examined over 19,000 uses of force incidents in eleven mid- to large-size cities in the United States found police used force against African American three times more than Whites, even when controlling for racial disparities in crime.[9] Another 2016 study by the National Bureau of Economic Research found racial disparities toward Blacks for nonlethal use of force during police encounters, including being pepper-sprayed, pushed to the ground, and handcuffed, even when time and place were controlled for.[10] These findings were corroborated by the Bureau of Justice Statistics (BJS), which found that Blacks were more likely to experience nonfatal force than both Hispanics and Whites.[11] Of those surveyed, nearly 87 percent believed the police behaved improperly, with approximately three-quarters feeling police were verbally and physically abusive.

Not all studies found racial disparities with police use of force. One 2017 study published in the *American Journal of Public Health* examined data from Dallas Police Department, examining over 5,500 use-of-force reports from 2014 to 2015.[12] When controlling for types of calls was considered, there were few discrepancies. For example, use of force was significantly higher for individuals under the influence of drugs or alcohol. However, the same study did find that 48 percent of White officers used force against someone who was not White, while only 3 percent of Black officers used force against a White suspect.

In recent years, with the emergence of the Black Lives Matter movement, the public discussion has centered around whether police show bias in using lethal force against certain minority groups. Studies examining lethal force show evidence that generally support this narrative. [13] For example, one 2015 study analyzing county-level data in the United States from 2011 to 2014 found that police were nearly three and a half times more likely to shoot an unarmed Black person than to shoot an unarmed White person. [14] More alarming perhaps, was a New York State Governor's task force study published in 2010 that examined three decades of data on police-on-police shootings that found Black and Latino off-duty officers risk mistaken identity by on-duty officers, and were more likely to be shot. [15] The study found that since 1982, nine out of ten off-duty officers killed by an on-duty officer were Black or Latino, suggesting strong bias, whether conscious or inherent.

Police bias, whether real or perceived by the community, is very problematic given the history of police brutality that has sparked a series of riots. Police bias exacerbates strained community/police relations in minority communities and makes the officers' jobs more difficult and possibly more dangerous. Areas that have an antagonistic relationship between police and citizens often undermine police efforts to fight crime, which can further widen the gap between police and the community and undermine community policing efforts.

FACTORS AND REASONS FOR VIOLENCE

There are several reasons proposed by the criminological research for the disproportionately high number of police brutality cases with minorities. Police researchers David Jacobs and Robert O'Brien looked at structural issues involving police violence, specifically the use of lethal force, and found that the political environment influences the rate at which Blacks are killed by police. [16] They found that cities with more Blacks and recent expansions in the Black population increased the rate of killings by police. They explain that the use of lethal force by police is used to preserve social order. Their structural analysis was backed by data showing that having a Black mayor reduced the killings, possibly attributing to policy direction regarding racial profiling and racial sensitivity.

Police use of force may be attributed to the level of perceived respect received by community members, and reciprocal respect levels given to the public by police. One 2002 study on policing neighborhoods found levels of respect to be a significant factor in contributing to police use of force. [17] The researchers observed over 3,000 police/citizen encounters in Indianapolis and St. Petersburg analyzing influences on respect, such as suspect behavior, suspect personal characteristics, and location of the encounter. They found that how a suspect behaved toward the officer was the most predominant determinant. Interestingly though, it was found that minority suspects experienced disrespect less often than Whites. Their findings, however, support

Jacobs and O'Brien's observations on policy influences, which showed that in St. Petersburg the Chief of Police prioritized eradicating police abuses. The findings also showed that the suspect's sex, age, income, and degree of neighborhood disadvantage were also significant factors in the chance of police brutality.

The main sociological theory on police behavior is criminologist Donald Black's explanation, which states that police action is a consequence of the nature of police/citizen encounters. Black asserts that police are less likely to take legal or coercive action when the accusers as well as the suspects are both of lower status.[18] Police are more likely to take action against lower-class persons when the accuser is of a higher status. Whether or not a police officer takes action is determined by the interaction between social class, race, and gender, as well as the seriousness of offense, nature of the relationship between suspect and offender, number of officers on the scene, and characteristics of the neighborhood. Black also explains that Blacks are more likely to be arrested because they frequently act disrespectfully toward officer.[19]

Some scholars explain police brutality as a manifestation of the personality of the officers themselves. One 1972 study found that officers, in general, tend to have "authoritarian" personalities which makes them more likely to use force.[20] Authoritarian personalities are the architype mindset of the professional police officer who must command absolute obedience and submission to the officer's authority. Recall Van Maanen's "asshole" who subjects himself to street justice when challenging this order. The authoritarian personality can be explained by the police subculture that fosters this command authority and weeds out individuals with a weak command presence.

REBUILDING COMMUNITY TRUST

Community trust, especially in poorer ethnic enclaves, is hard to come by as a result of decades of abuse that is often not reported or seen by the general public. This ranges from questionable stop-and-frisks, to racial profiling, to instances of brutality. This history of abuse has led to mutual distrust between officers and community members. This side effect of professionalization, which sought to ameliorate police corruption, has driven this large divide. Reestablishing community trust is often difficult.

Police have tried in recent times to implement cultural sensitivity training as well as hire women and minority officers. As mentioned in previous chapters, classroom activities that are not crime-control or law enforcement oriented are not taken seriously by recruits and the police subculture. Furthermore, women and minority officers share similar views and show little empathy for poor urban minority areas that are seen as a hegemonic cycle of creating the conditions of their own demise.

Another police implementation to try to improve police/citizen relations is community policing, which seeks to reestablish personal relations between police and the community. Walking patrols, bicycle beats, town halls, and informal encounters try to soften the image of the police as stoic and distant enforcers of the law. However, such efforts have had just limited success. We will explore community policing in much more depth in a later chapter.

SUMMARY

Police use of force remains a contentious and controversial issue in policing, not only because police are one of the only organizations legally sanctioned to do so, but also because of the how, why, and to whom force is used. When used improperly or excessively against certain minority groups, such as African Americans, whether real or perceived, it has historically triggered social upheavals. While police are not entirely to blame for these riots, which may be indicative of deeper rooted societal problems, such as racism and poverty, police are the visible manifestations of the state.

Explaining police use of force is complex and nuanced. Use of force is often based on the necessity of police to control situations. Losing this control and backing down is perceived as being determinantal to officer safety in current and future encounters by police. A strong police presence can deter dangerous situations. Therefore, challenges to an officer's definition of the situation can place a person at risk of street justice. Criminologists and social scientists have theorized what triggers use of force through officer mentalities as well as citizen interactions. Problems are compounded when use of force is used on minority groups that have a fractured and contentious history with police. In the next chapter, we look at another controversial issue: racial profiling.

NOTES

1. Max Weber, *The Theory of Social and Economic Organization*, translated by A.M. Henderson and Talcott Parsons (London: Collier Macmillan, 1947).

2. See www.theiacp.org.

3. See http://www.nij.gov/topics/law-enforcement/officer-safety/use-of-force/Pages/welcome.aspx.

4. "Christopher Commission Report," Report of the Independent Commission on the Los Angeles Police Department, 1991, http://www.parc.info/client_files/Special%20Reports/1%20-%20Chistopher%20Commision.pdf.

5. "Five Years Later: A Report to the Los Angeles Police Commission on the Los Angeles Police Department's Implementation of Independent Commission Recommendations," Report of the Independent Commission on the Los Angeles Police Department, 1996, http://

www.parc.info/client_files/Special%20Reports/2%20-%20Five%20Years%20Later%20-%20Christopher%20Commission.pdf.

6. Carl B. Klockars, "The Dirty Harry Problem," in *Policing: Key Readings* (Portland, OR: Willan, 2005), 581–595.

7. John Van Maanen, "The Asshole," in *Policing, CA: A View from the Street* (Santa Monica, CA: Good Year Publishing, 1978).

8. William Dunn, *Boot: An LAPD Officer's Rookie Year in South Central Los Angeles* (New York: iUniverse, 2007).

9. Phillip A. Goff et al., "The Science of Justice: Race, Arrests, and Police Use of Force," *Center for Policing Equity,* 2016, http://policingequity.org/wp-content/uploads/2016/07/CPE_SoJ_Race-Arrests-UoF_2016-07-08-1130.pdf.

10. Roland G. Fryer Jr., "An Empirical Analysis of Racial Differences in Police Use of Force," *National Bureau of Economic Research,* 2016, http://www.nber.org/papers/w22399.pdf.

11. Shelley S. Hyland, Lynn Langton, and Elizabeth Davis, "Police Use of Nonfatal Force, 2002–2011," *Bureau of Justice Statistics,* 2015, https://www.bjs.gov/index.cfm?ty=pbdetail&iid=5456.

12. Katelyn K. Jetelina et al., "Dissecting the Complexities of the Relationship between Police Officer-Civilian Race/Ethnicity Dyads and Less-than-Lethal Use of Force," *American Journal of Public Health* 107, no. 7 (2017): 1164–1170. doi: 10.2105/AJPH.2017.303807.

13. Geoffrey P. Alpert and Roger G. Dunham, *Understanding Police Use of Force: Officers, Suspects, and Reciprocity* (New York: Cambridge University Press, 2004).

14. Cody T. Ross, "A Multi-Level Bayesian Analysis of Racial Bias in Police Shootings at the County-Level in the United States, 2011–2014." *PLoS ONE* 10, no. 11 (2015). doi: 10.1371/journal.pone.0141854.\.

15. Christopher Stone et al., "Reducing Inherent Danger: Report of the Task Force on Police-on-Police Shootings," *New York State Task Force on Police-on-Police Shootings,* 2010, https://sites.hks.harvard.edu/criminaljustice-backup/publications/Police-on-Police_Shootings.pdf.

16. David Jacobs and Robert M. O'Brien, "The Determinants of Deadly Force: A Structural Analysis of Police Violence," *American Journal of Sociology* 10, no. 4 (1998): 837–862.

17. Stephen D. Mastrofski, Michael D. Reisig, and John D. McCluskey, "Police Disrespect Toward the Public: An Encounter-Based Analysis," *Criminology* 40, no. 3 (2002): 519–552. doi: 10.1111/j.1745-9125.2002.tb00965.x.

18. Donald J. Black, "The Social Organization of Arrest," *Stanford Law Review* 23 (1971): 1087–1111. doi: 10.2307/1227728.

19. Donald J. Black, *The Manners and Customs of the Police* (New York: Academic Press, 1980).

20. Robert W. Balch, "The Police Personality: Fact or Fiction?" *The Journal of Criminal Law, Criminology and Police Science* 63, no. 1 (1972): 106–119.

Chapter Eight

Racial Profiling

Police racial profiling has been arguably the most controversial issue in policing for the past few decades. Recently, racial tensions between the police and some minority communities have drawn a lot of attention. The divide between police and minority communities has visibly surfaced with the emergence of the Black Lives Matter movement, followed by the subsequent Blue Lives Matter movement. Issues of race and police brutality even sparked the protest in the NFL with some players kneeling during the playing of the national anthem, from 2016 to 2018.

Racial profiling is a complex issue, and is more than simply police being racist or racist officers. While racist police officers do exist, racial profiling is a manifestation of how police operate in a world they are not personally familiar with under professionalization: profiling can be interpreted as recognizing patterns. Drawing from group and personal experiences, recognizing patterns translates to managing the risks of a dangerous working environment. Race can be considered simply one factor that can be recognized in a pattern. Moreover, profiling, including racial profiling, occurs in virtually every profession, especially among service industries that have direct contact with the public. Ask any experienced barista and he or she will tell you with relative accuracy how certain people tend to order their coffee, or a waiter will know who the best and worst tippers are.

The combination of race with policing, however, is much more consequential. Whether racial profiling is purposeful or not, racial profiling is often discussed as an everyday reality is ethnic communities. Racial profiling is difficult to prove, and little research exists on its prevalence. Collective official data is hard to come by for traffic stops. For example, the UCR does not collect traffic stop data. Furthermore, many citizen/police interactions are not recorded, such as informal stop and talks with citizens. More invasive

stop and frisks by officers are often considered "consensual" police encounters that further muddy the prevalence of racial profiling, which may be
masked by probable cause. Whether real or perceived, racial profiling can
strain police/community relations and undermine efforts in community policing.

Several topics concerning racial profiling are discussed in this chapter:

1. The definition of racial profiling and its prevalence
2. Legal issues of racial discrimination
3. The prevalence of racial profiling
4. The minority experience
5. Racism and the police subculture
6. Alternative explanations of racial profiling

WHAT IS RACIAL PROFILING?

Racial profiling is the use of race as a determining factor by police on
whether to engage in law enforcement activity. These law enforcement activities usually involves police officers being proactive in looking for crime,
such as traffic stops, stopping pedestrians to talk, searching for contraband,
and placing certain racial groups under greater surveillance. While good
police practice involves identifying patterns of crime and group characteristics associated with the crime, racial profiling is the discriminatory practice
of identifying and associating crime with a racial group solely based on race,
ethnicity, and national original.

Racial profiling also includes "**discriminatory omission**." Discriminatory omission is defined as not providing adequate police services based on
racial or other forms of discrimination. The most blatant case of police discriminatory omission was witnessed during the civil rights movement of
1950s and 1960s. During that period in Southern states, sheriff deputies took
little to no action as Klu Klux Klan members harassed and terrorized Blacks.
In some cases, these acts included lynchings of Blacks that resulted in the
death.

Racial profiling is not new and is prevalent outside of official police
work. For example, many minority youths often find themselves being followed by store employees or security personnel in malls, who often suspect
them of shoplifting without any evidence or cause. However, public employees, such as police officers, cannot use race solely as a reason for a course of
action. Moreover, racial discrimination, constitutionally, is prohibited.

CONSTITUTIONAL LAW AND RACIAL DISCRIMINATION

The United States Supreme Court has ruled that racial discrimination is a violation of the Constitution. According to the law, race is considered a **"suspect classification."** This means that any time the state (government) wants to classify people according to race for differential treatment, it is very "suspect" or suspicious, without a very strong justification to do so. The state must meet a very high legal standard in order to justify the separation of the different races. These legal standards were shaped by two famous landmark cases.

Plessy v. Ferguson (1896): This landmark Supreme Court decision upheld the "separate but equal" standard, which justified separating groups based on race. In a seven to one decision, the Court upheld the 1890 Louisiana law (Louisiana Separate Car Act) that separated Whites and non-Whites in railroad cars. The Court upheld the decision citing that as long as the facilities were equal, there was no real discrimination in the act of segregation. However, it was shown that "Whites only" facilities were clearly better than for non-Whites. This case was later overturned in 1954 in the *Brown v. Board of Education* case.

Brown v. Board of Education (1954): The landmark Supreme Court decision ruled that separate but equal facilities were no in fact equal and violated the Equal Protection Clause of the Fourteenth Amendment of the Constitution. Specifically, the case involved public schools in Kansas, where White students were separated from non-Whites in separate but equal facilities. However, the Court ruled unanimously that this was "inherently unequal" and constituted racial discrimination. Brown's ruling overturned Plessy and set new standards for any type of racial discrimination.

Racial discrimination by the state is not illegal per se, but requires a high threshold for its justification. The legal justification comes in the form of a legal litmus test called **"strict scrutiny."** Strict scrutiny says that in order for some state organization to violate a Constitutional Amendment, it must (1) have a compelling government interest, (2) be narrowly tailored to accomplish this, and (3) use the least restrictive means. This means that if the state wants to suspend, for example, the freedom of speech (a First Amendment right), such as allowing someone to yell "fire" in a crowded theater, it must justify all three reasons.

The most often cited example is the proverbial yelling "fire!" in a crowded theater (Schenck v. United States, 1919). The Court ruled that the (1) compelling government interest was public safety, preventing people from being trampled in the ensuing chaos, (2) it was narrowly tailored to the specific word "fire" and within a theater, and (3) it was considered the least restrictive way of doing so. If, however, the state policy was to ban the word "fire" in a two block radius of the theater, it would be too broad and restrictive, and in violation of the Constitution.

Racial discrimination uses the same *strict scrutiny* standard, which is the highest legal threshold, to allow the state to justify its use. As mentioned, separating people by race is considered very suspect: people are born a certain race or ethnicity and there is no inherent justification for each group being treated differently. Therefore, there is no "compelling government interest" in doing so. This is not to say that separating the races is not justified under certain conditions. Take for example prisons, where the compelling government interest in separating races is the prevention of interracial violence, which has been historically true. Racial profiling, however, is a clear violation of the Equal Protection Clause of the Fourteenth Amendment and is simply constitutionally illegal without a compelling government interest.

In addition to violating equal rights protection, racial profiling violates the Fourth Amendment of the Bill of Rights. The Fourth Amendment prohibits search and seizure without probable cause. The law purposely limits the scope of police power to prevent a police state and to protect democratic freedoms of citizens. Pulling over a person based on race does not constitute probable cause, which is defined as a reasonable amount of suspicion to strongly justify a crime or criminal act having been committed. The standard can informally be thought of as—would a judge issue a warrant for a particular search based primarily on the race of the suspect. This would certainly not pass muster, again, rendering the stop illegal. If a person is stopped illegally in violation of the Fourth Amendment, all evidence is inadmissible in court even if illegal substances were found, such as illicit drugs. This also includes any confessions and further physical evidence that were obtained subsequent to the illegal stop, described in a legal metaphor as "fruit from the poisonous tree."

RESEARCH IN RACIAL PROFILING: MYTH OR REALITY?

There is no official centralized recorded data on racial profiling. Direct data on racial profiling is essentially nonexistent since it must be proven to be a case of racial profiling. Criminological researchers typically piece together data from a sample of direct observations, or make inferences about race and ethnicity using data collected from a handful of police agencies. According to the BJS, in 2001, there were only sixteen state police agencies that were required to collect race and ethnicity data for traffic stops. In 2004, twenty-nine state law enforcement agencies, such as certain highway patrols or troopers, required traffic stops to record race and ethnicity.[1] That was the last year that requirement took place.

Despite a large sample size from the twenty-nine state law enforcement agencies, the data collected is problematic. The methods used in determining a motorist's race differed amongst different departments. Twenty-seven agencies relied on the stopping officer's observations. Some agencies used the motorists' response to the question, while some departments relied on the Bureau of Motor Vehicle data listed on their driver's licenses. Officer observations may not be an accurate indicator of race or ethnicity. Officers may misidentify different ethnicities, especially with mixed races. Nevertheless, some researchers were able to measure for racial profiling using these data.

Despite incomplete official data sources, researchers have typically confirmed that Black and Hispanic motorists are disproportionately subject to police vehicle searches. A 2002 study found that Black drivers driving on Maryland's I-95 were twice as likely as White motorists to be stopped, and five times more likely to be searched.[2] A 2004 study found that bias against minorities accounted for at least 30 percent of all discretionary searches.[3] Additionally, the study found Black motorists are most at risk of biased police when travelling through areas where Blacks are a small percentage of the population.

One of the most comprehensive studies of racial profiling for traffic stops was conducted in 1996 by John Lamberth of Temple University. The study analyzed traffic stops in New Jersey and Maryland, comparing percentages of African American drivers who were stopped, ticketed, and arrested to their total numbers on the road crossing a turnpike.[4] The turnpike collected data such as driver speed, which showed abnormalities in speed differences between drivers pulled over. The study found that in New Jersey, over 73 percent of those drivers who were stopped and arrested were Black, but only 13.5 percent of the cars on the road were driven by Black drivers, leading to the conclusion that "the race of the occupants and/or drivers of the cars is a decisive factor or a factor with great explanatory power."

More recent studies of racial profiling have attempted to examine large data sets. Sociologist Joscha Legewie analyzed 3.9 million pedestrian stops in New York City by police and found race-based motivations for police action.[5] The study found that after the fatal shootings of two police officers by Black suspects, racial profiling and discriminatory use of force increased significantly for days after.

Not all data suggests racial profiling exists. Criminologists Anthony Vito, Elizabeth Grossi, and George Higgins looked at more than 40,000 traffic stops in Louisville, Kentucky, and found that overall, the decision to search is random, and racial profile was not a significant factor in the search decision.[6] Despite mixed quantitative studies, qualitative accounts of racial profiling paint a vivid account of perceived racial profiling whether or not it is a real phenomenon statistically.

THE MINORITY EXPERIENCE

Qualitative research on racial profiling uses ethnographies. **Ethnographical research** focuses less on the numbers, such as recorded incidents of racial profiling, and instead examines the cultural phenomenon and context through storytelling and narratives to reveal meanings behind actions. In principle, examining these details produces richer descriptions, values, and meaning based on the subject's perspective.[7] Psychologists Andrea Dottolo and Abigail Stewart interviewed thirty-eight middle-aged Black and White men and women high school alumni about their experiences with police encounters and found significant differences between races, with Black interviewees claiming to experience and witness discrimination far greater than White subjects.[8] One account, for example, shows the kind of rich descriptions of racial profiling:

> *I watch these guys, man, this, this kid pulled up in front of my house to drop somebody off. But before he could—I mean, the cops were all over us. This kid he'd never done anything wrong. They had him out of the car. I'm down there making a fool out of myself. 'What you doing like that.' But I couldn't under-stand why they had him handcuffed already. Man was sitting in his car. They tore his car apart. Couldn't find anything because, of course, he never did anything. And they, they said, 'oh, we're sorry,' and left. I mean, his door panels were off. Like that. He made a complaint. I don't know what happened then. But his, his dad went down there and almost got locked up for acting—but the kid never done anything.*

Many people are simply oblivious to racial profiling because it is something that does not affect them personally. They may read about it occasionally or see it on the news when a major incident breaks out, especially when the American Civil Liberties Union (ACLU) makes claims about illegal police racial profiling.[9] These claims are often explained by different narratives, for example, law enforcement may assert claims of racial profiling as a mis-understanding or an isolated incident. However, many racial minorities explain frequent encounters with police to be examples of racial profiling and normalized everyday racism.[10] These encounters can range from being stopped while walking down the street for a brief informal chat with an officer, to a being regularly pulled over for small or virtually non-existent infractions, such as a minor vehicle maintenance violation. The phenomenon of regular encounters with police for no apparent reason by African Americans is pejoratively referred to as **"driving while Black"** (DWB).

DRIVING WHILE BLACK

The ACLU gives an account of what that term, "driving while Black," means, with this example:[11]

> *On a hot summer afternoon in August 1998, 37-year-old U.S. Army Sergeant First Class Rossano V. Gerald and his young son Gregory drove across the Oklahoma border into a nightmare. A career soldier and a highly decorated veteran of Desert Storm and Operation United Shield in Somalia, SFC Gerald, a black man of Panamanian descent, found that he could not travel more than 30 minutes through the state without being stopped twice: first by the Roland City Police Department, and then by the Oklahoma Highway Patrol.*
>
> *During the second stop, which lasted two-and-half hours, the troopers terrorized SFC Gerald's 12-year-old son with a police dog, placed both father and son in a closed car with the air conditioning off and fans blowing hot air, and warned that the dog would attack if they attempted to escape. Halfway through the episode —perhaps realizing the extent of their lawlessness—the troopers shut off the patrol car's video evidence camera.*

More proof that the DWB phenomenon is real is when unlikely Blacks are pulled over for minor offenses by police, showing that class alone cannot explain the cause. In other words, police may identify certain older model, run-down (perhaps with slight damage) cars that poorer drivers may drive, to pull over. Many point to affluent Blacks being pulled over for no apparent reason. African American celebrities and athletes that claim to have been victims of DWB include Wesley Snipes, Will Smith, Blair Underwood, Le-Var Burton, Marcus Allen, and even O. J. Simpson's lawyer, the late Johnnie Cochran.

Cochran's encounter with law enforcement illustrates the experience that many Black drivers face. Before working on the Simpson defense, Cochran was a Los Angeles assistant district attorney. Cochran recalls a specific incident driving down Sunset Boulevard with his two children in the back seat when LAPD officers pulled him over with guns drawn. The officers claimed they believed Cochran was driving a stolen car and without any legal basis began to search it, but only found Cochran's official D.A. badge. According to Cochran, "When they saw my badge, they ran for cover."[12]

In 2017, two Orlando, Florida, officers drew widespread criticism when body cam video of a traffic stop was released by the Orlando Police Department, for pulling over the state's only Black elected state attorney, Aramis Ayala.[13] When the officers discovered her identity, they claimed to stop her for a dark tint on her vehicle and because her state vehicle information was masked by a confidential license plate number that did not allow information to be pulled up. They quickly released her without incident. However, most of the public felt the reasons given by the officers were bogus, and it instead, suggested racial profiling was the real motivating factor.

These types of real or perceived unjustified stops that have become routine for African American communities have many consequences that further strain community/police relations and undermine community policing efforts. The DWB phenomenon is often justified by some police departments as a byproduct of good police work that is not based on race but rather on suspicious activities, that nets positive results for police making arrests and taking drugs off the streets. However, the accumulation of these traffic stops results in deep cultural mistrust and cynicism by entire African American communities towards police and the entire criminal justice system. Moreover, innocent individuals getting stopped for no apparent reason produces fear, anger, and humiliation, as they often face being searched and handcuffed on a public street in plain view.

CRITICAL RACE THEORY: EVERYDAY RACISM

Claims of blatant racism by police are relatively few in today's world. However, the issues of racial profiling by police point to more subtle forms of racism that still exist and are often masked or do not draw critical public attention. One theoretical framework that explains this phenomenon is critical race theory. Critical race theory, which is a derivative of the larger law and societal movement of the late 1960s and 1970s, explains that racism has become normalized in American society. According to the theory, on the surface society appears to be fair—pointing to civil rights laws that passed in the 1960s, and other antidiscrimination efforts to create formal equal opportunity.[14] Virtually all company policies contain antidiscriminatory language, for example. However, critical legal scholars often argue this superficial fairness only serves to mask discrimination in practice.

Critical race theorists assert that racism has become more subtle and insidious. Formal equal opportunities serve to mask the realities of racism, such as DWB, to make it look "normal." Accordingly, racism is normalized in mainstream American society since Americans are placated by the appearance of fairness. However, critical race scholars point to the evidence of the inherent unfairness and discriminatory nature of the criminal justice system. For example, they draw attention to legal disparities produced and reinforced by the criminal justice and legal system between elite classes and poor minority classes.

Disparities in the law point to inherent bias in a system that appears to be fair and legitimate on the surface. The 1980s war on drugs focused primarily on the crack cocaine epidemic in poor ghetto neighborhoods. "Get tough" legislation resulted in federal sentencing guidelines, which specified five grams of crack cocaine netted a mandatory five year minimum prison sentence. Powder cocaine, a drug associated with the affluent but is of the same base elements as crack cocaine, required 500 grams in order to yield the five year minimum federal sentence. The 100:1 ratio finally changed in 2010 when Congress passed the Fair Sentencing Act, which reduced the disparity to eighteen to one. When coupled with biased policing of inner cities and street crimes, compared with affluent white-collar crimes, the picture of the experience of poor minority groups becomes clearer.

EXPLAINING RACIAL PROFILING AND THE NATURE OF POLICE WORK

While it is easy to dismiss racial profiling as a product of racist officers or a racist department, its explanation is much more complex. A primary function of police work is recognizing patterns and using these patterns to fight crime and minimize the inherent dangers associated with the job. Officers increase their ability to recognize patterns of behavior, criminal activity, environmental factors, and other possible correlates of crime, through experience. A seasoned veteran, for instance, may develop a "sixth sense" in recognizing something suspicious about a person, such as lying or other forms of deception. Experienced detectives may draw from patterns of previous cases to help solve a current case. In other words, profiling of all sorts can be considered a crucial element of good police work and a good officer.

Recognizing behavioral characteristics and basing judgement and predictions on those patterns for a group is essentially the definition of profiling. Associating behavioral characteristics with groups and treating those groups accordingly, or in other words stereotyping, allows officers to react to new situations based on past experiences. For many classifications, this may be good police work, such as recognizing suspicious behavior and things that may be out of place.

Most importantly, police officers operate in their world using stereotypes to assess those "types" of people who pose threats to them. Criminologist Jerome Skolnick describes these individuals as **"symbolic assailants."**[15] He explains:

> *The policeman, because his work requires him to be occupied continually with potential violence, develops perceptual shorthand to identify certain kinds of people as symbolic assailants, that is, as persons who use gesture, language, and attire that the policeman has come to recognize as a prelude to violence.*

Race is one of these factors that is part of the characteristic of assessing the symbolic assailant. According to Skolnick, "Factors that become important in determining danger are a person's actual behavior, language, dress, area, and in some situations, age, sex, and ethnicity." The act of stereotyping, which includes racial profiling, therefore, is not based on hatred or racism, but instead, can be considered a rational and logical act of survival for officers. In other words, the same pattern recognition skills that keep an officer safe and make him or her a good officer are also what makes an officer appear to be racist.

The most common justification for stopping a disproportionate number of Black drivers in traffic stops is explained through this rational lens. The argument goes like this: Blacks commit a disproportionate amount of certain crimes which justifies police focusing their efforts on African Americans. Legal expert David Harris writes of how one Maryland state police officer explains that it is not racism, but rather, it is good policing.[16] He states that racial profiling is "an unfortunate byproduct of sound police policies." In other words, finding patterns in crime helps police catch criminals; and since Blacks engage in a disproportionate number of those crimes, it makes sense to stop a disproportionate amount of Black drivers. In essence, many police officers and departments conduct activities that are unofficially based on race but do not consider themselves racist.

The culmination of police actions that produce racial disparities can be considered **institutional racism**, which is a subtle form of racism that is not reflected in official policies and procedures. A study of the British police describes the situation:

> If the phrase "institutional racism" had been used to describe not only explicit manifestations of racism at direction and policy level, but also unwitting discrimination at the organizational level, then the reality of indirect racism is more subtle, hidden and potentially more pervasive nature would have been addressed.

Sociologist John Lea categorizes institutional racism into three categories: (1) racism of overtly prejudiced individuals, (2) racism as conscious and deliberate policy, and (3) racism as unintentional or unwitting discriminatory practice in the mode of operation in organizations that are formally non-discriminatory.[17] The third type, it is argued, is the most prevalent amongst police and reflects the failure of an organization to detect and control such manifestations of race.

However, how can one claim institutional racism when there are African American police officers? Recall that the police subculture produces a unique worldview based on shared experiences. This homogenous worldview is galvanized during the selection process, training, and experiences. Through learning police work, recruits also inherently learn biases and patterns of behavior. These biases are learned by both White and minority officers. Even

African American police officers will share the same view of Blacks as their White counterparts.

Some officers, aware of official department policy against racism and prejudice, have subtle and creative justifications for probable cause in pulling over minority drivers. Questionable justifications include the stereotypical broken tail light and observed swerving. Some officers simply respond with the proverbial "it's not illegal to profile cars," referring to seemingly preferred vehicles driven by different minority groups, ranging from "low-riders" to modified Japanese import sports cars.

Racism does exist in police departments and it is not always subtle and covert. The LAPD came under harsh criticism after the subsequent investigation of the Rodney King beating, when officers were heard using racial slurs and epithets referring to Blacks. This reflects a larger culture that is at best, insensitive and tolerant of racism by some officers, and at worst, a racist organization. LAPD Sergeant Stacey Koon, on the day of the beating, described a domestic disturbance call involving Blacks, through his mobile data terminal as, "Gorillas in the Mist," referring to the novel and motion picture of the story of scientist Dian Fossey.

Another example is the high-profile LAPD, O. J. Simpson murder case, where LAPD detective Mark Fuhrman was taped bragging about beating Black suspects. Detective Fuhrman was recorded in an interviewing saying, "Yeah we work with niggers and gangs. You can take one of these niggers, drag 'em into the alley and beat the shit out of them and kick them. You can see them twitch. It really relieves your tension . . . we had them begging that they'd never be gang members again, begging us." He told the interviewer that he frequently told African American suspects, "You do what you're told, understand, nigger?" Fuhrman's and Koon's testimonies painted a picture of an organization that was tolerant of racism. However, while Fuhrman and Koon's cases are egregious and blatant racism, there are alternative explanations to police actions that can eliminate accusations of race.

ALTERNATIVE EXPLANATIONS

The first alternative explanation for racial profiling is the "rotten apples" explanation wherein every organization it is inevitable that there are a few bad individuals. Police, in this case, are no exception. Police departments are not racist organizations, as reflected by proactive minority hiring policies in virtually every department in the United States. However, taking into account the "blue wall of silence," one has to wonder whether silence by other officers equates to tacit acceptance of racism within the department.

Another view that can potentially mitigate the viewpoint of racial profiling and explain disparities in arrests is the fact that police are a reactive organization. This means that they respond to calls for service. Oftentimes calls come in with suspect descriptions in which the suspects are Hispanic or Black. Police, therefore, stop and question individuals matching these descriptions that are based on the call. This means that many Hispanic or Black males within a certain radius of the service call can be subject to a stop and search—which is a legitimate stop based on probable cause. Unfortunately, in ethnic enclaves, a 5'10" to 6' Black male wearing a dark shirt and blue jeans may fit the description of many individuals living in a neighborhood, putting police in the precarious position of stopping and questioning many Black males who are not the suspect.

In 2018, an incident in Philadelphia that swept across the Internet with millions of views, illustrates how police can be accused of and blamed for racial profiling. A Starbucks employee called 9-1-1 on two young Black men in the store, Donte Robinson and Rashon Nelson, who did not order anything but were waiting for an associate to arrive for a business meeting. The barista claimed the men violated store policy by using the restroom and not buying anything and therefore were trespassing and refusing to leave. The officers were recorded arresting the men to the protests of other patrons who shouted that the men did nothing wrong. While it was found that the officers, one of whom was Black, were following protocol, they drew sharp criticism and blame for being racially insensitive, when in fact one can place the blame on the Starbucks staff for implicit racial bias. The incident ended with settlements with Starbucks and the city of Philadelphia, along with apologies from the Philadelphia police chief and Starbucks CEO, who closed 8,000 stores for a day for racial bias training.

SUMMARY

Racial profiling continues to be one of the most controversial issues in policing that is neither easy to explain nor address. It is a complex issue and is not simply a case of the proverbial racist cop. Racial profiling often reflects the police subculture, neighborhood, and inherent dangers of the job. The officer is often confronted with the element of race and expected to delicately navigate and negotiate this volatile landscape. The officer is confronted with the contradictory expectation of being aware of race while at the same time ignore it completely.

Some acts of racial profiling can be explained as part of the larger rational function of recognizing and basing decisions on past patterns associated with crime, including race, to minimize the dangers of the job. However, institutional racism does exist, as is historically evident in the LAPD after external investigations found tacit allowance of racial slurs and brutality by some officers.

Racial profiling is not exclusive to police. Police, who respond to citizen calls, are sometimes blamed and accused of taking action based on race when they are simply responding to calls for service. In other words, perhaps citizens are to blame for many of the implicit biases that police deal with.

NOTES

1. Matthew J. Hickman, "Traffic Stop Data Collection Policies for State Police, 2004," *Bureau of Justice Statistics,* 2005, http://www.bjs.gov/content/pub/pdf/tsdcp04.pdf.

2. Samuel R. Gross and Katherine Y. Bames, "Road Work: Racial Profiling and Drug Interdiction on the Highway," *Michigan Law Review* 101 (2002): 651–754.

3. Ruben Hernandez-Murillo and John Knowles, "Racial Profiling or Racist Policing? Bounds Tests in Aggregate Data," *International Economic Review* 45, no. 3 (2004): 959–989.

4. Report of Dr. John Lamberth, "Plaintiff's Expert, Revised Statistical Analysis of the Incidence of Police Stops and Arrests of Black Drivers/Travelers on the New Jersey Turnpike from the 1988 through 1991," (State v. Pedro Soto, 734 A.2d 350, N.J. Super. Ct. Law. Div.), 1996.

5. Joscha Legewie, "Racial Profiling and Use of Force in Police Stops: How Local Events Trigger Periods of Increased Discrimination," *American Journal of Sociology* 122, no. 2 (2006): 379–424.

6. George E. Higgins et al., "Searches and Traffic Stops: Racial Profiling and Capriciousness," *Journal of Ethnicity in Criminal Justice* 10, no. 3 (2012): 163–179. doi: 10.1086/687518.

7. John Lofland et al., *Analyzing Social Settings: A Guide to Qualitative Observation and Analysis.* 4th ed. (Stamford: Cengage, 2005).

8. Andrea L. Dottolo and Abigail J. Stewart, "'Don't Ever Forget Now, You're a Black Man in America': Intersections of Race, Class and Gender in Encounters with Police," *Sex Roles* 59 (2008): 350–364. doi: 10.1007/s11199-007-9387-x.

9. "Racial Profiling: Definition," American Civil Liberties Union, 2005, https://www.aclu.org/racial-justice/racial-profiling-definition.

10. Kitty Calavita, *Invitation to Law and Society: An Introduction to the Study of Real Law* (Chicago: University of Chicago Press, 2010).

11. David A. Harris, "Driving While Black: Racial Profiling on Our Nation's Highways," *American Civil Liberties Union,* June 7, 1999, https://www.aclu.org/racial-justice/driving-while-black-racial-profiling-our-nations-highways.

12. Harris, "Driving While Black."

13. Emanuella Grinberg, "Florida State Attorney Pulled Over in Traffic Stop that goes Nowhere Fast," *CNN,* July 13, 2017, https://www.cnn.com/2017/07/12/us/florida-state-attorney-aramis-ayala-traffic-stop/index.html.

14. Richard Delgado and Jean Stefancic, *Critical Race Theory,* 2nd ed. (Philadelphia: Temple University Press, 1999).

15. Jerome H. Skolnick, *Justice without Trial: Law Enforcement in Democratic Society,* 4th ed. (New York: John Wiley, 2011).

16. David A. Harris, "The Stories, the Statistics, and the Law: Why 'Driving While Black' Matters," *Minnesota Law Review* 84, no. 2 (1999): 265–326.

17. John Lea, "The Macpherson Report and the Question of Institutional Racism," *The Howard Journal of Crime and Justice* 39, no. 3 (2002): 219–233. doi: 10.1111/1468-2311.00165.

Chapter Nine

The Politics of Police and Reducing Crime

Whenever crime rates or citizens' fear of crime is high, the same default, seemingly intuitive pattern often occurs that can worsen the situation:

1. Public calls for politicians and policymakers to address crime
2. Policymakers in turn resort to highly visible traditional crime control strategies, such as legislating more punitive laws and hiring more police officers
3. More officers make more arrests, resulting in higher crime rates
4. Courts and corrections become overwhelmed, resulting in more usage of probation, plea bargains, and early releases, which gives the impression that the overburdened criminal justice system is not punitive enough, or too lenient

The ramifications of this perception are that crime is not addressed at the root causes. Instead, arrested individuals get worse in prison, crime often continues from the **replacement effect** of another person fulfilling the role, and community resources are used to fight crime. According to criminologist Elliott Currie, communities with reduced resources lose control mechanisms that can drive up crime, leading to a perpetual cycle that can be difficult to break.[1]

Despite the public and political overemphasis of police in dealing with crime, police remain a vital component in controlling crime. This chapter examines the overall effectiveness of police to deter and stop crime.

Several topics that will be explored:

1. The philosophy behind police patrol under professionalism

2. The politics of policing
3. Police pursuits and other high-risk activities

VEHICLE PATROL VS. WALKING THE BEAT

Random patrols were an important aspect of policing during the reform era of policing that promised to reduce crime. Recall that one of the primary goals during professionalization was the eradication of corruption. Walking patrols, prior to the incorporation of automobiles and two-way radios, were blamed in part for contributing to corruption. However, beat officers in patrol cars resolved several issues. First, officers in patrol vehicles were insulated from the public so their encounters were brief and impersonal, making corruption much more difficult. Second, with crime-control-based measures of performance in place, officers were able to cover much wider areas. Third, randomized patrols, in theory, deter criminal activity.

Since potential wrongdoers could be spotted by a police officer in a vehicle at virtually any time and any place, there was a much greater chance of the criminal being spotted and caught. The officer, unlike the night watchman, was capable of traveling long distances in a relatively short time. The potential criminal, therefore, must assume that he would get caught so would think twice before committing a crime. Moreover, once spotted, officers could quickly apprehend the suspect and call for backup. The suspect therefore could not simply run away and hide, or plan criminal activities based on the officer's patrol schedule. Despite these apparent advantages of vehicle patrol, it is arguable that it is superior to walking patrols in all instances.

First, looking at the night watchman style of policing, where officers walked the beat, crime was relatively low. How could this be? By walking the beat, the officer becomes very connected with the community. He can sense tension and potential conflict before it escalates to a level that requires acute crime control intervention, such as use of force situations. By comparison, in the professional patrol model, officers only deal with the symptoms of larger community issues. The officer is reacting to the point of conflict. For example, an officer connected to a community can sense tension between rival gangs based on informal interactions with neighborhood residences, and may be able to gather information on this friction and intervene before violent breakouts.

Many researchers suggest that **reactive patrols** are not as effective as once believed. Severed police/community relations have been blamed for growing community tensions, lack of communication, and out-of-touch police officers. Moreover, insulation of police officers from the community can strengthen the "us versus them" mentality of officers who operate based on what police researcher Edwin Lemert describes as a "perpetual shorthand" of stereotypes of citizens. Likewise, community members also operate on stereotypes of police. Consequently, as officers rationally respond to unknown dangers based on many stereotypes using force, members of many impoverished minority communities feel targeted and ultimately respond to real or perceived police use of excessive force with social upheavals and urban riots.

In contrast, a more informal night watchman or community style can address issues and conflicts at the source of the problem often before use of force becomes necessary. The effectiveness of a close community style of policing, however, depends on one's definition of "success." Since peace keeping and order maintenance were the priority of the night watchman, a night where "nothing happened" was considered a good night. In other words, in contrast to the modern day police officer whose performance is based on crime control measures, such as number of citations or arrests and other factors defined by the UCR, the night watchman was not judged on such criteria.

A breakdown of the philosophy of direct supervision, a corrections operating philosophy based on proactive detention officers, offers insight into the advantages of using proactive versus reactive strategies in dealing with inmates that has parallels to the police world.

DIRECT SUPERVISION

In the world of corrections, conventional wisdom would reason that detention officers should be insulated from inmates. These are individuals convicted of crimes that one can reasonably assume to be potentially dangerous. Based on this reasoning, jails and prisons are designed for separating inmate populations from guards, in secure cells that protect officers from harm, which is by definition, incapacitation.

Two prison philosophies emerged on how to safely and effectively incarcerated convicted individuals. The first is the **Penn system**, based on the principles of the Quaker William Penn, stressed solitary confinement and corrections through penitence. The system was ultimately deemed to be ineffective in prisoner reform because of the ill psychological effects of solitary confinement and it was too expensive.

Alternatively, the **Auburn system**, based in Auburn, New York, modified the Penn-based facilities by eventually housing multiple inmates in larger cells. The facilities themselves featured long hallways lined with cells and guard towers posted at the perimeters of the facilities. Inmates, wearing the stereotypical black and white striped uniforms, marched in single-file lines, while silence was stressed among inmates to prevent learning bad motivations and deeds for criminal activity. Rehabilitation was implemented through learned discipline from inmates working during the daytime, producing goods ranging from garments to furniture.

While the Auburn system ultimately became widely adopted and evolved into modern-day facilities, both the Penn and Auburn system stressed separation of inmates from guards. Most of today's prisons, however, are considered violent and dangerous places. A UK-based study of prison violence found high levels of conflict and victimization among inmates.[2] The study found that violence often occurs because of unresolved escalating conflicts between inmates, where fights and assaults break out. Insulated guards are often unaware of rising tensions, exploitation, and other forms of interpersonal conflict that is prevalent in prison society.

Since the 1990s, however, prison reformers have introduced and adopted a different paradigm of prison operations, **direct supervision**, with positive results. Direct supervision, like community policing, stresses crime prevention through proactive measures that addresses a problem at the root causes, before it escalates to violence. Direct supervision includes both fundamental changes to prison design and the role of detention officers. Instead of a traditional style of facility where inmates and guards are separated, direct supervision facilities have guards and inmates freely moving about in housing units all day.

These housing units are specially designed with wide open spaces that allow inmates to spend the day in a recreation area, and cells are used essentially as bedrooms for sleeping, and not exclusively for incapacitation. Detention officers socialize with inmates daily to gather information and become sensitive to any tensions and interpersonal conflicts that may arise between inmates. The officers can intervene immediately before conflict escalates to violence. Moreover, like the night watchmen and later community policing, officers can build positive rapport with inmates.

When the design philosophy first gained momentum in the 1990s, it was criticized as not being punitive. The city of Santa Ana, California, for example, built a 40 million dollar jail with amenities for inmates that included fresh coffee, computers, and television. Critics dubbed these direct supervision facilities pejoratively as "glamour slammers," "Jail Hilton," and "Country Club Jails" that do not deliver justice.[3] Santa Ana's jail administrator Russell Davis, however, touted extremely low incidences of violence at the facilities that saved the city money. Davis explained, "In addition to patrolling the inmates, an officer's job is to befriend them. That way, the officer can better predict when there is tension and head off a confrontation."

While direct supervision jails and prison facilities can be criticized for potential corruption among officers, supporters argue that they are a better alternative to traditional facilities, citing both statistics showing lower rates of violence as well as more positive inmate and officer perceptions. Critics argue that likewise, the traditional style of professional policing, based on deterrence through random patrols, has been criticized for the same reasons.

PATROLS

If arrests, citations, and other crime control measures of success are prioritized, random patrols are a relatively effective mechanism to further that mandate. It is no coincidence that more proactive officers will find more crime. For example, officers actively looking for vehicle infractions will produce more citations. Vehicle patrols also produce faster response times, relative to foot patrols, which is another measure of success under the UCR. Moreover, randomized vehicle patrols can also, in principle, have deterrent effects. Would-be criminals who are cognizant that an officer can be anywhere at any time, may reconsider committing a crime. Moreover, individuals or groups committing crime may assume officers can arrive at a scene quickly, where they can be caught in the act. Despite these potential benefits, many scholars have called into question the overall effectiveness of random patrols.

Researchers have looked at the relationship between crime rates and the use of random patrols. The central question is whether increasing or decreasing the number of officers on patrols has an impact on crime. In 1974, police researchers George Kelling, Tony Pate, Duane Dieckman, and Charles Brown conducted a patrol experiment in Kansas City and found that in general, the answer is no.[4]

The widely-cited 1973 *Kansas City Preventative Patrol Experiment* debunked the notion that a highly visible police presence deters crime and makes citizens feel safer. Instead, the study found no discernable differences when police presence was increased and no significant effects on residential and commercial burglaries, auto theft, larceny, robberies, or vandalism. These crimes were still considered highly variable with police presence.

From 1972 to 1973, researchers from the Police Foundation conducted the experiment using officers from the Kansas City Police Department (KCPD) that compared different numbers of officers and types of patrols on any given beat. A total of fifteen beats were divided into three categories:

1. Five *reactive beats*: Officers only responded to calls of service and performed no "proactive" policing. This was done to indicate very little police activity and presence.
2. Five *normal beats*: Normal levels of patrol were maintained in order to serve as a control group for comparison. This is how KCPD patrols work without any type of experimental changes.

3. Five *proactive beats*: Two to three times the number of regular officers was used.

This indicated an intensified police presence and proactive strategy.

Citizens were then surveyed to gauge their level of fear of crime and
satisfaction with police. In addition, crime rates, arrest data, and other observations were used to measure the overall impact of police activity.

According to the Kansas City Preventative Patrol Experiment, citizen
satisfaction surveys did not show any differences between the different levels
of patrol. Citizens neither noticed changes in patrol presence nor felt any
more fear or safety from the increase or decrease in police presence. Moreover, researchers did not notice any changes in crimes that were thought to be
sensitive to visible randomized patrols. In other words, randomized patrols
did not have a deterrent effect on commercial and residential burglaries, auto
theft or auto break-ins, robberies, or vandalism. Despite these findings, the
study does not suggest that police have any deterrent effect, as later verified
by future studies.[5]

A 1995 study by criminologists Lawrence Sherman and David Weisburd
found that police can have a deterrent effect under certain conditions.[6] While
the majority of criminologists doubt the effectiveness of simply increasing
the number of police officers as an effective solution to crime reduction,
Sherman and Weisburd's study does show significant reductions in crime.
According to their study in Minneapolis, doubling the police presence in
crime in "hot spots," which are areas of elevated criminal activity, resulted in
a six to thirteen percent reduction in calls for service. The researchers compared fifty-five hot spots with increased presence to fifty-five hot spots with
normal levels of police presence. Their observations of over 7,500 hours of
police activity also showed significantly less signs of disorder, such as criminal activity in the open. They conclude that while general deterrence was not
achieved, which matched the Kansas City experiment conclusion, "micro-
deterrence" in hot spots were significant.

Despite questions brought forth by academics, engrained in the police
organizational culture and the mindset of most officers is that police serve as
a deterrent for crime. The use of force or potential use of force serves as a
deterrent. Deviations from police acting or taking no action, in most officers'
minds, could give incentive for suspects to challenge their authority. For
example, it may make it more dangerous for other officers if an officer being
challenged does not engage with a resistant suspect, oftentimes with the use
of force. In fact, many officers believe the use of overwhelming force deters
potential acts of violence towards police.

However, oftentimes this "don't back down" mentality may lead to more
harm. One controversial area is the use of high-speed pursuits. Despite the
regularity of police pursuits broadcasted live on television (especially infa-

mous on Southern California freeways, and with training officers), high-speed pursuits have resulted in severe harm, leading many departments to review and reconsider their use.

POLICE PURSUITS: DETERRENT OR DANGEROUS?

According to the data, using police as a deterrent for crime is marginal when increases in the police force reach points of diminishing returns. That is, no one is arguing that police have no effect on crime, but increases in the police force, to a certain degree, have very little impact. One particular area that is controversial relative to the effectiveness of police is the high-speed pursuit. In theory, police must pursue vehicles that fail to stop because failure to do so will have the opposite effect of deterrence. Drivers who know that police do not pursue cars will simply drive away. However, in practice, police pursuits often create dangerous situations for the officer, suspect, and general public.

According to the FBI:[7]

> Police pursuit records provide some frightening statistics. First, the majority of police pursuits involve a stop for a traffic violation. Second, one person dies every day as a result of a police pursuit. On average, from 1994 through 1998, one law enforcement officer was killed every 11 weeks in a pursuit, and 1 percent of all U.S. law enforcement officers who died in the line-of-duty lost their lives in vehicle pursuits. Innocent third parties who just happened to be in the way constitute 42 percent of persons killed or injured in police pursuits. Further, 1 out of every 100 high-speed pursuits results in a fatality. Research indicates that pursuits become dangerous quite quickly. For example, 50 percent of all pursuit collisions occur in the first 2 minutes of the pursuit, and more than 70 percent of all collisions occur before the sixth minute of the pursuit.

Looking more closely at the data shows the nature and potential harm of police pursuits. According to the Airborne Law Enforcement Association, fleeing suspects will drive an additional ninety seconds, fast and dangerously, before returning to a safe speed and safe driving manner. This is contrary to anecdotal evidence that drivers quickly return to safe driving manners after a terminated pursuit. A growing number of departments, out of concern for officer and public safety, as well as departmental legal liability, however, have implemented policies that mandate termination of pursuits when the risks are too great. According to researchers David Schultz, Ed Haduk, and Geoffrey Alpert, "the thinking behind this approach is to have the police not be part of the problem but part of the solution."[8] Their study showed that both suspects and officers believed that normal driving manners and speeds would resume relatively shortly after a chase had been called off, ranging from two to four blocks, or two to five miles on the freeway.

The big question remains whether the ends of catching the suspect justify the dangerous means; and is the threat of the pursuit enough of a deterrent to stop suspects from fleeing. Milwaukee police detective and police union president, Michael Crivello, when interviewed by *USA Today,* responded by saying, "When crooks think they can do whatever they choose, that will just fester and foster more crimes."

While no data exists to measure the deterrent effects of the decision-making process, finding the balance between the public safety and offender apprehension remains inconclusive, and has high stakes. Schultz, Haduk, and Alpert's study explained, "Perhaps the most compelling, ongoing, and logical reason for law enforcement's continued interest in high-speed vehicle pursuits has been its concern in balancing the values of crime control and offender apprehension with ensuring the safety of all parties who potentially might be involved—police officers, suspects, victims, bystanders, and the community."[9]

Looking at the impact of pursuits shows their potential hazards. The researchers' data reveals key points. First, most pursuits begin as traffic violations and misdemeanors. Second, high-speed pursuits average one death every day. Data shows that one percent of high-speed pursuits end fatally. While one percent may not seem high, *USA Today* reported that from 1979 to 2015, more than 5,000 bystanders and passengers were killed in police chases.[10] A total of over 11,000 people, including 6,300 fleeing suspects, have been killed. When adding injury statistics, that average number increases to over 1,700 yearly. Victims include small children, teen drivers, and the elderly.

Police officers are at major risk during pursuits. DOJ records show that over 139 officers have been killed during pursuits since 1979. To put things into context, far more dangerous police pursuits occur each year than do shootings. Some departments, such as Milwaukee and Orlando, have responded with policies that only allow officers to chase suspects with violent offenses, but most departments authorize complete officer discretion to engage in a pursuit.

The continued popularity and widespread use of police pursuits and the belief that it deters crime in the face of data showing its costs underscores the complicated politics of police work. Oftentimes policies that seem to contradict the research, as shown by the Kansas City Preventative Patrol Experiment, reveal the politics of police actions and policies.

THE POLITICS OF THE POLICE INDUSTRIAL COMPLEX

Police are often used in politics universally, as a panacea and solution for crime. This response to crime makes sense. Long-term policies focused on crime prevention are often trumped by the immediately visible and seemingly obvious solution of having more police officers. However,

Politicians, regardless of political affiliation, often take advantage of this situation because it fits well with a "get tough on crime" stance; when crime goes up, the solution is simply to add more police officers. Any deviation from this default solution can be politically disastrous for the politician, regardless of the research, as the Kansas City Preventative Patrol Experiment shows.

Police are symbolic of law and order and "getting tough" on crime. Inversely, any opposition to police as a solution will most likely carry the stigma of "soft on crime." This powerful notion highly influences criminal justice policy, regardless of data, which may suggest the opposite solution presented by the academic community and published research. In other words, any politician who suggests alternative policies that do not involve increasing the police force in an effort towards crime reduction, despite being backed by research such as the Kansas City Patrol Experiment, will most likely be perceived as soft on crime and fail to win their election or re-election.

The growth of the criminal justice system is no accident. According to authors Jeffrey Reiman and Paul Leighton, the growth in the criminal justice system is explained by **pyrrhic defeat theory**, defined as "a military victory purchased at such a cost in troops and treasure that it amounts to a defeat."[11] The pyrrhic defeat theory argues that the failure of the criminal justice system "yields such benefits to those in positions of power that it amounts to success." In other words, crime pays and can be quite lucrative for criminal justice actors. By casting the image of a losing war against crime, the criminal justice system continues to grow. Furthermore, criminal justice resources are needed and justified regardless of crime rates.

Police have used this political position to their advantage. According to the principles of pyrrhic defeat theory, when crime is up, more police are needed to reduce crime. When crime is down, more police are required to ensure crime does not go back up. While the authors discussed the theory in the context of class and power stratification in the United States, the police are an integral part of the criminal justice system that are often used as a political bargaining chips by policymakers and those in power.

Criminologist Elliott Currie discussed the devolving cyclical pattern that explains the exponential increased cost of policing and criminal justice in the United States since the 1970s. First, growing social disintegration leads to an increase in violent crime. The increase in violent crime causes widespread public fear of crime and a demand that politicians "do something" about the crime problem. Politicians respond with the default rhetoric and strategy discussed earlier, to "get tough" on crime. This means that money and resources that were meant for communities are reallocated to the criminal justice system, which includes police. For example, President Clinton passed a crime bill in 1994 that approved funding to hire 10,000 new police officers to tackle crime, with the ultimate goal of 100,000 new police officers. Consequently, the cycle repeats itself as money allocated to police is taken from crime prevention programs, which further deteriorates social conditions and leads to social disintegration.

Regardless of what the research shows, and political party's affiliation and agenda, politicians, at least the winning ones, will always advocate hiring more police officers. The public, generally unaware of the true impact of police on crime, usually supports this seemingly obvious proposition. This disjuncture between what the research shows (what we know) and praxis (what we do) is a longstanding concern with criminologists.

USING STATISTICS AND CLEARANCE RATES TO GAUGE POLICE PERFORMANCE

More generally, measures of police success come into question when looking at the impact of police on crime statistics. Police researchers James Q. Wilson and Barbara Boland noted major problems when employing clearance rates to measure police impact on crime.[12] First, departments differ on what is considered an actual clearance. For instance, some departments count an offense as cleared only when a suspect or suspects are taken into custody that they have enough evidence to bring forward charges. However, oftentimes suspects confesses to committing crimes other than the one they were arrested for. Some scholars have even pointed out that these confessions, which may boost clearance rates, are made by suspects wanting to please captors.

Second, the researchers find it difficult to draw conclusions of deterrence in which police directly caused the person to be arrested. According to researchers, police do not have control over a lot of factors that may lead a person to get caught, such as willingness of citizens to report the crime and identify suspects. In other words, if everyone started reporting crime and providing police with evidence that lead to an arrest, that would cause an increase in clearance rates. Third, researchers have difficulty drawing a connection between causal inferences of deterrence and the number of police officers per capita and crime. This was backed by the Kansas City Preventative Patrol Experiment.

SUMMARY

This chapter shows that oftentimes the intuitive solution of using police to address problems may have an opposite effect by worsening the situation. Several topics were shown to have little effect or even exacerbate issues, such as "get tough on crime" policies that contribute to revolving door justice and an increase in the number of police officers to deal with crime. However, a more cynical explanation may have to do with pyrrhic defeat theory, in which certain groups stand to benefit from seeming to be losing the war on crime, in the form of higher budgets, more equipment, more pay, and so on. This is described as part of a larger criminal justice industrial complex.

Using this lens, police measures of success based on crime-control statistics may be flawed by its easy manipulation and inconsistent recording practices. This distortion of crime and policing makes it very difficult for a public with minimal understanding of how police work, to support policies and strategies that may be more effective in reducing crime and do not directly involve investments in police.

NOTES

1. Elliott Currie, *Crime and Punishment in America,* 2nd ed. (New York: Picador, 2013).

2. Edgar Kimmett, Ian O'Donnell, and Carol Martin, *Prison Violence: The Dynamics of Conflict, Fear and Power* (Portland, OR: Willan Publishing, 2003).

3. Jeff Kass, "Inmates Find Privileges on Cutting Edge of Jails," *Los Angeles Times*, May 27, 1997, http://articles.latimes.com/1997-05-27/news/mn-62966_1_jail-officials.

4. George L. Kelling et al., *The Kansas City Preventive Patrol Experiment: A Summary Report* (Washington, DC: Police Foundation, 1974).

5. Richard C. Larson, "What Happened to Patrol Operations in Kansas City? A Review of the Kansas City Preventive Patrol Experiment," *Journal of Criminal Justice* 3, no. 4 (1975): 267–297. doi: 10.1016/0047-2352(75)90034-3.

6. Lawrence W. Sherman and David Weisburd, "General Deterrent Effects of Police Patrol in Crime 'Hot Spots': A Randomized, Controlled Trial," *Justice Quarterly* 12, no. 4 (1995): 625–648. doi:10.1080/07418829500096221.

7. John Hill, "High-Speed Police Pursuits: Dangers, Dynamics, and Risk Reduction," *FBI Law Enforcement Bulletin,* July 2002, 14–18.

8. David P. Schultz, Ed Hudak, and Geoffrey P. Alpert, "Evidence-Based Decisions on Police Pursuits: The Officer's Perspective," *FBI Law Enforcement Bulletin,* 2010, https://leb.fbi.gov/articles/featured-articles/evidence-based-decisions-on-police-pursuits-the-officers-perspective.

9. Schultz, "Evidence-Based Decisions."

10. Thomas Frank, "High-Speed Police Chases Have Killed Thousands of Bystanders," *USA Today*, July 30, 2015, https://www.usatoday.com/story/news/2015/07/30/police-pursuits-fatal-injuries/30187827/.

11. Jeffrey Reiman and Paul Leighton, *The Rich Get Richer and the Poor Get Prison: Ideology, Class, and Criminal Justice,* 11th ed. (London: Pearson, 2016).

12. James Q. Wilson and Barbara Bowland, "The Effect of Police on Crime," *Law and Society Review* 12, no. 3 (1978): 367–390.

Chapter Ten

Career Stages and the Mental and Physical Toll of Police Work

A career in law enforcement is a transformative experience that changes an individual's identity and how he or she perceives the world. An officer undergoes this transformation from the time he or she steps foot in the academy. However, the experience of the officer is not static; it is dynamic and changes throughout the officer's career. These career phases are not demarcated simply by promotion to higher positions, but relate to the internal changes to an individual's self-concept and corresponding attitudes toward himself or herself and others. The progression of changes to the officer ranges from an idealized perspective of police work as a rookie to cynicism and burnout.

For those who spend an entire career in law enforcement, the changes to the officer do not end with retirement. Self-conceptions and identity come into question as many retirees leave the force that has been perceived as a surrogate family. Many of these individuals face strong internal conflict with many ramifications.

This chapter explores the phases of an officer's career, highlighting the issues and conflicts with each phase. The progression of each phase also underscores the influence and permeation of the police subculture at each stage, including attitudes toward other officers and management. The topics covered in this chapter include:

- The rookie
- Midcareer officers
- Detectives and specialization
- Promotion and rank
- The veteran officer

- Life and death after policing

THE ROOKIE

Rookie officers are at the beginning phase of a life-changing profession. Even before starting work, these individuals are already different than the rest of the population. The career he or she is entering is full of hazards in more ways than just the risk of injury and death from the inherent nature of the job. In fact, the greater dangers are the ones they do not see, which include the physical and mental stresses of the job. Oftentimes these hidden dangers can range manifest in severe mental and physical health problems, ranging from heart disease to post traumatic stress disorder (PTSD), like in war veterans. In fact, more police officers die from suicide than are killed. In 2017, forty-six officers were fatally shot, compared to 140 who committed suicide.[1]

Two factors often distinguish the rookie officer from the public. The first factor is the attraction to the profession of policing and the hiring process, where like-minded individuals do very well, while weeding out those who do not fit in culturally. Recall that individuals attracted to the job have a strong interest in the crime control and law enforcement aspects of police work (arrests, marksmanship, etc.), as opposed to the order maintenance and peace keeping functions (crowd control, assisting motorists, etc.). Secondly, the police academy reorients the mind-set of the recruit from that of an individual to that of a selfless team member who can be trusted to aid other officers with his or her life. Ultimately, the blue brotherhood is reinforced, along with subcultural attitudes of "us versus them."

The process of police recruiting and training that leads to shared worldviews is not unique. The military and other organizations that rely on group solidarity and mutual trust as part of their identity foster similar virtual kinships and worldviews. In the case of the military and police, this solidarity is very important since they must trust and rely on each other in cases of emergency. This "blue brotherhood" is part of the allure of police work. Oftentimes trainees and rookie officers enjoy the camaraderie that develops during training. This group solidarity is an integral part of the academy experience. Departments use not only stress training to build relationships, but also symbolism, such as academy class numbers that distinguish the group from others. Academy classmates often build lifelong friendships and relationships. Joseph Wambaugh's classic fiction police novel, *The New Centurions*, highlights this brotherhood as his story arcs a group of LAPD academy classmates coming back together during a crisis and drawing from a bond that was never broken.[2] This brotherhood of likeminded individuals starts even before the officer is hired.

In interviewing applicants on why they want to become police officers, a *Los Angeles Times* article revealed a system that filters out those who do not fit the typical mold of the officer and consequently homogenizes the group.[3] For example, one applicant applying to a Southern California police agency stated, "I've always wanted to be in a shoot-out," while another applicant asserted, "I've never been able to hold onto a job: I'm going into police work to see if it will help me straighten out my life." These two applicants were quickly screened out of the process. Instead, departments generally desire and seek out individuals who want to help others and give back to the community.

Perhaps more importantly, departments desire individuals who have a passion for police work. In other words, they view policing as a "calling" in life, where some are philosophically destined to be officers. This theme is perfectly illustrated in a scene from an episode of the LAPD series *Southland* in which field training officer John Cooper is talking to his trainee, Officer Ben Sherman, right after the rookie (justifiably) shot a suspect and was questioning why he joined the police force and considering quitting:

Rookie Sherman: Taking a life is a big deal to me, okay?

FTO Cooper: What the hell did you think the gun was for, huh? Show-and-tell? Look, you'll get over it—all right, they'll send you to BSS, you'll do all that Buddhist "I love and revere all sentient beings" crap; then at o'dark-thirty, next time you're up, you will drag your weary, fried ass out of bed, you will put on your gun and your vest, and you will do it all over again. You know why? Because this is a front row seat to the greatest show on earth. Can you abuse it? Yes, sir—you can, and you will. I guarantee it. Because it is relentless, and it gets to you, and it seems like it changes nothing. But a day like today, with some interesting capers, and a few good arrests? That's good. But every once in a while, you get to take a bad guy off the streets for good . . . and that, my friend, is God's work. So now you wanna be a pussy and quit, you quit. You're a cop because you don't know how not to be one. If you feel that way, you're a cop. If you don't, you're not—you decide.

Police departments use psychological tests to screen out applicants who want to become police officers for the wrong reasons and who possess undesirable traits. For example, applicants who have overly aggressive personalities and strong prejudices may raise serious concern for hiring officers. For example, the same *Los Angeles Times* story interviewed one forensic psychologist who explained, "If [the applicants] are looking for this badge to give them self-esteem, there's going to be big trouble."

Successful applicants tend to be self-sorted by generally giving similar idealized answers for why they want to become police officers. These successful applicants often provide answers that embody a noble and altruistic vision of police work. Surveys conducted with recruits show the most common answer is the desire to help those in need. According to the *Houston Chronicle*, "They each want to be a hero, to face disaster and destruction with bravery and to help a community bond together. . . . Those who make it generally have a strong sense of right and wrong."[4] The top three answers given by successful recruits are (1) the opportunity to help others, (2) job benefits, and (3) job security.

The experience of the rookie officer has been documented in several nonfiction and fictional novels. As discussed, former police officer Joseph Wambaugh drew from his LAPD experience in his novel, *The New Centurions* about new officers.[5] One common theme among the rookie characters in the book was the difference in mentality between themselves and their field training officers. The rookies were ready and eager for action, contrasted by their FTOs who operated a deliberately slower pace. For example, one rookie, Roy Fehler, was disappointed and frustrated with his FTO who was older and wanted a much slower vision of police work that avoided risk and danger. Roy wanted a younger, more aggressive officer who, in his mind, did not shy away from real police work. This stark contrast of attitudinal differences does not represent personality differences, but rather changes to the officer through the course of their career.

Another popular book on the rookie experience is LAPD officer William Dunn's nonfiction, *Boot: An LAPD Officer's Rookie Year*, which documents activities during his first year, broken down into twenty-eight deployment periods.[6] Dunn's first deployment was to a volatile domestic family dispute call between two gay male cohabitants. While the situation warranted police intervention in the form of an arrest, he was advised to take no action since it often plays out where charges are dropped, and the arrest would be a "waste of time." Several more instances were discussed in which there is friction between the rookie and his FTOs, with the same theme of the rookie who wants to serve justice while the FTO is more cynically pragmatic and does not pursue police action. These experiences reflect career phase differences and a preview of changes to the officer. These FTOs written by Wambaugh and Dunn once started as the young idealistic officer.

In essence, almost all new rookie officers joined the force with a sense of justice and feel they can genuinely make a difference. We will see that this quickly changes as the new officer experiences cultural and structural blockages that keep him or her from accomplishing this feat. He will realize that he cannot change society, despite his best intentions and efforts. Moreover, administratively, it is better for new officers to not be too active and aggressive in order to minimize citizen complaints, getting in trouble with the brass, and perhaps the more hazardous, exposure to civil litigation.

One of the most common reasons why rookie officers do not get past their probation period, or quit policing altogether, is the lack of understanding of the true nature of the job. Many applicants draw their expectations from skewed entertainment media portrayals of police work in shows such *Law & Order* and even "reality" shows such as *COPS*. These shows, even reality shows, portray police work as very clear-cut moral paths, with obvious good guys and bad guys in easy to solve cases that end with high-speed pursuits and guns drawn. As discussed before, the reality of police work is much less action-oriented and has more to do with order maintenance and peace keeping than law enforcement and crime control. Consequently, when the realities of police work sink into the rookie officer, there are certain ramifications that affect officer attitudes and commitment to the job.

STAGES OF POLICE WORK: ATTITUDES AND COMMITMENT

Different stages of an officer's career are well documented and often mirror those of age-related stages in most professions. Psychologist Donald Super's Career Development Theory, written in the 1950s, defined three general career stages based on age: fourteen to twenty-four is considered the trial or exploratory stage, from twenty-five to forty-four years is the establishment phase, while forty-five to sixty is considered the maintenance stage, and sixty-one and older is the disengagement stage.[7] More importantly, these career stages represent self-concepts and realizations over time, described as "life rainbow," which arcs according to the status of an individual that progresses from child and student all the way to citizen, worker, and eventually homemaker or parent.[8]

Law enforcement careers loosely follow Super's arc and stages with slight changes that reflect the more compressed careers of officers who are eligible to retire relatively early. Law enforcement officers typically reach their mandatory retirement age in their mid-fifties. These stages, based more on experience rather than age, can affect job performance and attitudes toward police work.

The way an officer perceives his job can affect job performance. Psychologists James McElroy and Paula Marrow, along with Iowa police officer Wardlow, examined the levels of commitment to the job in accordance to age of the officer.[9] They conceptualize commitment with three definitions: (1) commitment to work as a valued activity, (2) commitment to one's career, and (3) commitment to one's organization. The researchers surveyed five police academy classes using questions based on the likelihood of them leaving their current department based on the aforementioned categories of commitment. They found that for the first category, deemed "affective com-mitment," officers showed lower levels during the trial stage and establish-ment stage of their careers. For the last two categories, career commitment and organizational commitment, younger trial stage officers showed statisti-cally significantly lower levels of commitment.

Lower levels of commitment amongst younger officers is not surprising given the high level of mobility for younger people who are typically freer of family commitments, such as children. Younger officers also cited alterna-tive employment opportunities, such as larger geographical jurisdiction, more specialized opportunities, higher pay, more promotion opportunities, and more action.

The research also shows that management can affect lower ranking offi-cers' commitment and job satisfaction. According to one study, officers feel more committed to an organization when his or her identities are more close-ly in line with the organization.[10] However, this commitment is highly influ-enced by management systems and practices, finding that commitment in-creases when officers are involved in the decision-making process, feel sup-ported by their superiors, and receive continual feedback on their job perfor-mance and expectations. Another study supported this view, which found organizational and management support to be positively correlated with posi-tive attitudes and commitment by lower ranking officers toward the depart-ment and the job.[11]

While the discussion has focused on the homogeneity of officers as a result of applicants and recruits being filtered out by the hiring and training process, many departments face issues with rookie officer voluntary attrition, if like-minded individuals are not hired. In the 1990s, the Tallahassee Police Department aggressively hired female officers as a response to class-action lawsuit for discriminatory hiring against women. The achieved critical mass of female officers was followed by a pattern of departures, as many of the new female officers who were not weeded out were put off by the nature of the work. Studies show the females who quit matched typologies that de-scribe those who have soured or burned out and do as little work as possible, described as "shirkers" and "avoiders."[12] Those who go on with police work face the same challenges of attitudes, often midway through their careers.

MID-CAREER OFFICERS: THE RISK OF
PSYCHOLOGICAL BURNOUT

Mid-career experienced officers have developed a personality that is unique to the profession. As reflective of the police subculture, the officer at this point has a very cynical worldview. The police subculture is infused with his identity and his experiences which reinforce this cynicism toward the public as well as management. The officer at this point typically does not trust non-police individuals and groups, while being fiercely loyal to fellow officers. The immersion into the police world and acceptance of police officer as his master status permeates his or her social spheres, where the majority of the officer's close friends are other officers. Moreover, given the mutual expectation to protect each other with their own lives, the officer considers fellow officers akin to immediate family.

Career-wise, the experienced officer is now a master of his or her domain. The fear and anxiety of dealing with the public becomes replaced by confidence and routinization. Most officers at this point have developed a "**sixth sense**" or acuteness for detecting things out of the ordinary, such as behavior and circumstances deemed suspicious. Some officers at this point have been promoted to specialized assignments, such as detective duties and mid-level ranks, such as corporal or sergeant. Note that these ranks are still considered more closely associated with line officers rather than management cops, or the proverbial "**brass**."

After a few years on the force, the officer has usually undergone several typical changes. First, his or her identity has been predominantly taken over by the police identity. The officer finds him- or herself closer with his police colleagues than friends he or she had prior to joining the police force. As discussed in previous chapters, this is due to cultural immersion, shift work, and shared experiences that only other officers can relate to. Second, the officer has developed a strong sense of cynicism toward the public, the criminal justice system, and even management. This is the result of a culmination of patrol experiences where police face constant deception by the public and disappointment with the criminal justice/legal system in meting out justice. Third, the officer in his or her mid-career is often besieged by stressors outside and inside the department and is at risk of burnout.

The nature of police work contributes significantly to officer burnout. A 2006 study by psychologists Arnold Bakker and Ellen Heuven likened police work to nursing, as being high-stress work.[13] They found both professions shared similar stressors:

1. Exposure to emotionally demanding interpersonal interactions, such as frequent confrontations with death and illness, violence, and victims of violence and accidents.
2. The suppression of feelings and emotions as part of their work role, despite the nature of their work being described as "emotional work."

Consequently, burnout, which is defined as occupational stress reaction, commonly occurs amongst officers. The study further typifies burnout as emotional exhaustion and depersonalization, in which officers cope by:

1. Emotionally distancing oneself from relationships.
2. Cynical and dehumanizing attitudes toward recipients, such as reduced empathy and "blaming the victim."

Other studies have found that the public was not the main source of burnout,
but organizational and structural stressors, such as workload and inadequate
systems of supervision and management.[14]

The paradox and conflicts of the nature of police work itself further
contributes to officer **burnout.** Officers must control their emotions and stay
neutral despite being constantly faced with emotionally charged, high-stress,
and possibly traumatizing situations. For example, officers constantly face
manipulation, conflicting situations, and aggression, but must maintain their
cool. Moreover, they are expected to show compassion and understanding
toward victims. Switching back and forth between professionalism and compassion is known as "detached concern."[15]

One possible exit from the stresses of patrol work is promotion, where
officers can escape from, to some degree, dealing with the public directly and
the acute dangers associated with being a line officer. Furthermore, promotions can allow officers to specialize in certain types of crimes and roles
within the department.

RISING THROUGH THE RANKS

Like most professions, policing has a promotion and rank system for officers.
Since police is a paramilitary organization, officers can choose to rise
through the ranks by applying and testing internally. For example, a sergeant
who meets the minimum qualifications can choose to apply to the next higher
rank. Depending on the nature of the department and the individual officer,
one can rise through the ranks relatively quickly. With each rank promotion
comes a different set of duties and responsibilities, which often involves
moving away from purely patrol duties.

Many officers choose to forgo rising through the ranks of the department
for a variety of reason. For some officers, patrol is the most rewarding
experience and the reason why they joined the force. For others, dealing with
more bureaucratic functions is not appealing. While for some officers, the
lack of a higher education, or even the lack of a graduate degree, is a limiting
factor. While the minimum education for the vast majority of departments is
a high school equivalent degree, more advanced positions require more education. For instance, most departments require a four-year bachelor's degree
for ranks higher than a sergeant, with many require a master's or higher for
the highest ranks, such as captain or chief.

DETECTIVES: SPECIALIZED POLICING

One step toward higher pay and ranks is becoming a detective. Detectives are police investigators that try to find a perpetrator after a crime has been committed and prepare the case for the prosecutor. They often arrive at crime scenes to conduct a more thorough investigation than the initial investigation conducted by the patrol officer. Their work often involves interviewing witnesses, looking for physical evidence, and even conducting sting operations. They can specialize in different areas, depending on the size of the department. For instance, they can range in specialization from homicide, to narcotics, to financial crimes. Detective experience is often a requirement for a promotion to sergeant or higher ranks.

THE RAMIFICATIONS OF HIGH RANKS: STREET COPS VERSUS MANAGEMENT COPS

In most occupations, a promotion in rank is seen as a positive and logical step in career advancement. It means the proverbial climbing of the corporate ladder. In police work, however, there are some ramifications to becoming or even aspiring to become a high-ranking officer, such as lieutenant, captain, or chief. It introduces officers to the politics of policing and can fundamentally change one's perceptions of the job. An officer ascending the ranks can find him or herself at odds and outcast by line officers and moreover, begin to question their police identity as the nature of their work no longer resembles the police work they joined the force for.

Police researcher Elizabeth Reuss-Ianni's 1970s and 1980s NYPD studies found a deep divide between regular beat patrol officers and high-ranking management cops.[16,17] The data suggested a growing divide between management and street officers stemming from bureaucratic frictions. What may look like a cohesive group from an outsider, as represented by the blue brotherhood, management and street cops often have divergent and conflicting incentives and loyalties. She found this sharp divide created split cultures, the "**street cop culture**" and "**management cop culture**." Management cops were found to be loyal to their social circle and political associations over line officers. She attributed this friction as having contributed to police/public strained relationships that led to urban rioting in the 1960s.

The police response to and involvement in urban riots and social upheavals in the 1960s, during which time police were heavily criticized for being racially insensitive and acting brutally, realigned high ranking officers with the viewpoints of politicians, and not fellow officers. High ranking officers post-riots primarily focused on reform, implemented a series of policies that affected police work. Officers feel these top-down policy changes, such as limitations to the use of force, have impeded effective police work. These management cops no longer hold the officers' best interest in mind, and are perceived by the force as bending to political will and political correctness—which is in clear violation of the unwritten police code. Consequently, you have two competing and conflicting cultures of street and management officers.

Regardless of the friction with management, an officer's perceptions begin to change when he or she is several years into his or her career as a seasoned veteran.

THE SEASONED VETERAN

As police officers advance toward the end of their careers, they are winding down police activity and looking toward retirement options. With years left before retirement, these seasoned officers tend to lie low and do not make waves, so to speak. Most have graduated from patrol work and moved on to more administrative positions. However, despite this being a relatively low-stress point in the officer's career, the cumulative effects of police work tend to take their toll at this point.

There are problems associated with late career stages of the officer. The police officer is beginning to feel the ill effects of the nature of police work, which are the intense fluctuations between boredom and acute stress. In other words, police work is very physically stressful and long-term stress can have lasting effects.[18] First, the boredom aspect of police work means patrol officers spend the majority of their time sitting and driving. Second, patrol officers generally eat unhealthy meals during their shifts, which include fast foods and restaurants. Third, shift work means that officers do not obtain proper sleep.

SLEEPING

Sleep is an often-overlooked aspect of overall health that can have severe effects for the officer's work performance. A 1997 Buffalo police health study found that nightshift work is significantly associated with snoring and a decrease in sleep.[19] This study was affirmed by a study published in the *Journal of American Medical Association* (JAMA).[20] The 2011 study of nearly 5,000 officers found that over 40 percent of municipal and state police officers from the United States and Canada suffer from sleep disorders that include sleep apnea and insomnia. Over one quarter of the officers were reported to have "excessive sleepiness" and falling asleep while driving at least once a month. Furthermore, the study found severe consequences of sleep deprivation, including serious administrative errors, safety violations attributed to fatigue, temperament issues, and falling asleep during meetings. These officers were also more likely to suffer from burn out, anxiety, and depression.

Controlled experiments with officers corroborate the JAMA study. Washington State University director of the Sleep and Performance Research Center, Dr. Bryan Vila, runs a simulation laboratory that can measure officer performance in driving using a 3-D simulator and reactions to different scenarios, including the use of firearms.[21] Multiple experiments have found fatigue due to shift work and restricted sleep severely adversely affects officer performance. Fatigued officers:

- Used more sick leave
- Used more inappropriate use of force
- Were involved in vehicle accidents more often
- Experienced more accidental injuries
- Had difficulties dealing with other officers from other agencies and community members
- Were more likely to die on duty, such as from fatal car crashes

Sleep deprived officers were found to compensate for fatigue by avoiding or minimizing work responsibilities, such as making fewer arrests to minimize court appearances. These issues are compounded in mid-career seasoned veterans, who tend to work more overtime jobs and tend to have more family responsibilities with younger children.

According to the NIJ, inadequate and improper sleep was shown to have significant health effects that include:

- Increased mood swings
- Impaired judgment
- Decreased ability to adapt to situations
- Heightened sense of threat
- Mental illness
- Reduction in hand-eye coordination
- Weight gain
- Chronic pain and lingering injuries
- Cardiovascular and gastro-intestinal problems

The stresses of police work coupled with the symptoms of sleep deprivation have led many officers to self-medicate in the form of alcohol and drugs. Most commonly, the police culture tends to promote drinking, leading to problems of alcoholism with some officers.

ALCOHOLISM

When coupled with the stress of police work, the officer begins to suffer health problems ranging from obesity to coronary heart disease. One manifestation of police cynicism and coping with stress is alcohol. Going drinking, as mentioned in previous chapters, serves as a social mechanism for officers to share their stories and bond with other officers. However, alcoholism has become a significant issue amongst many officers. A 2005 study published in a medical journal found that police officers consume alcohol and tobacco at higher rates than the general public due to prolonged exposure to stressors beyond the range of normal individuals.[22] Another study, published in 1993, explains that some officers use alcohol as a stress reliever for "professional role immersion," which police officers can suffer in the form of combat post traumatic stress disorder (CPTSD).[23]

FAMILY LIFE

Alcoholism as a coping mechanism for officers can be explained in part by the absence of sufficient family support. Police officers often suffer rejection by friends as part of their occupation, as mentioned, so often retreat to the presence and friendship of other officers. Most officers, however, do not spend enough time with their spouses to communicate their feelings and oftentimes mask their feelings. Moreover, they are unable to spend adequate time with their children (for example, due to shift work)—resulting in very authoritarian relationships with their families.

These family factors create a tremendous amount of stress for the officer who essentially has no outlet for their feelings and frustrations. Recall that police typically do not share their feelings with other officers because of a hypermasculine environment that only allows for storytelling. Sharing feelings is often perceived as a sign of weakness and the lack of mental toughness required for the job. Turning to professional psychological services is also not an option as civilian counselors and therapists are considered outsiders who are not to be trusted. Consequently, alcoholism and drug abuse has become an increasing problem among officers.

A short list of family related stress that contributes to strain at home includes:

- Shift work and overtime
- Spousal cynicism, not having control at home
- Not expressing feelings
- High expectations of their children
- Their kids are teased for being son/daughter of a cop

- Would rather spend time with other cops
- Perceived paranoia and overprotectiveness

These issues can also manifest in adulterous behavior by officers.

INFIDELITY AND DIVORCE

Despite the popular notion that police divorce rates are higher than the general population, there is little to no empirical evidence to support this claim. In fact, some studies have shown that police officers have a *lower* divorce rate than the general population. A 2010 study of police divorce examined US census data from 2000 and found that the police divorce rate is lower than the general population, even when accounting for demographic variables. [24]

Despite this claim by the study, the FBI contends using US Census data, that the law enforcement divorce rate is closer to 70 percent as compared to 50 percent of the general population. [25] They cite inflated, narcissistic, and self-involved personalities of police that alienate families. In addition, police researcher Jerome Skolnick asserts that officers tend to invest too much time in their "work family." Officers often perceive reality as being black and white on the job (clear right and wrong), which does not lend itself to dealing with personal family problems.

Infidelity, however, is a significant but understudied issue since one can imagine there is no official data and the data collection process can be near impossible. While there are no official statistics or data on police infidelity, there is plenty of anecdotal evidence and stories from police officers. Joseph Wambaugh, for example, writes frequently of the police lifestyle that attracts **"badge bunnies,"** a pejorative term for women who only date cops and can be seen hanging out around police stations hoping to score an officer. [26] A 2011 issue of a policing magazine writes: [27]

> *For the guys, sooner or later a badge bunny will approach you. Have you never heard of these creatures? Well, there are some females who are attracted to cops. Face it, you may not have movie star looks, but it's the uniform and your authoritative position in life that attracts them. It doesn't matter whether you're married, engaged or committed, you can still be in their sights.*
>
> *If you think this will never happen to you, think again. These groupies, badge bunnies, or holster sniffers seem innocent enough. They claim they're looking for a friend—a strong, handsome young man in uniform. Add to that description a good steady job, good pay, and benefits. Wait, I thought they were only looking for friendship. They want to hang around, show up in your life and sooner or later potentially ruin your career and life.*

PTSD AND SUICIDE

For some officers, police work, like soldiers experiencing the traumas and carnage of war, can lead to posttraumatic stress disorder (PTSD). A 2004 study looked at variables that led to suicide ideation, or thoughts of committing suicide, by officers, and found they were correlated with some characteristics such as depression, family discord, personal stress, and alcohol abuse.[28] The study, which surveyed 934 full-time sworn officers, cited 48 percent of male officers and 40 percent of female officers drank in excess and found that PTSD often led to higher levels of alcohol abuse. This alcohol abuse ultimately led to higher levels of suicide ideation, measured by the Scale for Suicide Ideation (SSI), a psychological test. PTSD was categorized by the following:

1. Homicide of another officer
2. Self-involvement in shooting
3. Abused children
4. Serious traffic accidents
5. Witnessing death
6. Seeing dead bodies
7. Serious assault victims
8. Homicide victims
9. Other disturbing incidents

RETIREMENT AND BEYOND

For many officers who make it to the age of retirement, it may seem that their lives could not get any better. They are often only in their mid-fifties, which is considered early for retirement and generally young enough to start a second careers. They are collecting a pension and other retirement benefits while having the option of not working or starting a second career. While for most professions this is an ideal situation, for many officers who have made "police officer" their primary identity, they can perceive retirement as essentially being ejected from the police force, which is essentially their work family. These individuals have become institutionalized and rely solely on their police identities and are asked essentially to sever ties with their working family.

Consequently, there are some ramifications for retiring officers. For most individuals, retiring from the police force does not mean retiring from work. In fact, early retirement is a considerable benefit for law enforcement. This allows officers to pursue second careers, often related to law enforcement. For example, some retired officers work on college and university police departments. A significant portion of college and university police officers are retired municipal or county officers. Other officers continue their education and even become college and university professors.

For a small percentage of officers, however, retirement is a difficult time in their lives. These officers have such a strong group/institutional identity that removing them from the force essentially destroys part of their identity. This friction can manifest in many ways, ranging from depression to alcoholism and drug abuse. One phenomenon that has been researched is police suicides after retirement.

Sociologist Emile Durkheim (1951) in his 1897 book, *Suicide*, explains suicide as a sociological phenomenon.[29] He classifies suicide into several categories based on the level of connectedness one has to the social environment, and looks at suicide *rates* in different forms of societies. One classification, **egoistic suicide**, is suicide based on the idea that a person no longer feels they are part of society. Weakened or non-existent social bonds translates into the individual not having a sense of purpose in life.

Using Durkheim's analysis, police officers who leave the force may suffer from the loss of identity that was once based on the groups'. We have seen this example of institutional identity with prisoners who cannot function once released. The ex-prisoner, and in this case, the former police officer, suffers from a state of moral disorder and cannot function, and therefore turns to suicide.

Despite the applicability of Durkheim's theoretical reasoning, the general research shows that police suicide in general amongst police is actually the same or lower than that of the general population. For example, a 2002 study examining NYPD data from 1977 to 1996 with 668 studied found that the police suicide rate is 14.9 per 100,000, compared to the New York City rate of 18.3 per 100,000, which is significantly lower.[30]

SUMMARY

The lives and careers of police officers are not static, therefore it is very difficult to support blanket statements about police officers. As officers evolve from rookies to their mid-careers and eventually to seasoned veterans and retirees, each stage presents new challenges and risks. The officer finds him or herself often suffering from the cumulative mental and physical stress of the profession with no avenue to share this stress, except in forms of self-treatment such as alcoholism. Moreover, these destructive behaviors manifest in health and wellbeing issues, such as sleep disorders.

The stresses of police work often have professional consequences as well. Mentally and physically, officers are more likely to physically harm themselves through traffic accidents and more likely to display behavioral issues, such as bad temperament and attitudes that lead to physical altercations.

NOTES

1. Christal Hayes, "'Silence Can Be Deadly': 46 Officers Were Fatally Shot Last Year. More than Triple That—140—Committed Suicide," *USA Today*, April 11, 2018, https://www.usatoday.com/story/news/2018/04/11/officers-firefighters-suicides-study/503735002/.

2. Joseph Wambaugh, *The New Centurions* (New York: Little, Brown, 1971).

3. Jerry Hicks, "So You Want to Become a Police Officer? Why?" *Los Angeles Times*, December 9, 1986.

4. Darlena Cunha, "Reasons People Become a Police Officer," *Houston Chronicle*, March 16, 2018, http://work.chron.com/reasons-people-become-police-officer-8994.html.

5. Joseph Wambaugh, *The New Centurions* (New York: Little, Brown, 1971).

6. William Dunn, *Boot: An LAPD Officer's Rookie Year* (New York: William, Morrow, 1996).

7. Donald E. Super, "A Theory of Vocational Development," *American Psychologist* 8 (1953): 185–190.

8. Donald E. Super, *The Psychology of Careers* (New York: Harper and Row, 1957).

9. James C. McElroy, Paula C. Marrow, and Thomas R. Wardlow, "A Career Stage Analysis of Police Officer Work Commitment," *Journal of Criminal Justice* 27, no. 6 (1999): 507–516. doi: 10.1016/S0047-2352(99)00021-5.

10. Beverly Metcalfe and Dick Gavin, "Is the Force Still with You? Measuring Police Commitment," *Journal of Managerial Psychology* 15, no. 8 (2000): 812–832.

11. Yvonne Brunetto and Rod Farr-Wharton, "The Commitment and Satisfaction of Lower-Ranked Police Officers: Lessons for Management," *Policing: An International Journal of Police Strategies and Management* 26, no. 1 (2003): 43–63.

12. William G. Doerner, "Officer Retention Patterns: An Affirmative Action Concern for Police Agencies," *American Journal of Police* 14, no. 3/4 (1995): 197–210.

13. Arnold Bakker and Ellen Heuven, "Emotional Dissonance, Burnout, and In-Role Performance among Nurses and Police Officers," *International Journal of Stress Management* 13, no. 4 (2006): 423–440. doi: 10.1037/1072-5245.13.4.423.

14. Ronald J. Burke, "Toward an Understanding of Psychological Burnout among Police Officers," *International Journal of Stress Management* 4, no. 1 (1997): 13–27.

15. Harold I. Lief and Renee C. Fox, "Training for 'Detached Concern' in Medical Students," in *The Psychological Basis of Medical Practice* (New York: Harper and Row, 1963), 12–35.

16. Elizabeth Reuss-Ianni, *Two Cultures of Policing: Street Cops and Management Cops* (New York: Taylor and Francis, 1983).

17. Elizabeth Reuss-Ianni and Francis A. J. Ianni, "Street Cops and Management Cops: The Two Cultures of Policing," in *Policing: Key Readings* (Thousand Oaks: Willan Publishing), 297–314.

18. Stephen Nordlicht, "Effects of Stress on the Police Officer and Family," *New York State Journal of Medicine* 79, no. 3 (1979): 400–401.

19. Luenda E. Charles et al., "Shift Work and Sleep: The Buffalo Police Health Study," *Policing: An International Journal of Police Strategies & Management* 30, no. 2 (1997): 215–227.

20. Shantha. M. W. Rajaratnam et al., "Sleep Disorders, Health, and Safety in Police Officers," *Journal of the American Medical Association* 306, no. 23 (2011): 2576–2578. doi: 10.1001/jama.2011.1851.

21. Bryan Vila and Dennis J. Kenney, "Tired Cops: The Prevalence and Potential Consequences of Police Fatigue," *NIJ Journal* 248 (2002), https://www.ncjrs.gov/pdffiles1/jr000248d.pdf.

22. Derek R. Smith et al., "Alcohol and Tobacco Consumption among Police Officers," *The Kurume Medical Journal* 52, no. 1/2 (2005): 63–65. doi: 10.2739/kurumemedj.52.63.

23. David F. Machell, "Combat Post-Traumatic Stress Disorder, Alcoholism, and the Police Officer," *Journal of Alcohol and Drug Education* 38, no. 2 (1993): 23–32.

24. Shawn P. McCoy and Michael G. Aamodt, "A Comparison of Law Enforcement Divorce Rates with Those of Other Occupations," *Journal of Police and Criminal Psychology* 25, no. 1 (2010): 1–16.

25. Daniel Mattos, "The Need to Promote Career-Long Vitality and Wellness in the Police Profession," *FBI Law Enforcement Bulletin,* October 1, 2010, http://leb.fbi.gov/2010/october/perspective-the-need-to-promote-career-long-vitality-and-wellness-in-the-police-profession.

26. Joseph Wambaugh, *The New Centurions* (New York: Little, Brown, 1971).

27. William Harvey, "The Dangers of Badge Bunnies and Holster Sniffers," *Police: The Law Enforcement Magazine,* August 8, 2011, http://www.policemag.com/blog/careers/story/2011/08/the-dangers-lurking.aspx.

28. John M. Violante, "Predictors of Police Suicide Ideation," *Suicide and Life-Threatening Behavior* 34, no. 3(2004): 277–283. doi: 10.1521/suli.34.3.277.42775.

29. Emile Durkheim, *Suicide: A Study in Sociology* (New York, NY: The Free Press, 1951).

30. Peter M. Marzuk et al., "Suicide among New York City Police Officers, 1977–1996," *American Journal of Psychiatry* 159, no. 12 (2002): 2069–2071. doi: 10.1176/appi.ajp.159.12.2069.

Chapter Eleven

Women in Policing

The sight of a female police officer performing patrol duties does not draw any attention these days. Nor should it, since women have been serving as police officers in the same capacity as their male counterparts since the late 1960s when the first female patrol officers, Betty Blankenship and Elizabeth Robinson patrolled the streets of Indianapolis. Looking further back, women have been in policing since the early twentieth century in various capacities and functions. Despite being in policing for over a century, controversial issues with women and policing still exist that warrant further exploration.

Despite efforts by virtually all police departments today to hire more females, they remain a relatively small percentage of the force. According to the DOJ, women make up approximately 13 percent of the nation's police force.[1] This number is greater in large cities, such as in Los Angeles, with 18 percent female officers, and relatively smaller in more rural departments, where female officers remain in the single digits.[2]

Nevertheless, women are making great strides in policing as they continue to slowly grow in number and take on higher ranks. One city is particularly noteworthy in the promotion of females in law enforcement. In 2018, the Dallas Police Department and the Dallas County Sheriff's Department were both led by a chief and sheriff who are female, Renee Hall and Lupe Valdez, respectively. Moreover, these two officers are women of color, and are joined by Dallas County district attorney, Faith Johnson, who is another woman of color.

Although most law enforcement agencies' efforts to hire more female officers and offer equality of job functions and roles between male and female officers, women in policing remains a contentious area. Specifically, research examining the experiences of female officers reveals the difficulty and contradictions of a female fitting in and performing well in a work environment steeped in a hyper-masculine culture.

Some of the major issues addressed in this chapter include:

1. The historic context of the original role and purpose of women in the police force.
2. The ways and reasons why women's roles changed in policing.
3. The attitudes and perceptions of male police officers toward female officers.
4. The effectiveness of female officers compared to their male counterparts.

HISTORIC CONTEXT

Women did not exist in the police department in any capacity during the political era. Recall that during this era, the night watchman was the predominant method of patrol. In the late nineteenth century during industrialization, police became increasingly corrupt, which sparked several groups to openly and harshly criticize the police for being incompetent and corrupt. One of these groups was the WASP (White Anglo Saxon Protestant) women who were inspired by Victorian values and took note of the corruption, and simply considered it unacceptable in a civilized society. Recall that these values included intolerance for crime and human cruelty, while promoting culture, arts, and education. In addition, these women crusaded to protect women and children from working in factories and from being outside of safer traditional domestic roles.

Legal reforms were aimed at protecting the growing number of migrant and immigrant women and children. Using their social status, considerable wealth, and political influence, reformers lobbied for laws that targeted their views of the moral ills plaguing society, especially in high-crime industrial areas. These reforms were essentially a war on vagrancy, with laws and policies that addressed activities that were deemed morally reprehensible, such as alcohol, gambling, and prostitution.

However, these reform women quickly realized that their legal reform efforts made little or no difference. These vices seemingly continued to take place openly and unfettered. They realized that lack of police enforcement undermined the newly passed laws. Concurrently, these values aligned with **temperance movement** in the 1920s that was spearheaded by evangelical and Catholic groups as well as other religious leaders and stakeholders, was gaining momentum in the United States. These groups blamed immoral activities that ruined families and weakened the moral fabric, such as police and political corruption, spousal abuse, prostitution, and the consumption of alcohol.

Amidst growing criticism, police reformers targeted corruption as the centerpiece of the reform era of policing. Recall reformers that include August Vollmer, O. W. Wilson, J. Edgar Hoover, and Richard Sylvester sought to professionalize police departments, fundamentally shifting the primary directive of police from enforcing norms to law enforcement. Reform era officers stressed strict adherence to crime control measures through standardized operating procedures, in stark contrast to the much more informal night watchman who through enforcement of community norms focused on peace keeping and order maintenance. The decree meant officers should not waste time with non-law enforcement service duties.

The functional shift to crime control left the door open for women in policing. Women at the time were interested in greater involvement in policing, and coincidentally the service component, which they felt was inadequate. Thus, women in policing began as a complementary relationship with the male officers.

THE FIRST POLICE WOMEN: PORTLAND'S LOLA GREEN AND LAPD'S ALICE WELLS

The first female police officers are not typical of officers we think of today. They functioned essentially as social workers working within departments with specialized tasks related to the service component of policing. Specifically, women officers focused primarily on dealing with women and children, populations that they considered vulnerable in an industrial environment that was increasingly dangerous and immoral. Guided by Victorian morality at a time of urbanization, vice crime, and corruption, these women sought to "cleanse" the city and focus on public health while restoring morality. These attitudes and ideologies spread throughout the United States during the Progressive Era, which would shortly lead to the temperance movement that targeted alcohol.

In 1908, the city of Portland, Oregon, hired its first female police officer, Aurora "Lola" Baldwin.[3] Baldwin was specially assigned as the superintendent of the Women's Auxiliary to the Police Department for the Protection of Girls. She was a proponent of crime prevention and focused attention on women and girls' issues over crime control, arrests, and incarceration while promoting the idea of women taking on larger and more important roles that included that of police officer.

One would assume that in the male-dominated world of policing during the reform era, which emphasized physical fitness, machismo, and crime control, departments would resent and resist having female police officers. It can be reasoned that female officers would undermine the image of the police officer as envisioned during the reform era of policing. This new officer was to have a physical presence and stoic demeanor to display professionalism. Instead, the first police women were openly accepted by male officers who viewed their service-orientation as complementary to their crime control mandate.

Shortly after Lola Baldwin was hired, in 1910, the Los Angeles Police Department hired its first female police officer, Alice Stebbins Wells. Alice Wells and other early police women sought to join the police force primarily to further their goals of protecting women and children. Prior to Wells joining the police force as an officer, earlier civilian women working in the department, for the most part, handled female prisoners and performed clerical duties. While Wells and other early policewomen were police officers by title, their roles and duties did not include law enforcement duties and activities. In fact, Wells stood only 5'2" tall and was an assistant pastor and social worker before joining the LAPD.

These female officers did not carry weapons or handcuffs, or make arrests. Instead the first female officers wore dresses with a badge and focused on work that the men considered "social work" and not "real" police work, such as the proverbial "catching bad guys." Male officers viewed the women as taking on the duties that were a distraction from real police work, which freed them to pursue crime control and law enforcement duties. When a skeptical member of the public disparagingly asked Wells, "How could *you* making an arrest?" She simply replied, "I don't want to make arrests. I want to keep people from needing to be arrested, especially young people."

Early police women's affiliation with police departments and status as police officers gave them the legitimacy and authority they needed to enforce vagrancy violations and directly oversee any mistreatment of women and children. Moreover, their presence in the police department appealed to police supervisors who used their oversight as evidence that the department kept corruption at bay, which was a major criticism of police during the political era. Women officers embraced their role as department "matrons" while the male officers were happy to offload non-crime control duties to focus on the new measures of performance under the reform era, such as response times, clearance rates, and other crime-control metrics.

Many police departments were so satisfied with the separation of crime control and service duties that they expanded their service capacity. The LAPD, for instance, created the City Mother's Bureau from 1914 to 1929, a subdivision for female officers that focused primarily on crime prevention. Each female officer had a caseload, like that of a social worker, where they would monitor and supervise children. The LAPD also created a juvenile bureau, in which the female officers were placed in control. This became the ideal arrangement for the LAPD, who freed up officers to handle "real" police work while the department "mothers" would handle non-police work. This mutually beneficial model, however, would not last.

CHANGING ROLES FOR FEMALE OFFICERS: BECOMING MORE LIKE THE MEN

Societal and cultural events led to fundamental changes in the roles of female officers. First, the Second World War in the 1930s and early 1940s meant that the men were needed to serve in the war effort. The shortage of men created increasing demands for women to step outside their crime prevention roles and perform some limited crime control duties that were once exclusive to men. Moreover, budgetary pressures placed more strain on the LAPD to provide more services with fewer resources. By the 1950s women began performing crime control duties out of necessity, such as issuing citations.

Second, the wave of professionalism that swept through policing in the 1950s created a singular paradigm of policing that focused all resources on crime control. This meant that police departments had little room for both social work roles and law enforcement to coexist. Instead, departments that were the vanguards for police professionalism, such as the LAPD under Chief William Parker, became exclusively crime-control oriented. The LAPD, and many other departments, began phasing out most social work duties. The department's City Mother's Bureau and Juvenile Bureaus were eliminated in favor of a single functioning law enforcement oriented force.

In 1925, the Los Angeles City Council considered a proposal to reclassify the women officers as civilian employees, which meant forfeiting a lot of gains and accepting a lower status. The existing female officers who joined the force to perform social work and crime prevention duties, like Alice Wells, were confronted with the choice to either become more like their male counterparts and reorient themselves as law enforcers or leave the force altogether.

Consequently, most female officers left the force. The increased pressures and responsibilities of law enforcement meant most women would need to abandon their reason in joining the force in the first place. Furthermore, most male officers resented the female encroachment into their world. This meant that female officers would have to try to fit into an increasingly male-dominated and openly hostile environment. The women that stayed were interested in adopting this crime control role and embraced the change as a career opportunity. This ushered in the second generation of women officers beginning in the 1930s, which lasted to approximately 1950.

Changes in LAPD personnel policies changed the type of women who joined the department. First, the city dropped its minimum age requirement of thirty for women joining the force. The department also dropped its marriage requirement for women. In addition, some departments in the 1930s began issuing firearms to the women and requiring uniforms that resembled more closely those of men. The LAPD began issuing guns to women in 1934. These changes resulted in a lot of the original pioneering women from the 1910s, to become disinterested in police work. They were simply becoming very similar to the men in both appearance and function—something they were explicitly not interested in doing. Note that women carried handguns in their handbags and not on their hips.

The masculinization of police women was a radical departure from the early days of Alice Wells and the mothers of the department. The process was accelerated during the war effort, during which the LAPD had over 500 openings for police officer in 1942 and 1943. This employment demand did not drastically increase the number of women on the force, which only increased from thirty-eight to fifty-seven during the war. However, it cemented the new role of women as crime fighters. Long gone were the days of crime prevention; the new female recruits did not differ significantly in terms of the mentality of the men. They joined the police force primarily for crime control and law enforcement, in stark contrast to the early women who intended to prevent crime and perform social work.

The role of female officers would be permanently changed to be virtually identical to male officers. Most male officers at the time, however, did not feel this was a good change, which created conflict within departments. Historian Janis Appier described this change using pejorative term from the viewpoint of the men as going from "City Mother" to "Sgt. Tits."[4]

POLICE WOMEN TODAY: JUST LIKE THE MEN

One can say that police women today have transformed completely, both in appearance and function. Gone are any remnants of Lola Green and Alice Wells' social work model of the matron police woman. Today's female officers wear the exact same uniform as the men. Women applicants must pass the same entrance tests as the men and make it through the police academy. As officers, most female officers even talk and think like the men. This homogenized group is both by design and self-selection.

Women who join the police force today join for the same reasons male recruits become police officers. While the standard answer given by most applicants is the desire to help others, both men and women applicants are primarily attracted to the law enforcement and crime control aspects of the profession. Most are interested in wearing the uniform, use of firearms, self-defense, and other crime control elements of policing. The mentality of female officers may be even tougher than those of men.

One of the reasons why female officers are recruited by police departments today is because it is felt that women officers benefited the department with their presence, and were more skilled at certain functions.[5] For instance, female victims tend to relate better to female officers. A study of abused women in Detroit area shelters found that there were significant differences in attitudes toward male and female officers.[6] The study found that in domestic situations, female officers were perceived more favorably because of their ability to calm a situation.

However, it is often the case that female officers are not sympathetic to female victims. The same Detroit study of abused women found that female officers did not automatically side with female victims. Moreover, oftentimes female officers treat female victims generally more harshly than their male colleagues. Female officers, who typically have a different mind-set than women in the general population, often find it very difficult to relate to the female victim of crime. For example, female officers often find it difficult to understand why women who are repeatedly victimized by their spouses or partners do not leave or take action. They see these women as inexplicably weak and wonder why they put up with the abuse, and consider them almost deserving of the abuse. The female officer cannot fathom allowing a male to dominate them in that way.

Female officers are a special type of person. They are not your typical female. Instead, most female officers who are hired and make it through training think and act like their male colleagues. Many find it difficult to relate to civilian females. However, this has created a dichotomy between officer and female that causes internal friction for many female officers that must be negotiated. The female officer often finds that she must negotiate and navigate femininity and her female identity with that of a police officer, a profession that is often characterized as hypermasculine.

BALANCING TWO IDENTITIES

Female officers balance their identities as a woman and police officer in a couple of ways. First, female officers, due to their unique dispositions, often find it difficult to maintain relationships with civilian men. Perhaps these men find having a female officer as a significant other emasculating, but female officers for the most part find that they are most compatible with male officers. You will find that most female police officers marry male police officers. This may be due in part to shift work, but it is a pattern found throughout the country.

Second, many female officers often hide their police identities to avoid stereotypes and biases. Moreover, they often feel overwhelmed by the police identity. Therefore, many female officers often answer questions about their occupation with vague answers such as, "I work for the city." Hiding their identity allows them to have somewhat normal lives. Some women participate in groups and clubs that engage in highly feminine activities where their police identity is never brought up, allowing them to be "normal" women. For example, some female officers may join book clubs.

FITTING INTO THE MALE WORLD, COPING WITH STRESS, AND TOKENISM

While seeing a female police officer is not considered a special sight these days and their presence in a police department is common, they still face considerable difficulties fitting into a male dominated profession. Police researcher Cortney Franklin outlined the many difficulties that female officers still face today in the workplace.[7] Female officers still face a hostile work environment and receive a variety of negative reactions such as:

- Women still face constant sexual harassment and discrimination in work assignments and promotion opportunities.
- Women officers still face doubt from their male counterparts who question their competency in handling tough situations. They face increased scrutiny compared with their male counterparts.
- Women still face derogatory remarks and references, which include labels such as "lesbians," "whores," "dykes," and they are often described as "bitchy" and "castrating."
- Women are further ostracized by their male counterparts and report feelings of group exclusion, lack of peer support and mentoring, and inappropriate job expectations based on gender.
- Male patrol officers often criticize women officers when they do not live up to their personal social and physio-social demands and expectations.

Consequently, gender stereotyping of women, perhaps due to chivalry or lack of confidence in female officers, results in women being systematically excluded from more masculine assignments. This results in women performing lower and even being passed over for promotions which are given to their male colleagues.

Fitting into the police culture is something women still have much difficulty doing. For instance, many female officers are often excluded from social activities where bonding takes place, such as social drinking. According to Franklin, social drinking serves three functions:[8] First, social drinking serves to objectify women by using alcohol as a disinhibitor by men to openly sexualize the social encounter. Second, women are viewed as outsiders if they are unable to or unwilling to cover up the wrongdoings of the male officers, including sexual harassment. Third, by ostracizing women from informal peer gatherings, such as drinking, women miss out on important bonding opportunities at the supervisory level.

Franklin concludes that the hypermasculine police subculture is ultimately a social structure that serves to degrade, subordinate, and oppress female police officers. Ultimately, women are reduced to "trophy status" by the men, who view them as sexual objects. Furthermore, the behavior is tacitly accepted by supervisors as being part of the culture, excusing them as "boys being boys."

Many female officers ultimately become disillusioned by policing. A study by police researcher Barbara Price found that many women cite the lack of opportunities for advancement, conflicts between shift hours and their personal lives, and the negative attitudes of men, for their disillusionment.[9] They feel the department they work for does not appreciate their unique attributes as a group and feel discriminated against in terms of work assignments, promotions, recommendations for promotions, and the availability of appropriate facilities.

Adding to feelings of disillusionment is the "**tokenism**" effect of being female. A study published by criminologists Carol Archbold and Dorothy Schultz, who interviewed women officers, found that while they were strongly encouraged by male supervisors to promote to higher ranks, they were ironically dissuaded by the encouragement.[10] This may suggest that many female officers are deterred by anticipatory feelings of disrespect and resentment by their male colleagues who they feel may perceive them as only receiving the promotion because they are female. This problem is compounded with race, as women of color find even more barriers to promotion.

These internal conflicts and external stressors can lead to female officer burnout. A variety of research has found sources of stress for police typically come from four categories: (1) the work environment, (2) the bureaucracy of the department, (3) availability of peer support and trust, and (4) accessibility of coping mechanisms. Female officers compound these stressors with unique factors. A study of women working in traditionally male fields reported elevated levels of stress derived from male hostility.[11] However, studies that compared men and women officers showed that females were better at coping with stress, using more constructive coping mechanisms than the men who tended to use more destructive ways to cope with stress.[12]

Nevertheless, a comparison between men and women officers showed that women faced more stressors that are risk factors of burnout.[13] The same study identified camaraderie and perceived unfairness as two additional sources of stress. The exclusion of women from the proverbial boys' club and inner-circle of some male officers, can lead to stress, especially in a profession where group solidarity and trust are critical during emergency situations.[14] Moreover, the general lack of women in the highest ranks in most police departments can be a stressor for female officers.

RACE AND GENDER

Issues of gender are sometimes compounded with issues of race. One study that looked at the impact of race and gender on police stressors found that female police officers had higher levels of stress than male officers, but race did not make a difference.[15] Nevertheless, the experiences of White female officers differ from those of Black female officers.[16] Price also found that 92 percent of Black female officers felt discriminated against compared to 57 percent of White female officers.[17] Black female officers reported the following discrimination:

- Black women feel they must demand respect while White women are put on pedestals.
- Black women report that their bosses don't send White women into high crime areas (but, by inference, do send Black women).
- Black women report they have no one to help them secure desired assignments, special training sessions or promotions; White women, they say, have "hooks" (connections).
- Black women report verbal racial insults.
- Black women say they have more trouble with racial discrimination from the cops than from the public.
- Black women claim that White women can get transferred inside to a warm job such as the switchboard on a cold night while they must remain on the street.

Price's findings are consistent with critical race theory and critical legal studies. Critical race scholars argue that the women's rights movement did not go far enough in addressing the "**double oppression**" of gender and race faced by women of color. Leading critical race scholars, such as Kimberle Crenshaw, underscore race consciousness and the experiences of Black women not as a singular experience, but as a collection of rich stories and experiences.[18] Therefore, storytelling is a key element in expressing racial identity and gender that allows for a pluralized view. In other words, one cannot lump together the experience of the White female officer with that of all female officers since it can be considered a privileged position.

Regardless of the racial differences, female officers have faced negative attitudes from their male colleagues since the shift toward crime control during the reform era of policing.

MALE OFFICER ATTITUDES TOWARD FEMALE COPS

There have been several perception studies on female officers by several groups. These studies may be dated, with more female officers joining the force, but their level of acceptance remains an issue. A 1994 study was conducted by police researchers Thomas Austin and Donald Hummer, which looked at male criminal justice students' perceptions of female officers.[19] Nearly half of their respondents held negative attitudes toward female officers. This is significant since according to a 1986 study by researchers Keren Pope and David Pope, a large component to female officers' success is determined by the degree to which they are accepted by their male colleagues.[20] However, in the 1980s, it was found that traditional role stereotyping was prevalent and kept a lot of women from being successful officers.

These studies however can be considered outdated in the fast-changing world of women and policing. Newer studies show that the current generation of female police officers is less affected by their male counterparts and gender barriers. One major hurdle that female officers face today is being subjected to male power. A 2009 study by researchers Philip Carlan and Elizabeth McMullan found that male officers promote the subordination of women, which can be a major stressor for female officers.[21] However, their large-scale survey found that police women today exhibit a lot of mental toughness, showing male-equivalent levels of professionalism, job satisfaction, stress, and confidence levels, suggesting policewomen are mentally tough and resilient to an oppressive and often hostile environment and can thrive in their careers.

Female officers' mental toughness may be an absolute necessity to survive in policing. A 2005 European study of female officers found policewomen face significantly higher levels of harassment and violence by their coworkers, superiors, and public encounters, compared to women in other occupations.[22] Attitudes toward female officers showed statistically significant findings in categories that include overprotectiveness, flirtatiousness, women's opinions being neglected, and women being criticized for minor mistakes. These perceptions by women point to a somewhat hostile work environment that privileges male officers.

Despite these negative attitudes, female officers have proven competent and able to perform all duties of their male counterparts. The means at which many female officers perform tasks, for example those requiring more physicality, however, may differ slightly.

WOMEN OFFICERS: DIFFERENT METHODS, SIMILAR OUTCOMES

There is no denying that female officers in general are not identical to their male counterparts. Despite the standardized training, progress toward acceptance, and other factors, there are still physiological differences from the male officers. First, males typically have stronger upper body strength and are larger in stature, which can be advantageous. One can argue that command presence is easier to establish with male officers compared to female officers. This command presence arguably can deter individuals from challenging the officer's authority, or dissuade them from potentially using force against the officer.

Female officers, however, can be and are equally as effective as their male colleagues. The methods in which they work, however, can differ slightly. During academy training, for example, female recruits typically lack the upper body strength of male recruits. When it comes to putting a 185-pound dummy in a car female recruits do not simply pick up the body and throw it into the back of a cruiser. Instead, one method commonly used is to pull the body from the other side of the vehicle. This produce has a similar outcome using slightly different methods.

It is found that female officers do not require as many physical altercations as compared to their male colleagues. As mentioned, it is argued that larger male officers can deter physical confrontations with their size and command presence. Female officers however, tend to be better communicators who can verbally deescalate a situation, which effectively produces the desired outcome with less liability. A 2000 study of both US and international female officers found that overall, female officers were:

1. Equally as competent as their male colleagues
2. Less likely to use excessive force
3. More likely to implement community-oriented policing
4. More likely to improve law enforcement's response to violence against women
5. Reduce problems of sex discrimination and harassment within a large agency with an increase in women officers
6. Can bring about beneficial changers to policy for all officers

SUMMARY

From their humble beginnings as station patrons or "moms" and meter maids, women have made great strides in the world of policing. Police women today are no longer the social workers they initially functioned as in the department, but full-fledged officers with all the rights and duties of their male colleagues.

While female officers have come a long way in becoming accepted as being a full-fledged police officers, women still make up approximately 10 percent of the total police force. However, the number of women in policing has increased significantly in the past few decades as police departments, cognizant of the benefits of having female officers, have actively sought to recruit women officers.

Despite these efforts and the desire to increase women in the force, most women in the general population are not interested in police work and do not join the force. The women who do enter into the profession tend to be a unique group that shares many values of policing in general, and are not very different from the men, ranging from their desire to help others to prioritizing the crime control and law enforcement aspects of the job. After academy and field training, female officers are virtually identical to male officers.

Yet, the reality is that women officers still operate within a male-dominated, hypermasculine environment and face unique challenges ranging from acceptance to harassment. They must also negotiate their work identities with social expectations of gender roles and feminism. This conflict is often compounded by work stressors that include not only the normal stressors of the work environment, department bureaucracy, peer support and trust, and coping mechanisms, faced by all police officers, but also with issues such as exclusion and tokenism.

Despite great strides in policing, many male officers and members of the public have a difficult time accepting the reality of women as police officers, especially when confronted with images of female officers being injured in the line of duty. Women in policing remains an important issue in policing today.

NOTES

1. United States Department of Justice, "Women in Law Enforcement," *Community Policing Dispatch* 6, no. 7 (2013), https://cops.usdoj.gov/html/dispatch/07-2013/women_in_law_enforcement.asp.

2. "Sworn and Civilian Personnel by CS Class, Sex, and Descent," Los Angeles Police Department, January 1, 2018, http://assets.lapdonline.org/assets/pdf/sr91jan18.pdf.

3. Gloria E. Myers, *A Municipal Mother: Portland's Lola Green Baldwin, America's First Policewoman* (Corvallis: Oregon State University Press, 1995).

4. Janis Appier, *Policing Women: The Sexual Politics of Law Enforcement and the LAPD* (Philadelphia: Temple University Press, 1998).

5. Kimberly A. Lonsway, "Hiring and Retaining More Women: The Advantages to Law Enforcement Agencies," *Feminist Majority Foundation,* 2000, https://files.eric.ed.gov/fulltext/ED473183.pdf.

6. Daniel B. Kennedy and Robert J. Homant, "Attitudes of Abused Women toward Male and Female Police Officers," *Criminal Justice and Behavior* 10, no. 4 (1983): 391–405. doi: 10.1177/0093854883010004002.

7. Cortney A. Franklin, "Male Peer Support and the Police Culture: Understanding the Resistance and Opposition of Women in Policing," *Women and Criminal Justice* 16, no. 3 (2005): 1–25.

8. Franklin, "Male Peer Support and the Police Culture."

9. Barbara R. Price, "Female Police Officers in the United States," in *Policing in Central and Eastern Europe: Comparing Firsthand Knowledge with Experience from the West* (Ann Arbor: University of Michigan College of Police and Security Studies, 1996).

10. Carol A. Archbold and Dorothy M. Schultz, "The Lingering Effects of Tokenism on Female Police Officers' Promotion Aspirations," *Police Quarterly* 11, no. 1 (2008): 50–73. doi: 10.1177/1098611107309628.

11. Barbara R. Price, "Female Police Officers in the United States," in *Policing in Central and Eastern Europe: Comparing Firsthand Knowledge with Experience from the West* (Ann Arbor: University of Michigan College of Police and Security Studies, 1996).

12. Ni He, Jihong Zhao, and Carol A. Archbold, "Gender and Police Stress: The Convergent and Divergent Impact of Work Environment, Work-Family Conflict, and Stress Coping Mechanisms of Female and Male Police Officers," *Policing: An International Journal of Police Strategies and Management* 25, no. 4 (2002): 687–708. doi: 10.1108/13639510210450631.

13. William P. McCarty, Jihong Zhao, and Brett E. Garland, "Occupational Stress and Burnout Between Male and Female Police Officers: Are There any Gender Differences?" *Policing: An International Journal of Police Strategies and Management* 30, no. 4 (2007): 672–691. doi: 10.1108/13639510710833938.

14. Renee Stepler, "Female Police Officers' On-the-Job Experiences Diverge from Those of Male Officers," *Pew Research Center*, 2017, http://www.pewresearch.org/fact-tank/2017/01/17/female-police-officers-on-the-job-experiences-diverge-from-those-of-male-officers/.

15. Ni He, Jihong Zhao, and Ling Ren, "Do Race and Gender Matter in Police Stress? A Preliminary Assessment of the Interactive Effects," *Journal of Criminal Justice* 33, no. 6 (2005): 535–547. doi: 10.1016/j.jcrimjus.2005.08.003.

16. Susan E. Martin, "'Outsider Within' the Station House: The Impact of Race and Gender on Black Women Police," *Social Problems* 41 (1994): 383–400. doi: 10.2307/3096969.

17. Barbara R. Price, "Female Police Officers in the United States," in *Policing in Central and Eastern Europe: Comparing Firsthand Knowledge with Experience from the Wes*. (Ann Arbor: University of Michigan College of Police and Security Studies, 1996).

18. Kimberle W. Crenshaw, *Critical Race Theory* (New York: New Press, 1995).

19. Thomas L. Austin and Donald C. Hummer, "'Has a Decade Made a Difference?' Attitudes of Male Criminal Justice Majors towards Female Police Officers," *Journal of Criminal Justice Education* 5, no. 2 (1994): 229–239. doi: 10.1080/10511259400083231.

20. Karen E. Pope and David W. Pope, "Attitudes of Male Officers towards their Female Counterparts," *Police Journal, 59* (1986): 242–253. doi: 10.1177/0032258X8605900309.

21. Philip E. Carlan and Elizabeth McMullan, "A Contemporary Snapshot of Policewomen Attitudes," *Women and Criminal Justice* 19, no. 1 (2009): 60–79. doi: 10.1080/08974450802586968.

22. Kaisa Kauppinen and Saara Patoluoto, "Sexual Harassment and Violence toward Policewomen in Finland," In *In the Company of Men: Male Dominance and Sexual Harassment* (Northeastern University Press, 2005). 195–212.

Chapter Twelve

Racial Minority and LGBTQ Cops

Like the controversies and difficulties faced by women in policing, racial minority and lesbian, gay, bisexual, transsexual, and questioning (LGBTQ) officers face similar issues. Accordingly, central to this chapter is the idea of dual identities that often cause friction and stress for both minority and gay and lesbian officers: one as a member of a minority group and another as a police officer. Minority officers have been exposed to and have faced open as well as more subtle forms of racism which they are expected to tolerate and tacitly accept as part of the *blue brotherhood* and adhere to the "blue wall of silence." For lesbian and gay officers, the hypermasculine and generally conservative police subculture often requires these officers to choose one identity while hiding another, or face consequences.

Ironically, members of these minority groups, along with women, are some of the most highly sought-after individuals by departments and agencies driven to diversify under community policing to ameliorate the strained relationship and racial tensions between the police and public under professionalism during the reform era. Police departments in response to increased attention from a history of social upheavals sparked by real or perceived police misconduct, from the Watts Riots in the 1960s to Rodney King in the 1990s, and more recently, Ferguson in 2014, have sought to hire officers that better reflect community demographics as the solution.

In principle, a more diversified police force will have a more profound effect on changing the police subculture. The subculture often manifests in racist, sexist, and homophobic attitudes among many officers, including management. For instance, the Warren Christopher Commission that investigated the Rodney King beating and ensuing Los Angeles Riots, found a culture of open racism that is tacitly accepted by the higher-ups at the LAPD. Having women and minority officers, it was thought, would make police departments more sensitive to those officers who would not tolerate such attitudes. In principle, a critical mass of minority officers from all groups would weaken and eventually dissipate the subculture.

The benefits of hiring minority officers, at least in principle, include:

- The minority officers better reflect the community which eases racial tension
- Minority officers can better relate to the minority community
- Removes language barriers
- Removes cultural barriers

Despite the apparent benefits of diversifying the department, changing the police subculture is much more complex and difficult. Increases in women, minority, and gay and lesbian officers has not been shown to weaken or eliminate the police subculture that has often been criticized for fostering racist, sexist, and homophobic attitudes. Ironically, these officers from minority groups have often adopted the police subculture and the same attitudes and worldviews as their colleagues, demonstrating the robustness of the police identity.

A SNAPSHOT OF POLICE RACIAL DIVERSITY

Police officers in the United States are predominately White. In fact, they are disproportionately White in many urban areas, which is significant when one looks at places with high degrees of racial tension. Ferguson, Missouri, for example, in 2015 had approximately 67 percent Black residents with a police force that was 94 percent White. Oftentimes it is the disparity between the dearth of minority officers in minority communities that is blamed as a major source of racial tension and possible social upheaval.

The significant disparity between racial minority officers in areas near metropolitan areas is a growing concern among large police departments. According to the Brookings Institute, both big cities and their suburbs exhibit the large diversity gap, with a 20 to 26 percentage point difference between the minority population and minority officers, respectively.[1] Meaning, police departments would need to increase the number of minority officers by at least 20 percent to match the population percentage of minorities. It was found that eighty-three out of 122 agencies surveyed, or 68 percent, had large diversity gaps. Some of the cities with the largest disparities between minority officers and percentage of minorities in the population included Allentown, Pennsylvania, which had a 49 percent difference, Sacramento, California, with over 41 percent, and Las Vegas, Nevada, with over 35 percent.

Progress has been made in recent decades at hiring more minority officers. According to the Bureau of Justice Statistics, one in six officers was a racial minority in 1987, which increased to one in four by 2007. From 2003 to 2007, Hispanic officers rose from 10 percent to nearly 16 percent of the police force. According to the Department of Justice, in 2013, racial or ethnic minorities accounted for over one quarter (27 percent) of officers in local police departments.[2] Hispanic officers accounted for the biggest gain from 2007 to 2015 with a 60 percent increase. In 2015, Black officers accounted for approximately 12 percent of local police forces while Asians, Pacific Islanders, and Native Americans accounted for approximately 3 percent of local departments. Despite these increases, minority officers are primarily concentrated in larger cities and overall, the police force does not truly reflect the demographics of the population.

Hiring minority officers remains difficult for most departments. A 1993 study of 356 Albany, New York, high school seniors found that race had a statistically significant effect on applying to police departments.[3] The seniors were asked whether they would accept a hypothetical police job offer. Black seniors were found to be less likely than White seniors to accept the job offer. When researchers broke down the variables that affected why Blacks were less likely to accept the hypothetical offer, it was found that it had to do with the culmination of negative experiences with and attitudes toward police as well as demographic variables. For example, Black seniors surveyed were less likely to report being stopped and questioned by police, they believed police treated minorities unfairly, and felt that Black and White officers did not get along on the job.

Despite the difficulties in hiring racial and ethnic minorities to the police force, efforts to recruit these officers by departments can be effective. Many departments in the 1990s paid for expensive television ad campaigns to attract women and minority officers, with limited success. This strategy later shifted to focusing on compensation and working conditions, such as time off and flexible schedules. A 2009 study confirmed this later strategy, finding that increasing starting pay resulted in more minority applicants but ultimately did not increase actual hires.[4] However, the study found that increases in recruitment budgets were effective in gaining more minority and women hires. Departments that used proactive and tailored recruitment strategies targeting minority applicants resulted in more hires, which included women. This is in contrast to traditional methods of general recruiting coupled with preferential treatment for minority applicants, which showed to be ineffective.

REALITIES OF RACIAL MINORITY OFFICERS

The idea of creating a diverse police force that represents the diversity of the community is a murky concept when one considers all the levels of diversity. Take for instance, women officers as discussed previously. While we discussed some of the difficulties of being a woman in a predominantly male field and being exposed to sexist attitudes, we did not consider the ramifications of being a Black policewoman.

An in-depth qualitative study of five large municipal police agencies by Susan Martin found 48 percent of Black female officers experienced both race and sex discrimination, compared to 17 percent of White female officers. Moreover, Black women found themselves competing and losing out against both Black male and White female officers even when even when affirmative action policies and rules intended to increase promotion opportunities for underrepresented groups were put in place. Overall, many Black female officers experienced both a structurally limited and culturally hostile work environment. One Black female officer described her experience with White male officers, stating:

> White males generally have very little respect for black females, especially if they don't know you. . . . If a white female is around and they start their cursing, they'll say 'excuse me.' If a black female is around they don't stop. Their attitude is, 'oh it is only a black female, who cares.' [5]

The reality, however, is that hiring minority officers often has very little impact on the issues that they are supposed to ameliorate. These issues include building instant rapport with the community and restoring or improving police/community relations, reducing institutional racial bias and racism, and other factors that are directly or indirectly related to changing the police subculture. Recall that the police subculture is characterized by various biases and stereotypes, cynicism, and an unwillingness to report other officers for misconduct.

The hiring of minority officers has seemingly neither significantly reduced engrained institutional racism in police departments nor reduced community tensions. Minority officers typically do not share the same view as the community but instead give their loyalty to the department. Black community perceptions of Black and White officers, for example, is sometimes contrary to principled beliefs that Black communities are more receptive and prefer Black officers.

A study published in the Journal of Criminal Justice by sociologist Ronald Weitzer who conducted 169 interviews with residents in three neighborhoods in Washington, DC, found that Black residents' interactions with White officers were less confrontational than expected by conventional wisdom.[6] The study found White officers to generally be more lenient than Black officers, by being more cognizant of accusations of being unfair and harassing in nature. In contrast, Black officers were perceived by Black residents as treating them more harshly, with one interviewee stating "[Black officers] seem to look down on their people. They kick them around." Adding, "It's amazing but White officers are far more courteous to Black people than Black officers are." Others explained the harsher behavior as a way to prove their loyalty to their White colleagues and worthiness of being police officers, which highlights the strength of the police identity and loyalty to fellow officers.

Moreover, the community often perceives these officers as "sell-outs" or betrayers of the community for joining an oppressive force. These minority officers frequently face hostility by the community who fail to understand why they are not given leniency by the officer. Furthermore, many Hispanic and Asian officers only speak English. When one considers all these structural and cultural factors, it becomes clear why hiring minority officers has relatively little impact on changing the police culture and public perceptions of police. One 2007 study by Megan O'Neill and Simon Holdaway interviewed Black British police officers who expressed the inner turmoil many racial minorities face in wanting to join the police force given these factors.[7] One officer stated:

> So you know, the decision to become a police officer for a black person is not necessarily a quick, easy decision as it might be for a white officer. . . . I had to look at where I came from, why I wanted to do it for the first instance and again saw the negativity. Because there is negativity out there about public services, police in particular. You know, so it was a big decision to make. . . .
>
> The police force has gone out there and said 'Right, target the young Asians to go and join the force', I've said 'It ain't gonna be that easy,' because 99 percent of those Asian youngsters will be dictated to by their parents. And if their elders don't want them to join, you ain't gonna get them to join. You need to be sort of talking to the elders and convincing them that there is a career to be made out of joining the police force and whatever else before they'll start encouraging their offspring. Because as far as Asian society is concerned, their views are you go into jobs such as accountancy, doctorates, lawyer, teachers and also the preconceived idea that anyone who's come from India has always regarded the police force over in India as being totally corrupt.

There is evidence, however, that shows qualitative differences between how Black and White officers handle conflict. A 2004 study showed that while Black officers were more likely than White officers to engage in activities during conflicts that were more supportive in predominantly Black neighborhoods, they were also found to be more coercive than White officers.[8]

Some scholars have argued that recruiting more ethnic minorities simply gives the illusion of progress but does little to change the organization. Police researcher Ellis Cashmore interviewed police officers in England and Wales of African Caribbean and South Asian backgrounds on their perspectives on efforts to enhance cultural diversity.[9] Some ethnic minority officers interviewed expressed cynicism toward "harmful" diversification efforts, calling them "window dressing" for only giving the outward image of action while not actually resulting in any changes to address institutional racism. These minority officers were very critical of both ethnic-based recruitment and diversity training. Moreover, the officers downplayed their token identity as "Black police officers" and stressed their main identity as regular "police officers."

Researchers Megan O'Neill and Simon Holdaway, in a follow-up study, looked at the perspectives from interviews with more senior and higher ranking Black Police Association members and found racial minority officers can make an impact on departmental policy and procedures and can serve as an impetus for cultural changes. These officers interviewed perceived their identities as "Black police officers," and not "police officers who happen to be Black." Reaching a critical population threshold of minority officers, it is argued, allows for race and being an officer to be non-mutually exclusive categories. Minority officers can acknowledge police injustices and bias without feeling disloyalty to the department. Despite these positive perspectives from high ranking Black officers, overall change has been difficult and slow in many departments.

There are several reasons why minority officers have had relatively little impact on changing the police culture and restoring community trust. As discussed in a previous chapter, the reasons include:

1. People attracted to policing and apply to policing jobs are specific types of persons. Regardless of race, sex, or even sexual orientation, recruits typically cite job security, career opportunity, family tradition of law enforcement, salary and benefits, a sense of adventure, and civic duty for joining the police force. Many individuals who do not share these values do not consider police work as a career.

2. The hiring process filters out individuals who do not fit the prototypical police mold. For those of you who are in policing or know of people who have applied to be in law enforcement, you know that the hiring process is quite extensive. Recruits not only must pass written and physical exams, but are subject to psychological screening and lengthy background checks. In addition, applicants are interviewed by multiple law enforcement personnel, whose primary goal is to make sure the applicant is "fit" to be a recruit. In policing, this means being able to trust that person. Recruits may be rejected if they do not quite

fit in to the value system that the officers in the department hold or if they are viewed as incapable of performing police duties. This process often filters out candidates who may have particular skill sets but fail to fit in with the system, resulting in a very homogenous group of individuals who are eventually hired.

3. Academy and field training further homogenizes the group by filtering out individuals who do not share core values. Successful academy cadets generally share the same viewpoint and belief about what is important in police work, physical training, self-defense, and marksmanship, considered "real" police work, while dismissing most lessons and activities not directly related to crime control. Individuals, for example, who may be excellent writers but do not see physical training as being of top importance, may find themselves eliminated. Stress training, where cadets are under constant scrutiny and an onslaught of verbal commands to put it gently, deemphasizes individuality for group identity.

Rookie officers are further scrutinized by field training officers who evaluate the performance, as well as "fit," of the individual. Furthermore, recruits must be receptive to **cultural transmission** in the form of **storytelling** by veteran officers. These "war stories" emphasize the dangers of the job while transmitting core values that new officers must internalize in order to be accepted into the group.

The culmination of the three processes during application and training results in a homogenous group that thinks and acts alike, regardless of the race of the officer. In other words, the blue brotherhood usually trumps ethnic identity.

LOYALTIES AND IDENTITY

Regardless of gender, race, sexuality, and other categories of identity, officers are expected to have a high degree of loyalty to fellow officers. Unlike the days of the night watchmen where officers relied on the community for direct assistance during emergency situations, today's officers are limited to fellow officers for help. These officer-needs-assistance calls are the most prioritized calls. Working under the constant threat of danger draws officers together and reinforces the "blue brotherhood," as characterized by the police subculture. This means loyalty to officers over loyalty to ethnic groups and other communities an officer may come from.

This expectancy of loyalty can put minority officers in a predicament. Minority officers are hired in part by the department, in theory, to change the organizational culture. Instead, these officers are usually incorporated into the culture but must patrol areas that expect them to be sensitive to their needs. For example, Black officers patrolling the inner-city minority neighborhoods are likely to encounter Black citizens who may expect a level of leniency. When such leniency is denied, they face hostility to a degree greater than what White officers would get, if they would get any at all. The same situation can be said about other racial minorities, including Hispanic and Asian officers.

Despite their loyalties to the police, minority officers often face an identity conflict. Recall our discussion of the police culture in which many police organizations, such as the LAPD during the 1980s and 1990s, have been shown to tolerate openly racist, sexist, and homophobic attitudes among some officers. This is problematic when there are racial minority, women, and gay/lesbian officers amongst their ranks. This puts many women and minority officers at odds with their fellow officers: Do they tolerate biases, or risk being alienated and ostracized by fellow officers that they must rely on during emergency situations? This quandary is faced by the small known numbers of officers who are gay and lesbian.

GAY AND LESBIAN COPS

While researchers, police management, and the public have focused mainly on women and racial minority officers as a point of progress in the world of policing, another sub-population of officers is often overlooked. Officers from the LGBTQ community face a unique set of challenges that have recently garnered the attention of departments and researchers.

Historically, attitudes toward gay and lesbian officers have reflected community sentiments. For one thing, gay and lesbian officers exist. The public generally does not associate gay men, for instance, as fitting with the hypermasculine and conservative working world of the police officer. Stereotypes of gay men as being weak and feminine, coupled with the fear of negative attitudes and ostracization by fellow officers has traditionally meant that gay and lesbian police officers have hidden their sexual identities. This hidden identity is not without reason. Like most victims of anti-gay and lesbian hate crimes who often do not report their victimization to police, lesbian and gay officers share similar fears of hostility, discrimination, and abuse.

For members of the public who are lesbian or gay, studies have shown occupational negative ramifications of coming out, or revealing their sexual orientation. For instance, self-reporting studies found openly gay or lesbian officers faced reduced salaries and more difficulties getting hired. For lesbian and gay officers, their fear of coming out can be attributed historically to the consequences of many that have revealed their sexuality, which ranges from simply being subject to lewd comments and being shunned by other officers to potentially life-threatening ramifications, such as calls for backup being ignored.

While there is little research in the area and even less public attention paid to this group, there are a small but significant number of homosexual officers nationwide. There is no estimate of how many are gay or lesbian since no official statistics exist, like they do with women and minority officers. Moreover, many of these officers have not disclosed their sexual orientation to fellow officers. However, there are some reports that show the presence of gay officers as well as their struggles of being gay.

Former Hollywood, Florida, police officer Mike Verdugo, for example, was fired in 2010 for not disclosing he was in a gay bondage film he had made in 1996. Verdugo, who served for ten years, argued that the city fired him solely on the film and did not take action for not disclosing working other jobs in the past.

In 2007, openly gay NYPD Police Officer Michael Harrington sued the department for discrimination and harassment. Harrington claims he was called "faggot" on numerous occasions by fellow officers who snubbed him at a Christmas party. He also claimed he was constantly bombarded with sexual innuendos about how he treats suspects. Finally, he was transferred from his patrol division to the West Village, a known gay neighborhood, to "be with his people."

Homosexual officers, the research shows, joined the police force for the exact same reasons given by straight officers. Researcher Roddrick Colvin found the following reasons for gay officers joining the police force: [10]

- Job security: 41 percent
- Career opportunity: 41 percent
- Family tradition: 17 percent
- Salary/benefits: 38 percent
- Adventure: 33 percent
- Civic duty: 41 percent

THE GAY AND LESBIAN OFFICER EXPERIENCE

Due to the strong police subculture, most homosexual officers hide their sexual identities in fear of discrimination and loss of trust by other officers. Remember, this trust is paramount since officers solely rely on each other for backup during life and death situations as part of the nature of the profession. The small number of officers who choose to share their sexual orientation often do so when they are feeling truly secure in the force.

Revealing one's homosexual identity can create a very hostile work environment, create social isolation, and subject one to intense harassment and homophobic talk.[11] Colvin's survey of gay and lesbian officers found wide-spread differential treatment by other officers and by the department, which include:[12]

- Outsider 51 percent
- Tokenism: 43 percent
- Social isolation: 48 percent
- Homophobic talk: 67 percent
- Repeated harassment: 34 percent
- Retaliation: 25 percent

Facing these consequences, many gay and lesbian officers do not share their sexual orientation. However, keeping one's identity secret creates inner friction between one's identity as a police officer and being a homosexual.

Concealment of a homosexual officer's sexual orientation can manifest in negative ramifications for the individual as well as the department. First, the individual may suffer psychologically with feelings of denial, self-homophobia, negative identity development, and feelings of being a fraud. Second, suppression of sexual identity inhibits organizational change and implicitly reinforces the openly homophobic environment.

Despite widespread social changes in attitudes of acceptance toward homosexuality in society, policing remains a slow-moving institution steeped in tradition and conservative values. Police departments were slow to incorporate women officers, who today still face similar issues, albeit less severe compared with homosexual officers. These women still work in a masculine profession that continually devalues their contributions and creates a losing predicament: live up to the prescribed male standards of performance that require women to exhibit masculine behavior to "fit in" but in doing so face the proverbial "she's a good officer, she must be lesbian" attitude that diminish that performance.

Lesbian and gay officers may keep their sexual identities secret based on perceptions that being openly homosexual may limit their opportunities. A survey of the professional support organization for lesbian and gay officers in New York, the Law Enforcement Gays and Lesbians International (LEGAL), found respondents cited possible promotion limitations (22 percent) and bad assignments (17 percent) as barriers to equal opportunity for homosexuals. Moreover, many respondents experienced homophobic talk (67 percent), being cast as an outsider (51 percent), social isolation (48 percent), repeated harassment (34 percent), and retaliation (25 percent) treatment at work.

FROM NEW YORK'S STONEWALL RIOTS TO
FORT WORTH'S RAINBOW LOUNGE RAID

Two historic police-led events contextualize the gay rights and policing that happened forty years apart. The first event occurred in 1969 at the Stonewall Inn in the Greenwich Village neighborhood of Manhattan, in New York City. The Stonewall Inn was a bar that openly catered to the LGBTQ community. It was one of the few establishments serving the LGBTQ community in a very strong homophobic social and political environment. However, the gay rights movement was gaining momentum from social turmoil and an atmosphere of change from the civil rights movement and protests from a counter-cultural movement of the Vietnam War and government corruption.

Amidst growing tensions between police and the LGBTQ community, it was common for gay establishments, particularly bars, to be targeted for raids. On an the early morning of June 28, 1969, police, including undercover agents, raided the Stonewall Inn to arrest patrons for violating public morality and alcohol restrictions. However, as over 200 bar patrons were led outside for arrest, many began resisting the rough treatment by police. This mistreatment by police sparked a large crowd of hundreds of neighborhood residents, many of whom were LGBTQ, to gather and lend support to the arrested bar patrons. Soon, the crowd began fighting back, which led to consecutive days of riots, sparking a pivotal milestone in the gay rights movement.

Emboldened by the Greenwich LGBTQ community that came to the aid of bar patrons, national protests against police raids targeting the LGBTQ community occurred in major cities. The Stonewall Riots shifted the gay rights movement from a hidden stance to one of gay pride and a willingness to fight back. However, despite growing public support for LGBTQ rights, legal changes did not ensue until decades later. This slow change is in stark contrast to two earlier movements that resulted in a societal sea of change: the civil rights movement in the 1960s that resulted in the 1964 Civil Rights Act, followed by the women's rights movement that peaked with the *Roe v. Wade* decision. Riding on the momentum of these previous movements, the gay rights movement, which was supposed to reach a tipping point in the 1980s, was set back by weaker public support and the emergence of the HIV/AIDS epidemic, which sparked a renewed wave of homophobia and stigmatization of the LGBTQ community.

On June 28, 2008, coincidentally the exact fortieth anniversary date of the Stonewall Riots, Fort Worth Police Department officers and Texas Alcoholic Beverage Commission (TABC) agents conducted an early morning raid of The Rainbow Lounge. The Rainbow Lounge, like the Stonewall Inn, was a bar that openly catered to the LGBTQ community. The targeting of the Texas bar on the anniversary of Stonewall Riots drew instant international attention, which prompted internal use of force investigations by both law enforcement agencies, and lawsuits to the city. Events such as Stonewall and the Rainbow Lounge serve to deter LGBTQ community members from joining the police.

The internal investigation resulted in some significant changes to the Fort Worth Police Department, thrusting the department located in one of the most conservative areas of the country to be a leading proponent of LGBTQ rights. Among other positive internal changes within the department, the department now recognizes and extends benefits to partners of gay and lesbian officers. The department also established the position of a LGBTQ liaison officer and actively recruits from the LGBTQ community.

In 2015, openly gay Fort Worth police officer Chris Gorrie appeared in a television ad that aired in advance of the 5th US Circuit Court of Appeals hearing on Texas' ban on gay marriage.[13] Other Fort Worth officers were also featured in the thirty-second ad in support of Officer Gorrie. In that same year, the US Supreme Court ruled in *Obergefell v. Hodges*, that gay marriage is legal in all fifty states.[14]

SUMMARY

Being a police officer is attractive to many people who like police work—in many cases it is an exciting, benevolent, and rewarding career. However, for those who are minorities, women, and homosexual, the career comes with difficulties. Women and minorities are a highly sought after demographic by departments that bring diversity into an institution that has historically and recently been steeped in controversy. Unfortunately, the goal of changing the institution from within has largely been unsuccessful. Instead of women and minorities bringing different perspectives to the police force, the institution has instead filtered out and changed these women and minorities to fit the existing culture, resulting in little to no change. This is especially problematic when that subculture includes, among other biases, homophobia and racist and sexist attitudes.

For LGBTQ officers, fitting in is especially difficult. These officers often maintain dual and conflicting identities as an officer and a homosexual. For the small numbers who are openly gay, they risk workplace discrimination that at best affects their morale but at worst could mean they face dangerous situations without being fully confident that other officers will quickly assist.

Despite these difficulties, progress is being made to hire and to incorporate more LGBTQ officers into policing. Significant policy and cultural changes have come about after the infamous raid on the Rainbow Lounge, in Fort Worth, Texas, which occurred forty years to the day of the Stonewall Inn Riots in New York City. Many department's management and officers no longer stigmatize and discriminate against LGBTQ officers. Nevertheless, most LGBTQ officers are wary of the social consequences of being a homosexual officer in a hypermasculine environment and remain closeted, so to speak.

NOTES

1. Alan Berube and Natalie Holmes, "Minority Under-Representation in City and Suburban Policing," *Brookings Institute*, 2016, https://www.brookings.edu/blog/the-avenue/2016/07/14/minority-under-representation-in-city-and-suburban-policing/.

2. "Percentage of Local Police Officers who were Racial or Ethnic Minorities Nearly Doubled Between 1987 and 2013," Department of Justice, May 14, 2015, https://www.justice.gov/tribal/pr/percentage-local-police-officers-who-were-racial-or-ethnic-minorities-nearly-doubled.

3. Robert J. Kaminski, "Police Minority Recruitment: Predicting Who Will Say Yes to an Offer for a Job as a Cop," *Journal of Criminal Justice* 21 (1993): 395–409.

4. William T. Jordan et al., "Attracting Females and Racial/Ethnic Minorities to Law Enforcement," *Journal of Criminal Justice* 37 (2009): 333–341. doi: 10.1016/j.jcrimjus.2009.06.001.

5. Martin, Susan E. "'Outsider Within' the Station House: The Impact of Race and Gender on Black Women Police." *Social Problems* 41, no. 3 (1994): 383-400. doi:10.2307/3096969.

6. Ronald Weitzer, "White, Black, or Blue Cops? Race and Citizen Assessments of Police Officers," *Journal of Criminal Justice* 28, no. 4 (2000) 313–324. doi: 10.1016/S0047-2352(00)00043-X.

7. Megan O'Neill and Simon Holdaway, "Examining 'Window Dressing': The Views of Black Police Associations on Recruitment and Training," *Journal of Ethnic and Migration Studies* 33, no. 3 (2007): 483–500. doi: 10.1080/13691830701234780.

8. Ivan Y. Sun and Brian K. Payne, "Racial Differences in Resolving Conflicts: A Comparison Between Black and White Officers," *Crime and Delinquency* 50, no. 4 (2004): 516–541. doi: 10.1177/0011128703259298.

9. Ellis Cashmore, "The Experiences of Ethnic Minority Police Officers in Britain: Under-Recruitment and Racial Profiling in a Performance Culture," *Ethnic and Racial Studies* 24, no. 4 (2001): 642–659. doi: 10.1080/01419870120049824.

10. Roddick A. Colvin, *Gay and Lesbian Cops: Diversity and Effective Policing* (Boulder: Lynne Rienner, 2012).

11. Mary Bernstein and Constance Kostelac, "Lavender and Blue: Attitudes about Homosexuality and Behavior toward Lesbians and Gay Men among Police Officers," *Journal of Contemporary Criminal Justice* 18, no. 3 (2002): 302–328. doi: 10.1177/1043986202018003006.

12. Roddick A. Colvin, "Shared Perceptions among Lesbian and Gay Police Officers: Barriers and Opportunities in the Law Enforcement Work Environment," *Police Quarterly* 12, no. 1 (2009): 86–101. doi: 10.1177/1098611108327308.

13. Frank Heinz, "Fort Worth Police Officers Make Case for Same-Sex Marriage in Statewide Ad," *NBC News*, January 5, 2015, https://www.nbcdfw.com/news/politics/FortWorth-Police-Officers-Make-Case-for-Same-Sex-Marriage-in-Statewide-Ad-287531621.html.

14. See https://www.supremecourt.gov/opinions/14pdf/14-556_3204.pdf.

Chapter Thirteen

Community Policing and Contemporary Strategies

The history of civil unrest that was sparked by real or perceived police misconduct since the 1960s can be attributed in large part to strained relations between police and minority communities. Conflicts between police and citizens can be considered an unintended consequence of the reform era of policing from the 1930s to 1970s, in which professionalism and crime control were used in part to ameliorate police corruption while enhancing the reputation, prestige, and pay of officers. In the wake of civil unrest and violence in the 1960s, growing tensions and riots sparked by police, such as the Los Angeles Watts riots in 1965, police reform and mending community relations was once again at the forefront of civil discourse.

Introduced in the 1970s and implemented in the 1980s, **community policing** offered a possible long-term solution to police-community relations. Community policing was introduced as a paradigm and approach to policing that focused on rebuilding police/community relations through a proactive, problem-solving approach that focused on the causes of crime and disorder.[1] Under this model, empowered citizens work collaboratively with police to identify and address underlying issues that ultimately relate to crime, even if these issues do not directly require crime control solutions. In principle, this is achieved not only through community policing approaches, but through better communications and contact with the public, such as via walking patrols and regular town hall meetings. However, community policing requires a fundamental shift in the mind-set of officers and police administrators to be more mindful of service and community needs.

Today, most police departments around the country have adopted community policing strategies and many have identified themselves as community policing departments. According to the BJS, over 90 percent of police

departments serving populations over 50,000 in 2013 had a mission statement that explicitly included a community policing component.[2] This return
to more community orientation is not without issues. While the idea makes
sense, overcoming public cynicism is difficult. Conversely, police must also
trust the public as more active participants in security. Overcoming these
deep-rooted cultural differences is difficult and controversial.

Some of the big questions and issues addressed include:

1. What is community policing?
2. How does the community policing model fit in with the grand scheme
   of policing?
3. Why is this policing model so popular?
4. How effective is community policing and specific strategies related to
   community policing (such as problem-oriented policing) according to
   the research?

COMMUNITY POLICING

Community policing is a paradigm of policing that reorients police to reconnect with citizens—a connection that was severed by design during the reform era of policing. Recall that one of the main criticisms of police during
the political era was corruption. Through professionalization, police were to
perform as impersonal actors. This impersonal contact between citizens and
nameless, faceless officers, who acted almost mechanically, created a series
of problems ranging from mutual distrust to racial tensions. Community
policing sought to involve average citizens in more active partnerships,
which empowered citizens by enlisting them as security partners.[3]

Criminologist Robert Trojanowicz, one of the leading experts that spearheaded the community policing model, compared community policing to
more traditional forms of police, stating:[4]

> *Traditional policing focuses on reducing crime by arresting the bad guys. Not
> only does this approach risk demonizing everyone who lives in high-crime
> neighborhoods, it requires relying on rapid response which makes it virtually
> impossible for the police to avoid being strangers to the community. This
> model also suffers from reducing the role of the law-abiding citizens in the
> community primarily to that of passive by-stander. Traditional policing must
> also, of course, deal with disorder. Yet it is clearly a lower priority than so-
> called "serious" crime, as evidenced by the fact that the fast track for promo-
> tions requires making high-visibility arrests. Bicycle thefts, domestic disputes,
> and low-level drug dealing, gambling, and prostitution are not the stuff of
> which top-flight careers are made.*
>
> *Community Policing takes a different approach to crime, drugs, and disor-
> der, one that can augment and enhance traditional tactics such as rapid re-*

sponse and undercover operations. One of the most obvious differences is that Community Policing involves average citizens directly in the police process. Traditional policing patronizes the community by setting up the police as the experts who have all the answers. In contrast, Community Policing empowers average citizens by enlisting them as partners with the police in efforts to make their communities better and safer places in which to live and work.

At the heart of community policing is crime prevention. Police can gather information and prioritize what the residents of a community ask of the police. Moreover, the citizens then become active partners, not just passive participants that provide information to police. This synergy between police and the community identifies early problems and root causes, and addresses the issues at the source instead of just reactively addressing the symptoms of the problem.

Community policing takes a holistic approach to crime prevention. Many crime issues may be addressed with a non-law enforcement solution. For instance, if residents notice that crime is high in a particular area, the police and community may go to the local junior high school to address the problem or perhaps identify that a particular dimly lit park may be the root problem. The solution can be to collaborate with city public works or parks and recreation departments to install adequate lighting. Or police and residents can meet with the school principal and discuss problem areas and strategies. Either way, arrests or other traditional forms of crime control measures are forgone in favor of more innovative approaches that address the problem at the root cause.

HISTORIC CONTEXT

To understand community policing, we briefly looked at its historic context which gave rise to its necessity. Recall that during the political era of policing, police officers were criticized for being corrupt, and rightly so. Night watchmen at the time, who were part of the community, mainly enforced community norms. This later led to Tammany Hall and the use of police as tools to further political ends. Unsurprisingly, police were criticized by reformers, mainly the WASPs, as being very corrupt. These WASP women, inspired by Age of Enlightenment ideals of intolerance for crime, fought for police reform.

Concurrently, in the early 1900s, police drew inspiration from other groups that had professionalized. By professionalizing, scientists and physicians gained higher prestige, more pay, and greater respect—all qualities that police strived for. Moreover, these professional groups, especially medical doctors, successfully shed their previous image of corruption.

This success was to a large degree replicated by lawyers who shed their reputations as "ambulance chasers" that take advantage of people at times of need and distress. Like physicians and scientists, the practice of law gained prestige with attorneys gaining respect. Legal scholars such as the Harvard Law School Dean championed reforms that in principle, pushed for the inductive reasoning of applied case law in a very systematic way, akin to the scientific method. This appearance of objectivity ameliorated perceptions of bias that had plagued the profession.

The professional model had unintended consequences that developed an antagonistic and even hostile relationship between police and certain impoverished minority communities. Severed ties with the police resulted in mutual distrust and ultimately the lack of respect. Police-community tensions began to develop because the reactive police force that primarily answered calls for service was not aware of tensions and problems until they reached critical levels.

The consequences of a police force that responds quickly and aggressively to crime in many urban areas resulted in urban riots and social upheavals being sparked by police. The Rodney King beating, for instance, was symptomatic of deep-rooted tensions between the LAPD and the residents of the Los Angeles inner cities.[5,6] Prior to the King riots, the Watts Riots occurred in the 1960s.[7] Police, it seems, acted as the impetus for racial tensions, class divide, and general resentment toward those in power.

The 1980s marked the peak and general phase out of the professional model of policing during the reform era. With the "war on drugs" in full swing and the all-out war with the inner cities, the professional model came under greater scrutiny and criticism. For instance, the LAPD's CRASH unit that drew national attention when overly aggressive officers blurred the lines between themselves and the supposed dangerous gang members they were after. Moreover, an internal investigation showed that some of Los Angeles' most elite cops were actual gang members and used their badges to intimidate others and not for serving the law.[8] With mounting political and social pressure on police to mend strained relations and soften their image, another reform was ushered in. Ironically, the solution for police was to reconnect with the communities they purposefully insulated themselves from.

By the 1990s, a new era of policing was taking shape: community policing. It was clear to police departments that the public must be incorporated as a partner to establish a long-term solution to crime. Police departments quickly embraced the new model, which they saw as a means to prevent future riots, mend broken relations with the public, and protect the department against lawsuits and accusations of racism. Some of the new principles under this new community paradigm of policing, which sought to ameliorate many of the trust and violence issues from the professional model of policing included:

- **Decentralization**: The monolithic bureaucratic structure of police was being retooled to be less intimidating and more responsive to citizens. The old model, which centralized police operations in one large department, was not conducive to citizens sharing information. The new community model emphasized smaller regional "storefront" substations that were inviting. The idea is that most citizens are too intimidated to stop by a large police department to report minor crimes or discuss growing tensions in the community. However, a person may drop by a smaller, police storefront office in a strip mall while shopping and share information with an officer in a more informal setting. These low-cost police substations allow officers to return to neighborhoods. When these storefront stations began appearing in the 1990s, residents responded positively. The *Los Angeles Times* interviewed residents in a higher-crime neighborhood and found positive results. For instance, one resident responded, "It felt like the police were ignoring us before, so we didn't call in problems. . . . Now we know they care. They really know the neighborhood. There's more trust than there was before."[9]

- **Personalization:** The one-size-fits-all strategy in professionalism did not work. Instead, the community dictates the priorities in the neighborhood. By addressing issues that concern the citizens most, police can increase customer satisfaction and build better rapport with the police. For instance, while police may feel it is not important to deal with teens in a local park, if residents have identified that as their most pressing issue, resolving that would bring about better feelings toward police. One particular forum for police is regular town hall meetings where citizens can voice their concerns to police representatives that actually listen and take action.

- **Service:** Under the community model, police emphasize citizen service and order maintenance over crime control and law enforcement. This may mean addressing issues that do not require direct law enforcement powers, such as cleaning up a public park. The customer-service model serves to rebuild community trust and satisfaction with the police force.

- **Proactive:** The key to community policing's success is for police to be proactive in finding out tensions and issues before they become major problems. Police build rapport with and ultimately the trust of citizens through familiarity of a walking beat and addressing issues quickly.

- **Solving problems at the cause—not necessarily crime:** Along the same lines with being proactive, police must "think outside the box" in terms of solutions and options available. In the old professional model, the choice was simple: arrest or not arrest. However, the community model requires a more nuanced approach to crime solutions, which may not involve crime control at all. The problem may be economic in nature or originate from problems at home. This may require a more holistic approach that involves teachers, social workers, counselors, and other support services. Officers should be open to working collaboratively to find long-term solutions that address root causes of the problem.

- **Empowering citizens and partnerships:** Under the professional model, citizens were passive actors in security. Their sole role was to pass on information to police, who were the crime control experts and could handle any situation directly and without direct citizen help. Under the community model, citizens are active security agents who can offer their resources in order to help police. Citizens are active partners who must be respected and should be seen as valuable resources.
- **Foot patrol, bike patrol, and citizen closeness:** Returning to walking beats may seem impractical under the professional model, but it is a key in reconnecting with citizens under community policing. By returning to walking/biking, police officers are no longer the nameless, faceless enforcers that patrol their streets. Instead, the officer now has a name, is familiar with the citizens, and is once again part of the community.

A list of some activities under community policing include:

- Bicycle and foot patrol
- Neighborhood town hall meetings
- Officers assigned to specific areas to get to know neighborhood
- Officers live in the community they patrol
- Crime prevention
- Informing citizens
- Allowing citizens to voice opinions and be active in shaping policy
- Citizens determine the importance of crimes and activities, some of which are not directly police related
- Neighborhood watches
- Storefront satellite stations
- Volunteer citizen patrols
- Surveys of community members
- Citizen oversight board

Criminologist David Bayley asserts that community policing share four main principles: (1) community-based crime prevention, (2) proactive servicing as opposed to emergency response, (3), public participation in the planning and supervision of police operations, and (4) shifting of command responsibility to lower rank levels. [10]

PIE IN THE SKY? PROBLEMS WITH COMMUNITY POLICING

Community policing makes a lot of sense to a lot of police administrators. However, there are many philosophical and practical issues that prevent it from reaching its full potential.

Community policing lacks a singular definition. While virtually all police departments today claim to be operating under the community model since the 1990s, community policing has different meanings to different departments. Their activities can range from full-fledged community models with citizen integration to merely handing out stickers to children, while maintaining all the previous professional policing duties. Some argue that not establishing a clear definition can be advantageous in allowing flexibility to implement new programs and activities. However, without a clear definition, community policing may be difficult to operationalize, interpret, enact, and evaluate.

There is general confusion over the word "community." There are countless ways to define the concept, which makes it very difficult to tie in with policing. According to police researcher Jayne Seagrave, "The link between police and community is complex involving the association of two sociologically dissimilar entities: with the police being a unitary, manageable occupational group, and the community being an amorphous elusive concept."[11] The lack of a clear definition results in few officers truly "buying in" to the policing philosophy.

Seagrave gives an example with her study of the Royal Canadian Mounted Police (RCMP). Her 1996 RCMP survey showed most officers held negative views of community policing. Their negative views were often derived from the general confusion of what specifically constitutes community policing. When asked to define the term and give their opinions, their responses included the following:[12]

- "Getting back to the public—useless!!!"
- "More paperwork."
- "Waste of time! We should concentrate on keeping the rats off the streets with all available members. Blockwatch (neighborhood watch equivalent) can be done with a handout!"
- "I'm unsure since I always hear the term but nobody is able to say exactly what it means."
- "This survey seems to assume that I know something about community policing. I do not."

Police measures of success are still based on standards from the professional model. During professionalization in the reform era of policing, police measures of success became based on crime control and law enforcement standards. Namely, the adoption of the FBI's Uniform Crime Report (UCR) established key measures of success. The UCR is broken up into serious Part I offenses, or index crimes, consisting of violent and property crimes, and less serious Part II offenses. The Part I index crimes include:

- Criminal homicide
- Rape
- Robbery
- Aggravated assault
- Burglary
- Larceny-theft (excludes auto)
- Motor vehicle theft
- Arson

The UCR's Part II crimes, considered less dangerous, include a variety of crimes that range from simple assaults, curfew violations, and loitering, to DUIs, drug offenses, and counterfeiting.

In the community policing model, arrests and other traditional measures of success are deemphasized in favor of looking for long-term solutions to crime and deviance. This leads to a lot of confusion and little incentive for officers to buy into community policing.[13] One of Jayne Seagraves' research subjects summarized the sentiment perfectly, stating that community policing means "more work and not getting credit for the job you're doing." In other words, an officer who is very good at community policing via establishing strong relationships with the community and problem solving can find him or herself being criticized for being too "lazy" to do what is considered by colleagues to be "real" police work that is crime-control related.

Community policing's measures of success are often at odds with current forms of policing priorities and outcomes, leading some researchers to recommend reorienting police entirely. Police researchers Nigel Fielding and Martin Innes recommended more innovative "qualitative" police performance measures over quantitative measures found in the UCR.[14] For example, some of these qualitative measures may come in the form of community or citizen satisfaction surveys over professional standards emphasized during the reform era, such as arrests and clearance rates. Many scholars have argued that police overemphasize crime statistics that are not a true reflection of crime. Social science researchers Jeffrey Reiman and Paul Leighton use the metaphorical "carnival mirror" to describe the distorted view of criminality as a derivative of crime policies and culmination of discretion from criminal justice actors instead of a true gauge of crime.[15]

In general, citizen satisfaction surveys show positive views of community policing. Studies show that citizens feel the positive impacts on crime and safety regardless of perceptions of actual crime rates and officer performance under community policing. Even if crime was statistically high, citizens still felt safer having a closer relationship with police under the community model. Moreover, community policing satisfies communities' desires to be active participants in justice. Criminologists Michael Reisig and Andrew Giacomazzi found that citizens were very receptive to the idea of co-producing order that addresses neighborhood crime areas. [16]

When measures of success are changed to accommodate community policing, it can have positive impacts on department morale. The Madison, Wisconsin, police department experimented with a community-oriented management style in the late 1990s. They found that "participatory management" was positively and significantly related to better work satisfaction amongst officers, higher levels of satisfaction with the organization and supervisors, improved perceptions of the significance of work, better task identity, and better work autonomy. [17] As a result, officers surveyed were more receptive to changes implemented by the department.

If community policing strategies are implemented in a department without changes to the existing structure and culture, a variety of issues can arise that undermine efforts to get officers to buy-into the new model. [18] Oftentimes the professional model of policing developed under the reform era is structurally and culturally incompatible with community policing. Mixed messages and divergent goals from community policing and professionalism can create strain on officers.

Several factors have been identified as potentially impacting the effectiveness of existing programs and undermining newly implemented community policing programs. A Vera Institute study examined eight community policing programs and found the following common issues: [19]

1. Many officers who did not participate in community policing projects saw them as simply community outreach and argued that it was not "real" police work because it appeared "soft" on crime. It was found that getting patrol officers to buy into the program was difficult.
2. The researchers found that "special unit status" given to community policing officers often exacerbated the conflict between the reform agenda of community policing and the paramilitary structure of police departments. Specifically, it perpetuated the distrust between line officers and management.
3. It was perceived by officers that community policing was simply a drain on resources and a "do-nothing" assignment.
4. Overwhelming demands of 911 service calls directly conflict with community policing desires to problem-solve.
5. Interagency cooperation and conflicts threaten to derail even the best organized and well-intentioned community policing programs. Many

citizens and politicians see community policing as a policing issue, not a city-wide participatory issue.
6. The most difficult issue facing community policing is establishing community partnerships. Many residents interviewed had very limited understandings of the program goals and their role specifically, in community policing. They were baffled by the idea of "partnerships" and could not explain what to do in these partnerships.

Part of the reason why some departments find it difficult to develop successful community policing is due to misconceptions about what it is. Many departments view community policing as a strategy or program instead of a holistic approach that encompasses philosophical, strategic, tactical, and organizational changes. According to criminologist Gary Cordner, common misunderstandings of community policing include:[20]

1. *The belief that community policing is a panacea to all problems facing a department.* Community policing does not immediately resolve police/community frictions.
2. *Community policing is not totally new.* Many officers feel that what they do is already a form of community policing, therefore no changes are necessary and police departments can simply claim to be a community policing department. However, there are aspects of community policing that are new and few departments can claim to implement all aspects.
3. *Community policing is a soft-on-crime, "hug-a-thug" strategy.* Many officers feel community policing is a superficial philosophy put in place to appease public pressure to change but has little to do with addressing crime. However, at its heart, community policing addresses crime and disorder in the long run.
4. *Community policing is a cookbook or a fixed checklist of activities.* Instead, community policing is a guiding principle without an exact definition or set of activities. It is intended to be flexible instead of a one-size-fits-all solution to crime in all areas.

One strategy of policing that is often categorized under community policing has been criticized for producing the opposite effect of the stated goals of community policing: *broken windows policing* adopts the broken windows theory that addresses "quality of life" issues that may lead to more serious crimes. This policing strategy is meant to draw police and citizens closer together through walking beats and close interactions, but the strict enforcement of misdemeanors has drawn controversy.

BROKEN WINDOWS POLICING

Broken windows is a theoretical concept developed by George Kelling and James Q. Wilson in the 1980s. The concept is based on the notion that little problems, if left unaddressed, become larger problems. Broken windows (a small problem), is a metaphor for abandonment, neglect, and the lack of guardianship. If left unfixed, a broken window signals to potential criminals that an area is not under surveillance and therefore, would be an acceptable place to commit crime, such as deal drugs.

Broken windows theory was empirically tested in 1969 by psychologist Philip Zimbardo, who compared the concept of broken windows with an experiment with two cars. Two cars were parked and indicated to be disabled (hoods up). One car was placed in the Bronx, a lower-class inner city located in New York, while the other car was placed in a suburban neighborhood in Palo Alto, California. Unsurprisingly, the car in the Bronx was immediately stripped and vandalized. However, the Palo Alto car sat unmolested for weeks. Only when Zimbardo smashed one of the windows, indicating the lack of ownership of the vehicle, did it suffer the same fate as the car in the Bronx. Zimbardo's experiment demonstrated that environmental factors can affect crime. Small things can become bigger things if left unaddressed.

The concept of broken windows was famously applied to policing by former NYPD transit police chief William Bratton, in the 1990s. Chief Bratton entered the department amongst high crime rates in the city, which was plagued by "quality of life" issues, such as urinating in public, panhandling, jumping turnstiles, and the general prevalence of "small" deviance. According to Bratton, this created an environment where there was no deterrence to or consequences for these actions. Specifically, the subways were considered unsafe places where these small crimes sent a signal that crime was tolerated by police, who were perceived to overlook or ignore such petty crimes. The danger under broken windows theory is that these small instances can escalate to robberies, rape, and murder.

Implementing broken windows policies, Chief Bratton ordered his officers to conduct "**quality of life policing**," in which small crimes, such as jumping turnstiles, loitering, and panhandling, were not tolerated. A noticeable difference in the cleanliness and feeling of safety in the New York subways was immediately felt. Crime dramatically fell in New York, leading many to give Bratton credit for implementing broken windows policing. Bratton later tried to implement a similar policing style at the LAPD with very limited results.

Bratton's success was not without criticism. The largest critique of Bratton's success was pointed out by many criminologists who pointed to the fact that violent crime fell everywhere during the 1990s, even in places where broken windows policing was not implemented. According to the National

Bureau of Economic Research, the increase in misdemeanor arrests has no impact on the number of murder, assault, and burglary cases.[21] Some scholars point to other factors during the 1990s, such as better policing in general, a deemphasis of the war on drugs, and even the latent effects of abortion stemming from the *Roe v. Wade* decision in 1973 (Zimring, 2006).

Perhaps the main criticism of Bratton's policing style, which was sold under the banner of community policing, was that it was more of a "**zero tolerance**" policing style which further drove the divide between the police and the community.

PROBLEM-ORIENTED POLICING

One community policing strategy that has shown a lot of promise is problem-oriented policing. Problem-oriented policing is an intelligence-based policing strategy that focuses limited police resources on addressing a particular problem. According to the Department of Justice's Office of Community Oriented Policing Services (COPS), problem-oriented policing is broken down into four components:[22]

1. *Scanning*: Identify recurring problems, prioritize problems, develop broad goals
2. *Analysis*: Try to identify and understand the events and conditions that precede and accompany the problem, narrow the scope of the problem, and identify the consequences of the problem for the community
3. *Response*: Brainstorm interventions, see what other communities have done, identify relevant data to be collected
4. *Assessment*: Identify any new strategies needed to augment the original plan and conduct ongoing assessment to ensure continued effectiveness

Problem-oriented policing shows promising results. An examination of Jersey City, an urban environment in New Jersey, using a randomized comparison between treatment conditions and non-interventions in different city blocks, showed focused policing reduced crime and disorder without any displacement effects.

Another study conducted in Santa Ana, California, in the late 1990s by University of California researchers, showed very promising results.[23] Interviews with community residents before and after problem-oriented policing policies have been implemented showed fewer citizen complaints about police and their neighborhoods.

POLICING HOMELESS AND MENTALLY ILL POPULATIONS

Community policing strategies are better suited to address longstanding complex problems, such as homelessness. As mentioned before, police have been called upon to handle all social ills and are expected to be a panacea for all problems. However, decades of growing poverty have produced an enormous homeless population, coupled with the erosion of social services, such as mental health institutions, represents a growing challenge for police who have been called upon to deal with them.

The booming national economy in the 2010s has been paralleled by a growing homeless population as housing becomes increasingly unaffordable. According to the US Department of Housing and Urban Development, in 2017, there were over 553,000 homeless people on any given night in the country.[24] Approximately one-third of those homeless were in unsheltered locations and one-third with children. Moreover, over 40,000 people were unaccompanied youths between eighteen and twenty-five years of age.

Homeless populations oftentimes encounter police for various reasons, ranging from committing direct criminal acts to communities considering them a nuisance and wanting officers to remove them from the area. For many police officers, especially those in smaller towns and cities with limited to no resources in dealing with the population, the homeless population represents a persistent frustration and burden. A survey of 100 police departments found little training and information provided to officers in dealing with skid row.[25] Earlier studies showed that as far back as the 1960s police only "managed" homeless populations and intervened only when laws were violated or when people were victimized.

Historically, police actions have been based on officer perceptions of homeless individuals. Police actions include strict enforcement such as frequent arrests, neglecting or ignoring them, and allowing petty crimes and the practice of "dumping," or transporting them to other jurisdictions. The frustration of police stems from the lack of department guidance coupled with the fact that living on the streets is not illegal per se, and attempts to pass anti-homeless laws that focus on vagrancy have often failed or were impossible to enforce. For instance, when NYPD transit police chief William Bratton tried to bring his crackdown to the massive homeless population in Los Angeles as the LAPD's police chief, his Safer City Initiative was criticized for simply displacing the population further away from resources.[26]

Part of the problem is that police management often does not view dealing with homeless populations as a major problem. A Police Executive Research Forum (PERF) study found that only a small percentage of departments surveyed had formal policies dealing with the homeless, and those that did, only addressed situations of severe weather, victim assistance, and other factors not related directly to the homeless population.[27] According to research conducted by criminologist Laura Huey, the homeless population is one of the highest populations at risk of victimization in often dangerous environments yet is the least served by police and private security services, making them "invisible victims."[28]

Compounding the problem of homelessness is a growing population with mental illness that police must deal with. Decades of deinstitutionalization have meant many individuals with no affordable professional services, such as the homeless population. As a result, police departments are recognizing the growing threat, both to officers and mentally ill individuals that has resulted in injuries and death to both officers and people with mental illness. According to the research, police officers typically do not feel adequately trained in dealing with these populations which results in high-risk encounters often with violent outcomes.[29]

PROCEDURAL JUSTICE AND IMPLICIT BIAS

In the wake of social upheavals, such as the Ferguson, Missouri, riots that ensued police/citizen interactions, renewed efforts have been taken to rebuild police/community relations. In 2014, the Obama administration created an eleven-member task force on twenty-first century policing that addresses core frictions that produce the conditions that lead to social upheavals.[30] The federal task force focused on three general areas: (1) *Local government* that should be more responsive to and give oversight directly to communities to explore the root causes of crime, (2) *law enforcement* who should review and update policies, training, data collection, increase transparency, and revamp hiring policies, and (3) *communities*, who should engage with law enforcement and be active participants in problem-solving at all levels, including schools and the political process, to reduce crime and improve quality of life.

Under renewed efforts to rebuild police/community relations and trust was the implementation of the *National Initiative for Building Community Trust & Justice,*[31] commonly referred to as "The National Initiative." The National Initiative project explored and addressed three key areas:

1. Procedural justice
2. Implicit bias
3. Reconciliation

The National Initiative used a $4.75 million grant to establish partnerships between the federal government, police departments, and academia. Participants included six police departments and research centers at John Jay College of Criminal Justice, Yale Law School, UCLA, and the Urban Institute, in addition to a board of advisors consisting of a diverse group of national law enforcement leaders, academia, and faith-based organizations.

The federal initiative focuses on restoring community relations and trust using a philosophy called **procedural justice**. Procedural justice examines the nature of interactions between police and the criminal justice system and the public, and how that interaction shapes public perceptions and ultimately, police/citizen relations. The key to procedural justice is promoting and enhancing the legitimacy of police through positive interactions with the public. According to the National Initiative, procedural justice is guided by four key principles:

1. Treating people with dignity and respect
2. Giving citizens a voice during police/citizen encounters
3. Police having neutral decision making
4. Conveying trustworthy motives

Procedural justice uses elements of community policing by encouraging collaborative relationships between the police and community that fosters voluntary participation in crime prevention and justice. Ultimately, the goal is to establish normative standards of law abiding and mutual trust. The relationship would be ideally evaluated by academia to produce evidence-based results in crime reduction.

A key element in establishing trust and respect between police and the community is addressing the issue of **implicit bias**, or stereotypes held by both police and the public. Implicit bias refers to automatic assumptions about persons or groups that are not bigoted but are often subconscious and manifest in biased actions without prejudicial intent. According to the National Initiative, it is a phenomenon by individuals and entire institutions, such as police departments, of "racism without racists." For example, some studies have shown that police tend to have **shooter bias**, where officers are more likely to shoot Black suspects than White suspects. These biases can include traffic stops, decisions to arrest, and other discretionary actions or inactions that cumulatively produce systemic bias that points to racism and prejudice.

Recent studies have shown the existence of implicit bias. A 2018 study by criminologists Justin Nix, Bradley Campbell, Edward Byers, and Geoffrey Alpert analyzed 990 police fatal shootings in 2015 and found Black civilians shot and killed were twice as likely as Whites to be unarmed.[32] The results suggest implicit bias in perceptions of danger of Black citizens versus Whites, by police officers. This conclusion is not to suggest police alone have implicit bias. A 2011 study published in the *Research in Organizational Behavior* journal confirms the existence of implicit biases that include race, ethnicity, nationality, gender, and social status among other characteristics, by not just police, but a wide variety of individuals and groups, ranging from students and doctors to employment recruiters.[33]

The National Initiative as well as the body of research has suggested additional focused training on procedural justice to recognize and address implicit bias. However, the question becomes whether police, an institution steeped in tradition and cultural transmission through storytelling and collective common experience, is able to unlearn these subconscious biases. A 2017 article by *The Atlantic* interviewed Salt Lake City training officers and showed very limited effects of training.[34] For instance, when asked about the disparate use of force against Black citizens, one officer reasoned that it was not due to implicit bias, but that Black people seemed to have a "higher degree of crime," but then admitted that he did have biases, but added, "Just like you, and every other person in the world." Others interviewed stated that it was unrealistic to be color-blind and moreover, oftentimes when the situation is acute, such as when officers are ambushed, it is impossible for the officer to think about race and bias. Researchers interviewed concluded that training falls short of bringing officers to the point of acknowledging their own biases.

More recently, police departments have recognized the need for addressing mentally ill individuals and formed crisis intervention teams that include mental health practitioners.[35] The crisis intervention team (CIT) model has been adopted by many departments with promising results. A survey of officers on attitudes about CIT found that most officers found the approach based on overall safety, accessibility, and officer skills and techniques, better prepared them in dealing with the situation and made their departments better.[36]

EMOTIONAL INTELLIGENCE

Progressive police departments around the country are beginning to incorporate concepts of **emotional intelligence** into their training regimen to combat implicit bias and its ramifications, including excessive force and racial profiling. The concept of emotional intelligence was introduced in the mid-1990s by Harvard psychologist Daniel Goleman, to mean the ability to understand, interpret, and manage self-emotions and the emotions of others.[37] Under this model, officers are trained to have acute self-awareness of their own mental state and mood during stressful situations while being empathetic to others. Accordingly, Goleman asserts five components: self-awareness, self-regulation, internal motivation, empathy, and social skills.

Emotional intelligence became popular when Goleman's best-selling book of the same title permeated the business world as a new paradigm in interaction within the company and with customers. This service model is currently being explored by police departments to change officers' cynicism toward non-police. This reorientation toward service and compassion is the goal of reestablishing trust and respect with the community. The impact of incorporating emotional intelligence into training can effectively instill empathy and officer buy-in, warranting further research into this new area.

SUMMARY

For the past few decades, community policing and its variations, such as problem-oriented policing, has been the predominant paradigm in policing. When done correctly by focusing on problems and community concerns, it shows a lot of promise. For example, successful programs in Santa Ana, California, and in Jersey City, New Jersey, are a testament to its potential.

Trying to introduce new policies and concepts, however, requires police officers to buy-in as participants. Unfortunately, police is a slow-moving bureaucratic organization that is steeped in a strong subculture and crime-control oriented structure. As such, community policing efforts have been undermined and dismissed as "superficial" and are not considered "real" police work.

Looking at the past few decades of data, we see that there are some "dos" and "don'ts" when it comes to community policing. A Department of Justice Office of Community-Oriented Policing Services report shows police should focus on community concerns over internal policing concerns: finding the best response versus merely improving current responses and systems, focusing on community problems for which the police should assume some responsibility, looking for root causes and underlying conditions, and analyzing data.

The reality of community policing and problem-oriented policing is that police are working with limited resources and the core functions of police will always take priority. It remains a competing model that has not gained full acceptance from the two groups that matter the most: the community and patrol officers. In addition, high ranking executives and mid-level managers need stronger direct involvement in implementing these programs. If not, community policing remains more rhetoric than actual practice.

A more recent manifestation of community policing is addressing officers' implicit bias through procedural justice. While efforts are being taken to train officers and departments to rethink their mentalities through realizing their own biases, these efforts largely have fallen short of the stronger undercurrents of institutional culture and cultural transmission. Getting officers to buy-in wholeheartedly to procedural justice practices, as recommended by the National Initiative, requires them to acknowledge and accept their own biases. This is a difficult task given the paradox of police work: *What keeps officers safe* (recognizing patterns and preemptively acting on those patterns) *is what can make officers biased.*

NOTES

1. Gayle Fisher-Stewart, "Community Policing Explained: A Guide for Local Government. US Department of Justice Office of Community Oriented Policing Services," 2007, https://cops.usdoj.gov/pdf/vets-to-cops/cp_explained.pdf.

2. Brian A. Reaves," Local Police Departments, 2013: Personnel, Policies, and Practices," *US Department of Justice Bureau of Justice Statistics Bulletin,* May 2015, https://www.bjs.gov/content/pub/pdf/lpd13ppp.pdf.

3. "Understanding Community Policing: A Framework for Action. Community Policing Consortium, US Department of Justice," Bureau of Justice Assistance, August 1994, https://www.ncjrs.gov/pdffiles/commp.pdf.

4. Robert C. Trojanowicz and Bonnie Bucqueroux, "Community policing and the challenge of diversity," *Board of Trustees, Michigan State University,* 1991, https://www.ncjrs.gov/pdffiles1/Photocopy/134975NCJRS.pdf.

5. Jerome H. Skolnick and James J. Fyfe, *Above the Law: Police and Excessive Use of Force* (New York: The Free Press, 1993).

6. "Report of the Independent Commission on the Los Angeles Police Department," Independent Commission on the Los Angeles Police Department (Christopher Commission Report), 1991, http://www.parc.info/client_files/Special%20Reports/1%20-%20Chistopher%20Commision.pdf.

7. John A. McCone et al., "Violence in the City: An End or a Beginning?" (McCone Commission Report on Watts Riot: 1965)," *The Governor's Commission on the Los Angeles Riots,* December 2, 1965, https://archive.org/details/ViolenceInCity.

8. Randall Sullivan, *Labyrinth* (New York: Grove Press, 2003).

9. Andrew D. Blechman, "Communities Buy into Storefront Police Sites: Law Enforcement. Substations Offer a Low-Cost, Effective Antidote to Crime by Getting Officers Out of Squad Cars and Into Neighborhoods," *Los Angeles Times,* July 23, 1995, http://articles.latimes.com/1995-07-23/local/me-27032_1_police-officers.

10. David H. Bayley, "Community Policing: A Report from the Devil's Advocate." In *Community Policing: Rhetoric or Reality* (New York: Praeger, 1998), 225–237.

11. Jayne Seagrave, "Defining Community Policing," *American Journal of Police* 15, no. 2 (1996): 1–22. doi: 10.1108/07358549610122476.

12. Seagrave, "Defining Community Policing."

13. Mary A. Wycoff and Wesley G. Skogan, "The Effect of a Community Policing Management Style on Officers' Attitudes," *Crime and Delinquency* 40, no. 3 (1994): 371–383. doi: 10.1177/0011128794040003005.

14. Nigel Fielding and Martin Innes, "Reassurance Policing, Community Policing and Measuring Police Performance," *Policing and Society* 16, no. 2 (2006): 127–145. doi: 10.1080/10439460600662122.

15. Jeffrey Reiman and Paul P. Leighton, *The Rich Get Richer and the Poor Get Prison: Ideology, Class, and Criminal Justice,* 11th ed. (New York: Routledge, 2016).

16. Michael D. Reisig and Andrew L. Giacomazzi, "Citizen Perceptions of Community Policing: Are Attitudes Toward Police Important?" *Policing: An International Journal of Police Strategies and Management* 21, no. 3 (1998): 547–561. doi: 10.1108/13639519810228822.

17. Anthony A. Braga et al., "Problem-Oriented Policing in Violent Crime Places: A Randomized Controlled Experiment," *Criminology* 37, no. 3 (2006): 541–580. doi: 10.1111/j.1745-9125.1999.tb00496.x.

18. "Understanding Community Policing: A Framework for Action. Community Policing Consortium, US Department of Justice," Bureau of Justice Assistance, August 1994, https://www.ncjrs.gov/pdffiles/commp.pdf.

19. Susan Sadd and Randolph M. Grinc, "Issues in Community Policing: Problems in the Implementation of Eight Innovative Neighborhood-Oriented Policing Programs," *Report submitted to the National Institute of Justice*. New York: Vera Institute of Justice, 1994.

20. Gary Cordner, "Community Policing: Principles and Elements," *National Center on Domestic and Sexual Violence,* 1996, http://www.ncdsv.org/images/communitypolicingprincipleselements.pdf.

21. Hope Corman and Naci Mocan, "Carrots, Sticks and Broken Windows," *Journal of Law and Economics* 41 (2005): 235–266. doi: 10.3386/w9061.

22. Michael S. Scott, *Problem-Oriented Policing: Reflections on the First 20 Years. Office of Community-Oriented Policing Services* (Washington, DC: US Department of Justice, 2000).

23. Paul Jesilow et al., "Evaluating Problem-Oriented Policing: A Quasi-Experiment," *Policing: An International Journal of Police Strategies & Management* 21, no. 3 (1997): 449–464. doi: 10.1108/13639519810228750.

24. Meghan Henry et al., "The 2017 Annual Homeless Assessment Report (AHAR) to Congress," *US Department of Housing and Urban Planning,* December 2017, https://www.hudexchange.info/resources/documents/2017-AHAR-Part-1.pdf.

25. Robert H. McNamara, Charles Crawford, and Ronald G. Burns, "Policing the Homeless: Policy, Practice, and Perceptions," *Policing: An International Journal of Police Strategies and Management* 34, no. 3 (2012): 357–375. doi: 10.1108/13639511311329741.

26. Duke Helfand and Richard Winton, "Bratton Admits Skid Row Displacement," *Los Angeles Times*, October 4, 2007, http://articles.latimes.com/2007/oct/04/local/me-skidrow4.

27. "The Police Response to Homelessness," Police Executive Research Forum, 2018, http://www.policeforum.org/assets/PoliceResponsetoHomelessness.pdf.

28. Laura Huey, *Invisible Victims: Homelessness and the Growing Security Gap* (Toronto: University of Toronto Press, 2012).

29. Randy Borum, "Improving High Risk Encounters between People with Mental Illness and Police," *Mental Health Law and Policy* 28, no. 3 (2000): 332–337.

30. Charles H. Ramsey et al., *Office of Community Oriented Policing Services. The President's Task Force on 21st Century Policing Implementation Guide: Moving from Recommendations to Action.* (Washington, DC: Office of Community Oriented Policing Services, 2015).

31. See https://trustandjustice.org/.

32. Justin Nix et al., "A Bird's Eye View of Civilians Killed by Police in 2015," *Criminology and Public Policy* 16, no. 1 (2018): 397–417. doi: 10.1111/1745-9133.12269.

33. John T. Jost et al., "The Existence of Implicit Bias is Beyond Reasonable Doubt: A Refutation of Ideological and Methodological Objections and Executive Summary of Ten Studies that no Manager Should Ignore," *Research in Organizational Behavior* 29 (2011): 39–69. doi: 10.1016/j.riob.2009.10.001.

34. Tom James, "Can Cops Unlearn Their Unconscious Biases?" *The Atlantic*, December 23, 2017, https://www.theatlantic.com/politics/archive/2017/12/implicit-bias-training-salt-lake/548996/.

35. Amy C. Watson and Anjali J. Fulambarker, "The Crisis Intervention Team Model of Police Response to Mental Health Crises: A Primer for Mental Health Practitioners," *Best Practices in Mental Health* 8, no. 2 (2012): 71–79.

36. Natalie Bonfine, Christian Ritter, and Mark R. Munetz, "Police Officer Perceptions of the Impact of Crisis Intervention Team (CIT) Programs," *International Journal of Law and Psychiatry* 37, no. 4 (2014): 341–350. doi: 10.1016/j.ijlp.2014.02.004.

37. Daniel Goleman, *Emotional Intelligence: Why It Can Matter More than IQ* (New York: Bantam Books, 2012).

Chapter Fourteen

Policing the New Age of Crime

Terrorism, Cyberspace, White-Collar Crime

Police in the twenty-first century have expanded their roles into new areas of crime and new crime types, some of which police are not entirely equipped to handle. These contemporary avenues and crimes include: policing complex white-collar crimes, terrorist activities, and criminal activities that occur online. However, with new responsibilities and demands for service come a new set of challenges. This chapter examines the difficulties in policing these relatively new areas of crime and the challenges that law enforcement face.

Part of the challenge in dealing with more complex crimes is asking more from local police, which is an institution steeped in tradition and bureaucratic rules. As explored in previous chapters, individuals who become officers generally come from similar backgrounds, have similar levels of education with similar majors, are interested in police work for similar reasons, and prioritize similar policing activities. These backgrounds, interests, and priorities center on street crimes, which are the original mandate of police. More abstract forms of crime that require technical knowledge, experience, and expertise, such as advanced accounting and computer networks, may be beyond the scope of local law enforcement. Moreover, structural and cultural bounds may inhibit effective policing.

One can argue, however, that the American criminal justice system is divided functionally and jurisdictionally, working in tandem to address different crime types. For instance, crimes that are traditionally federally handled include bank robberies and mail fraud. These crimes violate federal law that is often necessary in a practical sense for addressing inherent issues of jurisdiction with certain crime types. However, when considering that state and local law enforcement officers vastly outnumber federal agents, it makes sense to utilize more state and local personnel and resources. According to the BJS, there were 120,000 full-time sworn federal law enforcement officers in 2008 compared to over 750,000 full-time sworn state and local officers in 2012.[1,2] These numbers are higher today, nevertheless showing the large discrepancy.

Topics covered in this chapter include:

- The expansion of police roles and power
- The post-9/11 Homeland Security era
- Challenges of policing cyberspace
- The balance between privacy and crime control
- System capacity theory
- The challenges of policing white-collar and corporate crime
- An expanding world for police

Recall that police, through professionalization during the reform era, essentially became experts in crime control and law enforcement. Extensive training coupled with specialization resulted in a transformative function of police from proactive peace keepers, like the night watchmen, to reactive law enforcers. As metrics of performance evolved and departments focused on minimizing response times coupled with the convenience of dialing 9-1-1 for assistance, so too did public expectations. Officers were expected to respond quickly and effectively in dealing with crime, as well as peace keeping and order maintenance matters, such as the proverbial cat stuck in the tree. Police under professionalism ironically became victims of their own success as they became the de facto panacea, or "cure-all," for all societal problems. Social changes have also contributed to the expanded role of police.

As society has progressed through modernization and population growth, it has become too complex and crowded for informal social controls to work effectively. Recall that informal social controls are social sanctions applied by informal agents of social control, such as family, friends, clubs, churches, and other non-police groups. Dense urbanization since the industrial revolution meant two factors that contribute to crime: (1) cities full of strangers made it difficult to settle disputes and (2) cities serving as social hubs meant a more heterogeneous population with differing and often divergent norms, creating a state of what sociologist Emile Durkheim describes as "anomie," or normlessness. The breakdown of informal social controls placed a greater need and reliance on formal social controls, or police, and the criminal justice system overall.

Adding to the greater reliance on police are the historic erosion and loss of service institutions. Since the early 19th century, psychiatric hospitals were places to treat individuals suffering from mental disorders and illnesses. These "asylums," adopted from European enlightenment ideals, promised humane treatment of patients who would eventually be cured of their illness, by fostering a moral and rational mental state. These institutions were intended to provide peaceful and gentle means of mental rehabilitation free from prison-like restraints.

By the turn of the century, however, it was clear that asylums were ineffective, harmful places of sedation and lobotomies, and financially unsustainable. Public support virtually disappeared when a 1970s exposé broadcast showed widespread patient neglect and abuse in New York. The final death knell for "**insane asylums**" came with the 1975 release of the critically acclaimed and Oscar-winning *One Flew Over the Cuckoo's Nest*, which starred Jack Nicholson as a mental patient.

Consequently, psychiatric asylums were abandoned with the promise of **deinstitutionalization**. Deinstitutionalization meant the process of replacing large monolithic psychiatric institutions with smaller, tailored community mental health centers to take their place. The deinstitutionalization movement, however, never materialized. Instead, mental patients were released with little recourse and planning, resulting in many committing crimes and eventually ending up in the criminal justice system. This meant that mental illness became a de facto policing matter. Today, the nation's largest mental institution is the Twin Towers county jail in downtown Los Angeles, which houses 1,400 inmates suffering from mental illness or disorders.

The 1970s also saw a greater reliance on police and the criminal justice system with the widespread abandonment of rehabilitation programs coupled with massive investments in criminal justice. The highly influential 1974 meta-analysis of prison rehabilitation by sociologist Robert Martinson titled "What Works?" concluded essentially that "nothing works."[3] This study sparked prison reform divestments in rehabilitation programs and investments in incarceration, leading to the explosive growth of a stable inmate population of approximately 200,000 prior to the 1970s, to nearly 2.3 million today. Without adequate in-custody treatment and reentry support, police today must handle ex-offenders with high recidivism rates.

Concurrently, police professionalization during the early 1900s meant that police sought to be the exclusive experts in crime control. By design, police have taken on a greater role in society—part of which has to do with expanding the power, prestige, and respect of policing as a profession. Recall the benefits of professionalism enjoyed by scientists and doctors, which means higher pay, prestige, and respect by society.

Today, if and when new problems arise (both law enforcement related and non-law enforcement related), police are called by default. Police heavily advertised the 9-1-1 system as the default number to call in dealing with emergencies in the 1980s period of emphasis on crimes statistics. This meant that police responded to a variety of disturbance calls, even when it was outside their power to take meaningful action. Since then, police have scaled back their support of everyone calling 911 by default, offering non-emergency numbers and services.

Adding responsibilities is not all bad news for police. Greater responsibilities meant an expansion of police duties and powers. Police can justify greater budgets, staffing, and expanded jurisdictions. This was part of the goal during professionalization during the reform era. Through professionalization, police have gained autonomy (the ability to hire and fire their own, for instance), gotten higher pay, garnered a better reputation, and acquired much larger budgets. The emergence or reemergence of different crime types in the twenty-first century has led to changes in police.

A 4TH ERA OF POLICING: THE POST-9/11 HOMELAND SECURITY ERA

The September 11, 2001, terrorist attacks have reoriented police to prioritize terrorism activities, especially at the federal level. Some researchers have dubbed this a fourth era of policing, the post 9/11 era that prioritizes homeland security. Criminologist Willard Oliver noted the drastic cuts in grant funding from Community Oriented Policing Services (COPS) while Homeland Security budgets have grown significantly, demarcating the end of the community era.[4] Moreover, police have shifted away from intimate, community relations and again toward professionalism. The nature of police activities, once again, prioritizes crime control, in the form of police operations centers and information systems over foot patrol and problem solving.

Today, state and local law enforcement agencies have adopted many strategies based on military threat models and train extensively for terrorist activities. The 2013 Boston Marathon bombings showed the degree to which police have adopted paramilitary strategies, tactics, and equipment. The search for bombing suspects Tamerlan and Dzhokhar Tsarnaev showed images of Boston police utilizing tactical gear, vehicles, and working collaboratively with other agencies to coordinate emergency and information management. This display showed the real threat of terrorism in today's world and how police must respond.

The militarization of police, however, has come at a cost. Police have once again prioritized and embraced the paramilitary model at the expense of community policing that was prevalent throughout the 1990s. The threat of domestic and international terrorism has once again furthered the professionalization agenda of crime control and law enforcement, justifying higher budgets, more equipment, and personnel. While this is not to say that these are not mutually exclusive functions of police, where officers can be responsive to community needs while staying hypervigilant toward threats, it can send mixed messages to the public.

The trend toward militarization of police did not start, however, post-9/11 terrorist attacks. The trend began to accelerate during the 1980s with the war on drugs and advent of paramilitary special weapons and tactics (SWAT) teams. The creation and use of SWAT teams increased exponentially during the 1990s, increasing from 3,000 annual deployments in the 1980s, to over 40,000 in 2001, and over 60,000 today. The acceleration of SWAT creation and deployment was attributed in part to a 1994 law that authorized the Pentagon to donate surplus military equipment to local and state law enforcement.

The importance of being prepared was highlighted in 1997 in the North Hollywood district of Los Angeles, California. Two heavily armed bank robbers were confronted by LAPD officers as they exited a Bank of America branch with loot in hand, leading to one of the most infamous shootouts in history. The two suspects, Larry Phillips and Emil Matasareanu, fired automatic weapons at police, who returned fire with their service pistols and shotguns. The outgunned officers struggled to take down the armored suspects with their weapons and the robbery played out like a scene from a movie or video game. Ultimately, SWAT officers, along with other officers that resorted to borrowing more powerful AR-15 rifles from the local gun shop, were finally able to kill the suspects. In the end, twelve officers and eight civilians were injured. This event underscored the justification for police to adopt military weaponry and strategies.[5]

More recently, in 2016, the militarization of police was necessitated by the shootout between Dallas police officers and Micah Xavier Johnson. Johnson, a war veteran and activist against police shootings of Black men, ambushed a group of officers during a protest event. Five officers were killed, and nine others were injured by Johnson who was heavily armed and fortified in a corner of a parking structure on a college campus. Eventually Johnson was killed by an explosive device deployed by police. The event underscored the need for police to adequately arm themselves.

Despite their expanded powers and military equipment, not all state and local police agencies are entirely comfortable with, or accepting of, expanding their role in handling counterterrorism and homeland security. One particular area of contention has been the enforcement of borders and illegal immigration. Federal agencies as well as politicians have called upon local law enforcement to take a larger active role in border security and immigration enforcement. However, with the recent politically oriented border controversies, such as zero-tolerance enforcement and separating illegal immigrant children from their parents, many police agencies have resisted expanding their roles in this area.

However, state and local law enforcement has in many cases outright refused to cooperate.[6] Police agencies have expressed that such work constitutes bad police work and undermines several decades of community policing. Making citizens safe, they argue, depends on intelligence gathering, which in turn depends on the types of relationships between the police and the community. They point to the irony that strict border enforcement actually makes it *less safe* from potential terrorist attacks by undermining the information network that has been built.

Overall, the impact of terrorism post-9/11, on state and local agencies, has been limited. This is due in part to the nature and function of state and local law enforcement, which has more localized agendas. However, researchers have found that larger metropolitan departments and state agencies have implemented changes to their internal structures, namely the creation of counterterrorism units.[7]

The policing of terrorism, in general, is a compatible and comfortable mandate for police. There are clear potential victims and "bad guys" that are universally understood by the law enforcement community. Moreover, the crimes associated with terrorism, such as exploding bombs, hostage taking, threats, and so on, are easily understood by law enforcement that have the necessary skillset and equipment to handle escalating situations. Agencies can relatively easily apply, expand, and modify existing resources, such as increasing tactical training and expanding SWAT teams and specialized investigators, to counterterrorism efforts.

Other forms of crimes, however, challenge traditional functions of police, their technical abilities, and jurisdictional limitations. In the past couple of decades, computer crimes have emerged as a real and growing crime that challenges the existing paradigm of police.

POLICING CYBERSPACE

With the ubiquity of the Internet comes a whole new set of challenges for state and local law enforcement. Cyberspace represents a new medium for crime. Some criminologists argue that it represents the proverbial "old wine in new bottles," meaning that traditional crimes such as theft are merely occurring in a new environment. Criminologist Peter Grabowsky explained:

> *I suggest that "virtual criminality" is basically the same as the terrestrial crime with which we are familiar. To be sure, some of the manifestations are new. But a great deal of crime committed with or against computers differs only in terms of the medium. While the technology of implementation, and particularly its efficiency, may be without precedent, the crime is fundamentally familiar.*[8]

Others have echoed this opinion by showing that despite the high-tech nature of police portrayed on television in shows such as *CSI: Crime Scene Investigation*, the nature of policing has not fundamentally changed and remains relatively low-tech.[9] Moreover, they contend that even cybercrime, something that is inherently high-tech and technical in nature, merely requires one step (linking an abstract **internet protocol "IP" address** to a physical location) that is relatively technical.

Legally, cybercrime also falls within familiar territory. Legal scholar Susan Brenner asked, is there such thing as "virtual crime?" in her legal analysis of cybercrime.[10] She found that when broken in to its core legal components, one can reclassify cybercrime by more traditional classifications and categories, such as vandalism, stalking, forgery, fraud, pornography/obscenity, and burglary/criminal trespass. Moreover, legal reasoning can be applied by simply analyzing four primary legal considerations for cases: (1) **actus reus** (criminal act), (2) **mens rea** (criminal intent), (3) attendant circumstances (legal rule), and (4) harm.

Despite these assertions that cybercrime can be perceived as an easily understood crime, it does pose some unique challenges to law enforcement and the criminal justice system. First, digital evidence is very time consuming and expensive to process. Computer forensics requires special equipment and expertise. Digital evidence, which can be easily and inadvertently altered by merely viewing the content, requires investigators to image, or make, an exact replica of the contents of the drive before any search or forensic work can begin to preserve original timestamps.

The careful preservation of potential evidence means agencies must purchase large drives to store data, purchase expensive forensics software that can recover deleted data, and certify and continuously train digital forensic investigators. Even tech-savvy officers without proper training who may be able to find evidence on computer systems and networks may alter the evidence enough to where a defense attorney can claim the evidence was tampered with. Therefore, only larger departments are equipped to handle digital forensics in-house. These departments have one or more trained and certified technicians who can process digital evidence. Smaller departments must wait for overburdened regional digital crime labs to assist in their cases.

Second, structural and cultural impediments also make policing cybercrimes problematic.[11] Police officers typically do not have backgrounds in digital investigations and evidence gathering. Instead of hiring more technically savvy individuals as digital forensics experts, police organizations that value patrol experience make it a point to train existing officers as special detectives that work on cybercrime. They reason that this saves time because experienced officers "know what they're looking for." This process takes nearly a decade as officers start on patrol and promote their way to the detective division that deals with high-tech crimes.

Another structural challenge with computer crimes is at the prosecutorial level. Prosecutors tend to typically avoid time-consuming complex cases.[12] Digital evidence does not only come from computers. Today, digital evidence can be stored on a variety of personal digital devices and services, including smartphones and web-based storage. Collecting, preserving, sorting, and processing this information for court is a very time-consuming activity that requires time, expertise, and resources.

Added disincentive for police departments to significantly invest in digital forensics teams is often undermined by the financial and legal process. Many victims of certain crimes are reimbursed by companies. Moreover, many tech companies are reluctant to cooperate with investigators. For instance, when the FBI demanded that Apple create software to help unlock their iOS operating system that powers their devices in the wake of the 2015 San Bernardino terrorist attacks, Apple refused to do so in an open letter vowing to keep their users' information private. For other companies, an intrusive police investigation that requires seizing company equipment, such as hard drives and servers, is simply not an option. These factors, among many others, give police little incentive to aggressively pursue computer crime cases.

Compounding financial and legal factors are jurisdictional issues. Police have historically functioned to enforce territories and regulating spaces. Crime control technologies have furthered this end. According to geographer Steve Herbert, officers frequently govern citizenry through controlling predefined spacial parameters. [13] Moreover, an officer's competency is measured by how well they manage activities within their respective spaces of responsibility.

Computer crime suspects and victims can span across legal jurisdictions, including international borders. This creates major disincentives for prosecutors to pursue cyber cases, creating what are known as **"free zones,"** where prosecutors require minimum loss thresholds (such as $10,000 minimum losses) in order to file for cases. Free zones are created when minimum thresholds do not reach this level and criminals are free to operate with impunity. This in turn affects police activities.

Not all cybercrimes are policed the same way. Police typically pursue cases with clear villains and victims. State and local law enforcement typically avoids more complex cyber cases, such as hacking (unauthorized access to computer systems) and intellectual property violations, such as copyright infringement cases. These cases require more technical expertise, have diffused victimization, and are very time consuming. Hacking cases in particular often require extensive computer network knowledge, with perpetrators often taking active steps to mask their locations. Moreover, these perpetrators often reside internationally in countries with lax laws, making evidence gathering and prosecution very difficult and often a political process.

Consequently, law enforcement and most state and local prosecutors tend to prioritize street crime cases that have translated over to the cyber environment. State and local police have primarily focused on cases of child predators and child pornography. These crimes are easily understood and have clear victims and villains. Police investigators often masquerade as child victims in order to meet the perpetrator and ultimately arrest them. These arrests are easier to prosecute and bring positive reputations to the officers and departments since child predators are considered a universally disdained group. However, having a clear victim does not always mean local and state law enforcement will pursue cases.

Cyber bullying is a growing phenomenon that is a challenge for many law enforcement agencies to adequately address. Cyber bullies make online threats and harass a victim, often resulting in emotional distress that can end in more significant physical harm. According to a study published in the *Journal of American Medical Association Pediatrics*, victims of cyber bullying were 2.5 times more likely to commit suicide, and children who were taunted by bullies were three times more likely to have suicidal thoughts.[14] While lawmakers are actively enacting cyber bullying legislation due to some high-profile cases involving teen suicide, police are still lagging when it comes time to act.

Many police investigators in the past, having little recourse on teenage bullying, have simply told victims to log off the Internet. In recent years, however, new legislation specifically addressing online harassment and bullying have placed higher penalties on the act. In 2009, for instance, the state of Texas passed Penal Code 33.07, which addressed online harassment. The statute classified online harassment as either a Class A misdemeanor punishable by up to one year in prison and fined up to $4,000, or a third degree felony, which is punishable by two to ten years in prison and a fine up to $10,000. The Dallas Police Department Computer Crimes Unit has published a guide that outlines the penalties and types of cyber bullying that it considers serious offenses.

Despite growing legislation addressing cyber bullying, in general, police largely consider it a form of cybercrime that does not warrant their full attention or police resources. Legal scholar Marc Goodman gives a good summary of "why the police don't care about computer crime," stating:[15]

- That's not why I became a cop!
- It is difficult to police the Internet
- The lack of resources
- The police cannot do it alone
- Lack of public outcry

These reasons given by Goodman mainly involve structural and cultural issues on why police are reluctant to prioritize computer crimes. Similarly, complex financial and white-collar crimes also share much of the same reasons for why state and local police do not pay adequate attention to them.

POLICING FINANCIAL AND WHITE-COLLAR CRIMES

Other complex crimes that state and local law enforcement and prosecutors tend to avoid are complex white-collar and financial crimes. Similar to cybercrimes, white-collar and corporate crimes are often dealt with by larger departments in special financial crimes divisions. Since there is a lot at stake in terms of financial losses, police departments and prosecutors find it difficult to ignore such large-scale crimes. However, the nature of white-collar crimes makes them very difficult to police.

White-collar crime was coined by renowned sociologist Edwin Sutherland in his 1939 American Society of Sociology (ASA) annual meeting as "crime committed by a person of respectability and high social status in the course of his occupation."[16] The term drew attention to corporate criminals who were essentially getting away with large-scale embezzlement while avoiding any type of public and governmental scrutiny or stigma. The context of Sutherland's presentation and publications was relevant since the public and academics were focused on street crime while the industrial "robber barons" that were deliberately committing crimes drew little attention and instead were often heralded as the "titans of industry" that played a part in rescuing the country from the Great Depression.

Contemporary white-collar crime scholars have given different reasons why it is not prioritized by lawmakers and the public and consequently is difficult to police. One of the most significant reasons includes white-collar crime's hidden nature, which is often hidden in the complexity of corporate structures and transactions. White-collar and corporate crimes are often hidden in nature and often only discovered by chance or by whistleblowers, but never by random police activities as is found with street crimes. Moreover, the structure of the corporation buries illegal activities within a web of complex relationships and diffused responsibilities. This is often referred to as the "**corporate veil**," which masks illegal activities with overly complex structures.

In addition to its hidden nature, the lack of a universal definition of white-collar crime has meant no universal means to record and gauge the magnitude of the crime. Sutherland's original definitional two components of white-collar offenders, the high social status and occupational requirement, have been challenged by criminologists. For instance, questions of whether an ordinary accountant who is not of high social status can commit white-collar crime, is debatable. Consequently, without an agreed upon definition, white-collar crime is not included in official crime statistics, such as the UCR, making it difficult, if not impossible, to accurately gauge its magnitude. As a result, there is little public outrage or demand for policing and legal action.

White-collar crimes often deter legal action. Prosecutors, for instance, must decipher and prepare financial evidence, requiring understandings of complex accounting. For most state and local prosecutors this simply takes too much time and effort, and is considered too costly. Instead, plea bargains are often the norm, in which corporate executives plead guilty for much reduced charges, commonly referred to pejoratively as "discounted justice." This in turn affects how police deal with white-collar crimes.

Larger police departments use specially trained financial crimes units to handle white-collar crime. These units, while effective, are often overworked with large caseloads.[17] According to criminologist Michael Levi, investigators are often deterred by two factors: (1) the social status of some suspects who often have vast financial and political resources to fight any charges, and (2) the relative inaccessibility of most offenses to routine observation and to normal police informant strategies.[18]

The policing of financial crimes brings forth longstanding tensions within police departments. A study conducted by criminologist Anne Alvesalo found that economic crime investigators have developed tensions with officers on traditional assignments as they jockey for increasing resources.[19] Integrating economic crimes units and functions into the everyday culture and function of police remains contentious and rocky at best, which marginalizes economic crime investigators who are seen as not doing "real" police work. Focusing strictly on police without addressing other pertinent parts of the criminal justice system, however, cannot curtail white-collar crime.

SYSTEM CAPACITY THEORY

Criminologist Henry Pontell's **system capacity theory** argues that the ability or overall capacity of the criminal justice system to mete out justice is dependent upon the smallest limiting factor.[20] An easy way to think about this theory is to imagine a series of pipes in a house that lead from the house to the city's sewer system. The overall ability of the house to drain water quickly depends on the capacity of the smallest pipe. It does not matter if the house has been recently renovated with new plumbing if it connects to a smaller pipe from the city's sewer system. This bottlenecking effect occurs in the criminal justice system between police, courts, and corrections.

When crime is on the rise, the public as well as politicians, usually push for hiring new police officers. However, simply hiring more police officers without increasing the capacity of other parts of the criminal justice system does not increase the capacity to mete out justice. For instance, more arrests require more prosecutors to file the charges, which require more judges, which require more prisons and jails, and so on. For instance, the 2018 issue of illegal immigration became a political focal point with more agents being hired and pressure on agencies to deport individuals. However, one of the largest bottlenecks that slowed down the process was not the lack of border agents, but the courts. In 2018, there were more than 700,000 cases that needed to be processed. In a news interview, Ashley Tabaddor, president of the National Association of Immigration Judges, explains the caseload backlog, stating:[21]

> Imagine a one lane highway and one exit ramp and you now double or triple the lanes and still keep the same exit ramp, you are going to have traffic, you're going to have this bottleneck. And that's where we find ourselves is that for years and years of neglect, we have not had the budgeting.
>
> So I believe based on that alone, it's quite evident that for the numbers to work out, you need more judges to be able to handle the influx of the cases particularly now where the emphasis on enforcement of the law is at its maximum level. . . . It's not only an issue of hiring a judge. When a judge gets hired, there needs to be a team—a support team also hired with that judge. So you need to have the courtroom space, the office, that file space, then you need the technological support.

The consequence of not increasing the overall capacity of the system and only increasing one element, such as hiring more police officers, undermines the deterrent effects of the criminal justice system. As the immigration model demonstrates, having more police officers making more arrests simply backs up the court system as prosecutors, judges, and other legal actors struggle to keep up with the increased workload. As a result, prosecutors rely more heavily on efficiency tools, such as plea bargains, instead of focusing on serving justice.[22] Consequently, arrested individuals are released quickly with little punishment, leading many to criticize our system as a "revolving-door" that undermines any type of deterrent effect of the system. Ironically, this fuels a cycle where the public demands more police action.

In complex white-collar crime cases enforcement is severely limited by the capacity of agencies to process the crime and coordinate experts and law enforcement agencies. Criminologists Henry Pontell, Kitty Calavita, and Robert Tillman explain that the enforcement of white-collar crime and corporate fraud is "limited by the complexity and the massive scale of thrift crime relative to available resources and to the level of coordination possible among agencies."

SUMMARY

We have just barely scratched the surface of exploring the nuances and complexities of policing complicated crimes such as financial and cyber-crime. The one-size-fits-all policing model that we currently operate under makes it very difficult to train or hire highly specialized experts who may not be police officers. Current efforts to police these crimes are marred by structural and cultural issues that undermine inner and interagency collaboration. Moreover, police activities are often dictated by prosecutorial and criminal justice priorities, which in turn are affected by public opinion.

According to sociologist Edwin Lemert, public opinion is a vital factor in prioritizing and allocating resources to fighting financial crimes.[23] He blames ambivalent attitudes produced by a "generalized culture conflict which affects such a large majority of the population that little consistent action is possible," adding, "community tolerance is precariously stabilized just short of a critical point in the tolerance quotient at which collective action is taken." Without collective outrage against extremely costly white-collar and computer crimes, necessary legislation and law enforcement efforts fall short and victimization continues to soar.

NOTES

1. Brian A. Reaves, "Federal Law Enforcement Officers, 2008," *US Department of Justice Bureau of Justice Statistics,* June 2012, https://www.bjs.gov/content/pub/pdf/fleo08.pdf.

2. Duren Banks et al., "National Sources of Law Enforcement Employment Data," *US Department of Justice Bureau of Justice Statistics* , October 4, 2016, https://www.bjs.gov/content/pub/pdf/nsleed.pdf.

3. Robert Martinson, "What Works? Questions and Answers about Prison Reform, *"The Public Interest* (1974): 22–54.

4. Willard M. Oliver, "The Fourth Era of Policing: Homeland Security," *International Review of Law, Computers and Technology* 20, no. 1 (2007): 49–62. doi: 10.1080/13600860600579696.

5. Radley Balko, "A Decade After 9/11, Police Departments are Increasingly Militarized," *Huffington Post,* September 12, 2011, http://www.huffingtonpost.com/2011/09/12/police-militarization-9-11-september-11_n_955508.html.

6. David A. Harris, "The War on Terror, Local Police, and Immigration Enforcement: A Curious Tale of Police Power in Post-9/11 America," *Rutgers Law Journal* 38, no. 1 (2006): 1–60.

7. Daniel E. Marks and Ivan Y. Sun," The Impact of 9/11 on Organizational Development among State and Local Law Enforcement Agencies," *Journal of Contemporary Criminal Justice* 23, no. 2 (2007): 159–173. doi: 10.1177/1043986207301364.

8. Peter N. Grabowsky, "Virtual Criminality: Old Wine in New Bottles?" *Social and Legal Studies* 10, no. 2 (2001): 243–249.

9. Johnny Nhan and Laura Huey, "'We Don't Have These Laser Beams and Stuff Like That': Police Investigations as Low-Tech Work in a High-Tech World," in *Technocrime, Policing and Surveillance* (New York: Routledge, 2013), 79–90.

10. Susan. W. Brenner, "Is There Such a Thing as 'Virtual Crime?'" *Berkeley Journal of Criminal Law* 4, no. 1 (2001): 1–72.

11. Johnny Nhan, *Policing Cyberspace: A Structural and Cultural Analysis* (El Paso, TX: LFB Publishing, 2010).

12. Johnny Nhan, "Criminal Justice Firewalls: Prosecutorial Decision-Making in Cyber and High-Tech Crime Cases," in *International Perspectives on Crime and Justice* (New Castle, UK: Cambridge Scholars, 2009), 520–540.

13. Steve Herbert, "Territoriality and the Police," *The Professional Geographer* 49, no. 1 (1997): 86–94. doi: 10.1111/0033-0124.00059.

14. Mitch Van Geel, Paul Vedder, and Jenny Tanilon, "Relationship between Peer Victimization, Cyberbullying, and Suicide in Children and Adolescents: A Meta-Analysis," *JAMA Pediatrics* 168, no. 3 (2014): 435–442. doi:10.1001/jamapediatrics.2013.4143.

15. Marc D. Goodman, "Why the Police Don't Care about Computer Crime," *Harvard Journal of Law and Technology* 10, no. 3 (1997): 466–495.

16. Edwin H. Sutherland, "White-Collar Criminality," *American Sociological Review* 5, no. 1 (1940): 1–12.

17. James Meeker and Henry N. Pontell, "Court Caseloads, Plea Bargains, and Criminal Sanctions: The Effects of Section 17 P.C. in California," *Criminology* 23, no. 1 (1985): 119–143. doi: 10.1111/j.1745-9125.1985.tb00329.x.

18. Michael Levi, "Policing Financial Crimes," in *International Handbook of White-Collar and Corporate Crime* (New York: Springer, 2017) 588–606.

19. Anne Alvesalo, "Economic Crime Investigators at Work," *Policing and Society: An International Journal of Research and Policy* 13, no. 2 (2003): 115–138.

20. Henry N. Pontell, *A Capacity to Punish: The Ecology of Crime and Punishment* (Bloomington: Indiana University Press, 1984).

21. Ben Schamisso, "How to Reduce the Immigration Case Backlog? Depends Who You Ask," *Newsy*, July 18, 2018, https://www.newsy.com/stories/trump-and-immigration-judges-disagree-on-how-to-cut-backlog/.

22. Henry N. Pontell, Kitty Calavita, and Robert R. Tillman, "Corporate Crime and Criminal Justice System Capacity: Government Response to Financial Institution Fraud," *Justice Quarterly* 11, no. 3 (1994): 383–410.

23. Edwin Lemert, *Crime and Deviance: Essays and Innovations of Edwin M. Lemert* (Lanham, MD: Rowman and Littlefield, 2000).

Chapter Fifteen

The Police and Social Media

Over the last decade, the use of social media use by police has exploded. In 2014, the International Association of Chiefs of Police (IACP) Center for Social Media found that over 95 percent of police agencies surveyed used social media.[1] This widespread adoption of social media use on platforms, primarily Twitter and Facebook, makes perfect sense for law enforcement agencies: Social media provides an avenue for police to further their reliance on information. In other words, agencies can use social media to quickly and easily gather and disseminate information, ranging from informing the public of road closures to soliciting information on a criminal case.

Social media use by law enforcement, however, is not as simple as it may seem. There are controversial issues and unforeseen complexities to its use.[2] For example, do departments allow for open public feedback? Public interaction can be useful but it can also serve as a platform for open criticisms which may or may not be true. What information should departments disseminate? Who exactly should be able to post on social media and what should that person's qualities and qualifications be? These are questions that departments today are grappling with as they are expected to participate in a space that does not have rules but has many risks.

Among the many other functions of social media, perhaps the most important for police is the humanizing effect of social media. Social media can essentially be a *virtual* space for community policing. One of the key pillars of community policing is establishing a relationship with the public to put a face on officers that were painted as nameless and faceless during professionalization in the reform era of policing. This has traditionally been done by putting officers back on walking beats and bicycle patrols. This method is often difficult in large cities spanning over vast geographic spaces. Therefore, these activities are limited to larger departments with more resources, and are deployed strategically, often in transient tourist locations, but without a presence in actual residential communities. Social media can establish this presence.

Social media also makes an officer's profession much more hazardous. The ubiquity of cameras coupled with virtually instant uploads to social media can create narratives that "go viral" out of critical incidents, such as an interracial use of force, that have real consequences. An officer accused or even acquitted of racially charged misconduct can be in real physical danger from being "**doxed**," (sometimes spelled "doxxed"), the unauthorized public disclosure of private information, such as one's home address, which can potentially ruin an officer's career and life.

This chapter explores issues of social media use by police, while high-lighting more contentious and potential hazards of social media use including:

- The world of social media and the social media world
- Police involvement in social media
- Police legitimacy
- The nature of interaction between police and citizens on social media
- The benefits and hazards of crowdsourcing
- Off-duty use of social media

THE WORLD OF SOCIAL MEDIA AND
THE SOCIAL MEDIA WORLD

To say that there are a lot of social media users on the Internet today is an obvious understatement. To give you the scope of social media use and the Internet in 2018, consider these estimates from the 2018 Global Digital Report: there are an estimated 4.021 billion Internet users worldwide and of those users, 3.196 billion, or nearly 80 percent, use social media, which represents a 13 percent increase from 2017, with Facebook being the most predominant and fastest growing social media network.[3]

Most people view social media as a tool to connect people, sharing media such as pictures and videos, and self-expression. This view is based mostly on the nature of the services available, which started with MySpace and evolved to Twitter, Facebook, Instagram, Pinterest, YouTube, and so on. Each service offers a variety of entertainment and professional functions, ranging from primarily sharing pictures and chatting to making industry connections and finding employment, such as with the popular LinkedIn. Social media has been criticized for variety of issues ranging from fostering a culture of vanity to cyberbullying, and more recently, issues of privacy and spreading false information.

In recent years, social media platforms have played an increasingly consequential and impactful role in society.[4] The Arab Spring uprisings showed some of the power of social media.[5] In 2011, young Middle Eastern protesters took to social media sites such as Twitter, YouTube, and Facebook to organize and mobilize resources that led to the eventual overthrow of Egyptian President Hosni Mubarak by hundreds of thousands of protestors, in hopes of establishing a democratic regime. These platforms served as a surrogate for the lack of free press and allowed the outside world an unfiltered glimpse into a world that had resisted open communications. While democracies were not established in the region, the movement, often referred to as the "Twitter uprising" and "Facebook revolution," showed the potential power of social media.[6]

While social media can be a powerful tool for connecting people and groups for noble causes, it can be misused, with some real consequences. One infamous story involved senior director of corporate communications at media company IAC, Justine Sacco. During a 2013 trip from New York to Cape Town, thirty-year-old Sacco jokingly made some racially insensitive tweets to her 170 followers.[7] For example, in addition to mentioning the body odor of the German passenger sitting next to her on her flight and Londoners' teeth, she tweeted, "Going to Africa. Hope I don't get AIDS. Just kidding. I'm white!" This was meant as a joke to her friends but before the last leg of her flight landed, and unbeknownst to her, Sacco's tweet had gone viral and was trending as the number one tweet in the world with users calling for her firing and contacting her bosses. She tried to delete the tweet, but one Twitter user commented, "Sorry @JustineSacco, your tweet lives on forever." An interview with Sacco some time later revealed the lasting impact of getting fired and the public shaming and humiliation.

The Arab Spring uprising and Sacco's story illustrates the power as well as the hazards of social media use. Law enforcement also took notice of the power of social media platforms for broadcasting and communications, as well as criminal investigations.

THE INTRODUCTION OF POLICE TO THE SOCIAL MEDIA WORLD

Several major incidents in the United States and abroad demonstrated the power of social media as a tool for law enforcement. In 2010, students in the United Kingdom used social media to organize a protest for free education amidst a global recession. Police could use the same social media sources to monitor the movements and conduct surveillance. In 2011, thousands of people began rioting in London, with looting and violence spreading throughout the entire country. Police triangulated data from social media sites, such as Facebook and Google Maps to track and identify the looters, some of whom were taking "selfies" with looted items. Similarly, in 2011 when the NHL team, the Vancouver Canucks, lost the Stanley Cup, rioting took place in the city. Police, aided by members of the public who were angered by the damage, took to Facebook and YouTube to identify suspects.

In 2013, Boston police solicited help from social media outlets to help identify and locate the Boston Marathon bombing suspects. Social media was used by people on-scene to provide news updates and serve as a photo repository for investigators. While police were able to use more traditional means to locate the suspects, the sheer volume of photos and videos available showed the potential of **crowdsourcing**. Crowdsourcing is the collective mobilization of a large group for a common goal.

Crowdsourcing criminology has garnered attention as an emerging field in recent years and has sparked organic collaborations between the public and law enforcement. Police as well as criminologists have taken note of the potency of collective knowledge and resources.[8] For example, a study of the Boston Marathon bombing showed parallel investigations by online forum members, such as from the popular social aggregate news site Reddit, who scrutinized photos to identify every tiny clue to report to the police.[9] These social media sites also helped Boston police and other agencies broadcast information to calm nerves as well as request information.

POLICE USE OF SOCIAL MEDIA

Today, law enforcement agencies in the United States have found the usefulness of social media a powerful tool, not just in an investigative capacity, but also as an invaluable and powerful tool to connect with the community. For example, social media complements community policing agendas and can serve as virtual town halls that allow active interaction with the community, which is a nearly impossible task on foot or bike in large metropolitan areas. An article published in the *Proceedings of the European Conference on Social Media* identified six main uses identified by policing agencies:[10]

1. As a source of criminal information
2. To push information to the public
3. To support police IT infrastructure
4. To leverage the wisdom of the crowd
5. To extend community policing in online environments
6. To show the human side of policing

One noteworthy benefit of departments using social media is the humanizing effect of social media. Recall that during police professionalization during the reform era, officers were mandated to minimize fraternization with members of the public to prevent corruption. This Joe Friday "just the facts ma'am" impersonal demeanor, coupled with reactive patrols in cars, contributed to police/community tensions.

Social media allows departments to portray a more positive and personable image of police. Some departments tweet pictures of officers assisting in non-police matters or at community events. This "softer" side of policing is rarely newsworthy, but social media allows agencies to present narratives that are not purely negative and directly crime related in nature.

In recent years, many departments have gained public praise and support for producing videos that have gone viral on social media. For example, in 2016, Detroit Police Department officers participated in the Running Man dance challenge posted on YouTube, and called out Philadelphia, Cincinnati, and Chicago police departments to do the same. Countless other departments accepted the challenge, including Pittsburg, Lawrence, Raleigh, and Bloomfield, to name a few.

More recently, in 2018, law enforcement organizations have been challenging each other in "lip-sync challenges" on Facebook and YouTube. The Norfolk Police Department's video went viral when hundreds of thousands of viewers watched officers across police department offices, and a few firemen, lip-sync and dance to Bruno Mars' "Uptown Funk." The video was so popular that the officers in the video were invited to appear on national news and shows, including NBC's *Today Show*, NBC *Nightly News*, and *CBS News*.

One of the most successful uses of social media was a series of recruitment videos produced by the Fort Worth Police Department that featured *Star Wars* characters. One of these viral videos that were featured in *USA Today* and other news outlets, with nearly a million views, showed a Stormtrooper at the police academy shooting range with terrible marksmanship, in true *Star Wars* fashion. Another *Star Wars*–themed recruitment video featured in *Fox News* featured Chewbacca as a rookie officer with his FTO. Mixing humor, popular culture, and police officers, not only served as a great recruitment tool for the department but humanized the officers and the profession.

A 2016 IACP and Urban Institute survey found a variety of uses of social media by member departments.[11] These include:

1. Notifying public of public safety concerns (91 percent)
2. Community outreach and engagement (89 percent)
3. Public relations (86 percent)
4. Notifying public of non-crime issues (traffic) (86 percent)
5. Soliciting tips on crime (76 percent)
6. Monitoring public sentiment (72 percent)

7. Intelligence gathering for investigations (70 percent)
8. Recruitment and application vetting (58 percent)
9. Communicating with government agencies (29 percent)
10. In-service training (6 percent)
11. Other (3 percent)

The study also found that most departments used only one social account, with the majority opting for Twitter. Nineteen percent of departments that used two or more accounts generally used the accounts for different purposes and to reach different audiences. Some personnel within the departments, such as the chief of police, can have separate official accounts that have a different tone and focus, such as community engagement and department vision.

Two growing areas of police social media use of information posted by users. First, according to the IACP, the majority of departments have contacted or presented warrants to social media companies to search user information for evidence in an investigation. Facebook, for example, has served as an invaluable tool in mapping criminal networks ranging from gangs and prostitution to human trafficking and sexual predators. According to the FBI, more sexual predators are luring children through social media.[12]

Second, in a similar fashion, departments are scouring social media accounts of applicants, looking for disqualifying activities and associations, such as photos ranging from excessive drinking and illicit drug use to involvement with hate groups. While these are more extreme examples, many applicants are disqualified based on an assessment of character through their social media accounts. For example, a background investigator may find racist jokes or a lifestyle that contradicts the narrative the applicant is presenting, raising issues of trust.

POLICE LEGITIMACY

One of the biggest benefits of social media use is perhaps the increase in police legitimacy. According to criminologists Steven Chermak and Alexander Weiss, "a critical aspect for acquiring and preserving legitimacy is being able to manipulate and manage their external environment."[13] Traditionally, police have used public information officers (PIOs) to advocate for and promote the organization in the media. The researchers assert that trained PIO's interaction with the media can effectively control news images by taking advantage of being the gatekeepers of information. Police legitimacy was highly influenced by how the media perceived how helpful law enforcement was in helping to provide information to create a story quickly and to generate public interest in the news story. However, this relationship was often contentious and depended on how effectively police were able to explain and legitimize actions taken to the media.

Social media allows the organization direct control of narratives without media filtration. Police can take active steps in crafting and shaping organizational identity, such as ameliorating implications of racial bias and increasing legitimacy through transparency from direct discourse with the audience. These functions are critical during crisis situations where different narratives are presented not only by the media, but by social media users and organizations.

Researchers have examined the nature of police interactions with the public or community to see if efforts at increasing police legitimacy are effective. Some researchers have dichotomized the nature of interactions into two categories: broadcast versus interaction. It is argued that direct police broadcasting of information, while helpful, does not notably affect police legitimacy. Two Netherlands researchers, Stephan Grimmelikhuijsen and Albert Meijer, found police use of Twitter, which is more broadcast in nature, had an overall negligible effect on perceived legitimacy.[14] They conclude that "overall, the findings suggest that establishing a direct channel with citizens and using it to communicate successes does help the police strengthen their legitimacy, but only slightly and for a small group of interested citizens."

A comparison between Twitter, a more broadcast-based social media platform, and Facebook, which is more interactive, underscores how police-community interactivity can affect police legitimacy. A comparison between North American police departments social media use by researchers Albert Meijer and Marcel Thaens has classified this as a "push" (broadcast) versus a "pull" (interactive) strategy and a third, "networking" strategy.[15] The push strategy used by the Boston Police Department via Twitter tended to be the least effective, with media outlets vying to write the worst stories that portrayed the department in a negative light.

In contrast, the Metropolitan Police Department in Washington DC, employs a "pull" method which draws in the community with interaction through Twitter and Facebook. According to the researchers, by doing so, it resulted in "strengthening the image of the department and building good relations with citizens are considered to be of value but more important is the direct contribution to police tasks." This has resulted in much improved police/media relations as well as better recruitment of officers, which is a clear indication of organizational legitimacy.

The third strategy employed by the Toronto Police Department, the networking strategy, showed the most positive effect on police legitimacy. Community members were encouraged to be actively involved and assist in ongoing investigations, in addition to interactions through social media. Citizens were encouraged to call Crime Stoppers as well as assist in traffic services using different social media platforms, including YouTube. More-over, the department allowed for different officers assigned to specific divi-sions to manage their own social media accounts instead of a singular point of broadcast through a PIO. This resulted in a greater humanizing effect for officers as well as greater public satisfaction in serving in a more active role.

Similar conclusions were drawn by other researchers about the nature of interaction and use of social media by police. An examination of Twitter usage by Cisco researcher Jeremy Crump found the overly cautious approach by police due to a strong culture of resistance to change meant the platform was underutilized. [16] Crump concluded that the broadcast nature of Twitter, coupled with police reluctance to interact and follow back users who have followed the department account, meant limited opportunity to have a dis-course. Other researchers comparing different social media platforms have confirmed the qualitative differences between the interactions on Twitter versus Facebook.

Despite evidence showing the positive impact on police-citizen relations which ultimately boosts police legitimacy, allowing active crowd participa-tion, such as in crowdsourcing, has its risks for police.

THE DANGERS OF CROWDSOURCING

Crowdsourcing, or collaborative policing with the public, in principle, seems to be ideal for criminal investigations and police work. The public volunteer their time and diverse expertise to aide police with investigations. At mini-mum, the public can serve in a passive capacity by being an extra set of "eyes and ears" for law enforcement. The popular, and one of the longest running television shows, *America's Most Wanted*, for example, can be considered a form of crowdsourcing. Each show featured the crime, an active fugitive, and ended with a number that viewers could call. When the show aired, it claimed to have aided in the capture of fugitives.

In the Internet age, the police can potentially expand this passive role and tap into a pool of diverse expertise for investigations. For example, during the Boston Marathon bombing Reddit community members, often tracing it back to their own occupations ,were able to identify and share information on very specific items of interest, ranging from the pressure cooker that was suspected to be used in the bombing, to specific caps worn by different people in the crowd who were suspected of being the bomber. While this breadth and depth of expertise can seem useful, experience has shown that it also comes with a set of risks and liabilities.

Internet users and communities have made errors in identification and have carried out illegal forms of vigilante justice. For example, the Reddit community that organically formed its own investigation misidentified Sunil

Tripathi as one of the Boston bombing suspects and spread his name throughout the Internet. Tripathi, as it turns out, was a missing Brown University student at the time, and was eventually found dead in an apparent suicide. However, Tripathi's identity as a Boston bombing suspect was picked up by some mainstream news outlets, such as *ABC News,* as well as popular Internet aggregate news sites, such as the digital news site BuzzFeed. This misidentification resulted in angry calls to his family and posts on the Facebook page dedicated to finding him.

An in-depth study of police usage of Twitter and Facebook found errors were common when law enforcement engaged the public through social media. Temple University graduate researcher Lauren Mayes found that even routine posts on social media soliciting public assistance can be problematic.[17] For example, when one department posted a surveillance shot of two men suspected of a crime, it was a picture of the wrong men. One officer interviewed by Mayes explained:

> *One time, I posted a picture of two guys in the ATM that we're trying to identify. It turns out, the bank, we got them identified but it was the wrong people. The bank gave us the wrong footage. Ultimately, it was the bank's fault and nobody knew. . . . The very next day when I found out about this . . . I put a post, hey everybody, just so you know, these kids, this wasn't them.*

In addition to the potential for errors, well-intentioned Internet users and community members can cross the line and become potential criminals when they pursue suspects. In 2011, Internet users outraged at the destruction of their city, not only identified rioters but shamed and harassed them online. Furthermore, threats of violence were made against the identified rioters, prompting Vancouver Police to plead with citizens not to engage in vigilante justice.

Compounding issues of misidentification and vigilante justice, crowdsourcing and social media may interfere with emergency response management and coordination. Social media users often create new accounts with official sounding handles or user names, during large-scale emergencies, such as in riot situations. These official-sounding handles can get mistaken for the actual official police handle. For example, London Metropolitan Police and Greater Manchester Police faced difficulties tracking the emergence of different users and groups during the 2011 Manchester Riots.[18] According to researchers, the public was confused by the proliferation of new users, such as @IDRiotors and @ManchesterRiots. The two agencies found it difficult to track these new users and to differentiate between official law enforcement handles and ones created by Internet users and community members.

THE IMPACT AND HAZARDS OF POLICE OFFICER
USE OF SOCIAL MEDIA

Like most people, individual police officers participate in social media and have personal accounts with sites such as Twitter and Facebook. Many of these officers join dedicated pages for law enforcement. For example, there are pages ranging from Police Lives Matter and Blue Blood Brotherhood that offer support, to forums for promoting officer interests in a group dedicated to hobbyists who collect police challenge coins.

Off-duty police use of social media has resulted in numerous officers who have gotten in trouble for issues of indiscretion, with real consequences. According to researcher Andrew Goldsmith, police indiscretion and careless use of social media use has resulted in off-duty officers getting in trouble with the department, and some even fired.[19] Many officers are seduced by a celebrity-like status as public figures. For example, in 2015, San Jose police officer Phil White was fired after drawing national attention for antagonistic tweets at Black Lives Matter.[20] One tweet read, "Threaten me or my family and I will use my God given and law appointed right and duty to kill you. #CopsLivesMatter." While White was reinstated by an independent arbitrator, these tweets were condemned by the police department, police union, city leaders, and social justice groups.

Other officers have been disciplined or fired for tweets with racial undertones, highlighting the hazards of police use of social media. For example, an officer from Nashville, Tennessee, was fired for commenting that he would have shot Philando Castile, an African American who was controversially shot by an officer when reaching for his driver's license and disclosing he was armed, more times than he was already shot. One New Rochelle Police Department officer was suspended for posting a racially charged comment, stating, "It's fine to be anti-police, but be 100 [percent] about it. Don't call the police when your world is in disarray to help deal with the worst 10 minutes of your life. Figure it out yourself or better yet call Shaun King and Black Lives Matter for help."

Controversial posts by officers have prompted police departments to acknowledge the public figure roles of officers and develop policies to serve as a general guideline for off-duty social media use. For example, in 2015, the Seattle Police Department, in light of high-profile incidents of officers posting racially charged social media posts, issued guidelines on off-duty social media use. Under policy guidelines, officers are not to post speech that negatively impacts the department's ability to serve the public, which includes comments that support the ridiculing, biases, or that disrespect any protected classes, such as race, religion, sex, gender, and national origin. Baltimore Police Department has similar guidelines, with penalties that include termination from the department.

Restrictions on personal social media use for officers bring up issues of free speech. The courts are seeing more legal challenges to the restrictions on free speech by off-duty officers and other public employees. For example, a Petersburg, Virginia, police department issued a policy that prohibited any negative comments about the department, prompting a 4th circuit three-judge panel to rule that the social media policy was too broad (see *Liverman v. City of Petersburg*). According to the American Bar Association, the conflict arises because online speech is made when a public employee is not engaging in official, job-duty speech.[21] However, the ABA comments that "If the speech touches on matters of public concern, then the court balances the employee's right to free speech against the employer's interests in an efficient, disruption-free workplace." Typically, the courts have deferred to an employer's judgment, which sets up the potential for future legal challenges and development of legal standards that balance public employer/employee free speech concerns.

THE IMPACT OF MEDIA AND THE "FERGUSON EFFECT"

Part of the reason why many officers feel it is necessary and appropriate to express their feelings on social media platforms is because they feel media coverage of officers and policing situations to be negative and biased against them. These officers often feel that official positions by police departments and PIOs do not adequately defend the officers, contributing to subcultural feelings of "us versus them" between police and the media. Officers then turn to social media to vent their frustrations.

Experts examining this antagonistic relationship between police and the media have dubbed it the **"Ferguson effect,"** in reference to the Ferguson social unrest from the shooting of Michael Brown in 2014. The Ferguson effect, coined by *Wall Street Journal* journalist Heather MacDonald, is when crime rates rises from public agitation of police derived from the culmination of negative stories of police misconduct.[22] A study by criminologists Justin Nix and Justin Picket of perceptions of officers found that most officers were firm believers in the Ferguson effect, noticing an increase in crime rates from negative media coverage contributing to hostile public attitudes.[23] However, there were no findings of a significant rise in crime rates in large metropolitan areas from the Ferguson effect, showing a disjuncture between perceptions and actual effects on crime rates.[24] Nevertheless, officer perceptions are based on real and perceived threats to officers who have been accused of misconduct or wrongdoing.

One phenomenon that has emerged as a significant threat to officers accused of misconduct is the doxing of officers' personal identities. One of the worst fears of every officer is that their private information, such as home address, is released to the public. This information may put the officer and his or her family at risk. Many officers go to great lengths to mask their personal information, including special arrangements with motor vehicle departments that shield their personal vehicle's license plate information from any search inquiries. However, Internet sleuths and other outlets, including the media, have managed to dox officer identities for high profile cases, which further exacerbates subcultural feelings of "us versus them" by police.

There are many examples of officers' personal information being released online to the public. Officer Darren Wilson, who was accused of shooting Michael Brown, which led to the Ferguson riots in 2014, was doxed by Internet users who published his Missouri marriage license with home address. In 2011, NYPD officer Anthony Bologna, who appeared to be pepper spraying peaceful protesters on a viral video, was doxed by "hacktivists," or politically motivated hackers. Bologna, who was initially unidentified, was targeted by an organized dox, resulting in his name, precinct, personal phone number, last-known home addresses, names of his relatives, high school, and a record of a lawsuit against him, being published on different forums and websites.

In 2016, hacker group *Anonymous* doxed the personal information of fifty-two Cincinnati police officers, including the police chief, in retaliation for the controversial shooting of Paul Gaston, a Black man armed with a BB-gun. The hacker group released a statement to police that said, "You lost. While we release your officers' information, we will hold no responsibility of the actions of those that see the information." Doxed officers often live in fear of harm, which requires many departments to provide around-the-clock security at the officers' homes. Many of these residences have become staging areas for protestors and some news media, in high profile cases.

Officers who have not been directly involved in cases of misconduct are also at risk of doxing. Hackers have doxed entire department's officers' identities. For example, in 2016, hackers gained access to a government database and published the names, phone numbers, and email addresses of over eighty officers from several Miami departments. These hostile acts towards officers, even those not directly involved in any wrongdoing, shows the often-contentious relationship between police and some Internet users and groups that perceive law enforcement as a group instead of as individuals. Furthermore, these types of actions can also reinforce the police subculture by furthering police mistrust of non-police entities and the "us versus them" siege mentality.

The issue of doxing has become a prevalent and important issue among police departments. In 2018, the Chicago Police Department released an internal training document on social media surveillance and being doxed.[25] The department began coaching officers on avoiding potential exposure of personal information from various technologies. For example, it warned officers who upload photos or messages through social media that their exact locations can be extracted from embedded information on mobile devices. This GPS information can be used to pinpoint an officer's home address. Ironically, many of these methods and technologies are used by police to monitor and surveil suspects.

The policing community has also warned fellow officers of the risks of being doxed. A 2016 article posted on PoliceOne, a popular policing site, warned officers that doxed information can be used for a variety of malicious activities, ranging from physical stalking and harassment to extortion and coercion.[26] These potential harms have sent a chilling effect across the law enforcement community and ad to the uncontrollable hazards of police work.

SUMMARY

Social media has become an important tool that police departments around the country have incorporated into their many functions. Platforms like Twitter and Facebook have become important investigative tools as well as serving as direct broadcasting tools. Social media has also allowed departments and agencies to present their narratives that have historically been surrogated by media outlets and community members that may present false or misleading information.

Perhaps more importantly, social media allows police to reconnect with the community more effectively. While most departments have implemented community policing activities that range from walking beats and bike patrols to holding community town halls, they can only directly connect with a fraction of the community they serve. Social media allows for greater access to police officers in a more personal manner, which humanizes the officers and legitimizes the police force. This humanization effect is important to police in general, who have severed community relations by design from professionalization. Moreover, the public can potentially directly assist officers, with a broad range of expertise.

Despite the positive impact of social media, it has many negative aspects and presents some hazards to police departments and individual officers. Departments often feel that social media falsely creates and amplifies negative narratives which may result in greater hostility towards officers, and higher crime, out of spite, known as the Ferguson effect. Furthermore, off-duty use of social media has created a predicament for departments that cannot prevent officers from personal social media use, but need to regulate officers' posts that run counter to the department's image and reputation, which creates legal challenges. Finally, officers are now exposed to their own personal information being exposed and published online.

These increased hazards and instances of malicious activities, such as doxing, have resulted in officers drawing closer to each other, which reinforces the police subculture while potentially undermining community policing efforts. The contradictory nature of social media use remains an emerging controversial issue in the world of policing.

NOTES

1. KiDeuk Kim, Ashlin Oglesby-Neal, and Edward Mohr, "2016 Law Enforcement Use of Social Media Survey," *International Association of Chiefs of Police,* February 2017, http://www.theiacp.org/Portals/0/documents/pdfs/2016-law-enforcement-use-of-social-media-survey.pdf.

2. Petra S. Bayerl et al., "Who Wants Police on Social Media?" in *Proceedings of the European Conference on Social Media* (UK: Academic Conferences and Publishing International, 2014).

3. See https://wearesocial.com/blog/2018/01/global-digital-report-2018.

4. Stephen Owen, "Monitoring Social Media and Protest Movements: Ensuring Political Order through Surveillance and Surveillance Discourse," *Social Identities* 23, no. 6 (2017): 688–700. doi: 10.1080/13504630.2017.1291092.

5. Heather Brown, Emily Guskin, and Amy Mitchell, "The Role of Social Media in the Arab Uprisings," Pew Research Center, 2012, http://www.journalism.org/2012/11/28/role-social-media-arab- uprisings/.

6. Brown, "The Role of Social Media in the Arab Uprisings."

7. Jon Ronson, "How One Stupid Tweet Blew Up Justine Sacco's Life," *The New York Times,* February 12, 2015, https://www.nytimes.com/2015/02/15/magazine/how-one-stupid-tweet-ruined-justine-saccos-life.html.

8. Antonio Vera and Torsten O. Salge, "Crowdsourcing and Policing: Opportunities for Research and Practice," *European Police Science and Research Bulletin* 16 (2017): 143–154.

9. Johnny Nhan, Laura Huey, and Ryan Broll, "Digilantism: An Analysis of Crowdsourcing and The Boston Marathon Bombings," *British Journal of Criminology,* 57, no. 2 (2015): 341–361. doi:10.1093/bjc/azv118.

10. Petra S. Bayerl et al., "Who Wants Police on Social Media?" in *Proceedings of the European Conference on Social Media* (UK: Academic Conferences and Publishing International, 2014).

11. Kim, "2016 Law Enforcement Use of Social Media Survey."

12. Jeff Reeves, "More Sexual Predators Using Social Media to Lure Children, FBI Says," *CBS News,* July 21, 2016, https://www.cbs17.com/news/more-sexual-predators-using-social-media-to-lure-children-fbi-says_20180327091622773/1082780184.

13. Steven Chermak and Alexander Weiss, "Maintaining Legitimacy Using External Communication Strategies: An Analysis of Police-Media Relations," *Journal of Criminal Justice* 33 (2005): 501–512. doi: 10.1016/j.jcrimjus.2005.06.001.

14. Stephan G. Grimmelikhuijsen and Albert J. Meijer, "Does Twitter Increase Perceived Police Legitimacy?" *Public Administrative Review* 75, no. 4 (2015): 598–607.

15. Albert J. Meijer and Marcel Thaens, "Social Media Strategies: Understanding the Differences between North American Police Departments," *Government Information Quarterly* 30, no. 4 (2013): 343–350. doi: 10.1016/j.giq.2013.05.023.

16. Jeremy Crump, "What are the Police Doing on Twitter? Social Media, the Police and the Public," *Policy and Internet* 3, no. 4 (2011): 1–27. doi: 10.2202/1944-2866.1130.

17. Lauren Mayes, "Law Enforcement in the Age of Social Media: Examining the Organizational Image Construction of Police on Twitter and Facebook,"(PhD diss., Temple University, ProQuest, 2017), https://search.proquest.com/openview/36486ef26ad6da61b0e7b9e1002ea802/1.pdf?pq-origsite=gscholar&cbl=18750&diss=y.

18. Sabastian Denef, Petra S. Bayerl, and Nico Kaptein, "Social Media and the Police: Tweeting Practices of British Police Forces during the August 2011 Riots," in proceedings from Conference on Human Factors in Computing Systems, CHI 2013, April 27–May 2, 2013, Paris, France.

19. Andrew Goldsmith, "Disgracebook Policing: Social Media and the Rise of Police Indiscretion," *Policing and Society* 25, no. 3 (2015): 249–267. doi: 10.1080/10439463.2013.864653.

20. Robert Solanga, "San Jose Police Officer Fired for Combative Tweets on Black Lives Matter," *The Mercury News*, October 21, 2015, https://www.mercurynews.com/2015/10/21/san-jose-police-officer-fired-for-combative-tweets-on-black-lives-matter/.

21. David L. Hudson Jr., "Public Employees, Private Speech: 1st Amendment Doesn't Always Protect Government Workers," *American Bar Association Journal,* 2017, http://www.abajournal.com/magazine/article/public_employees_private_speech?icn=most_read.

22. Heather MacDonald, "The New Nationwide Crime Wave: The Consequences of the 'Ferguson Effect' are Already Appearing. The Main Victims of Growing Violence Will be the Inner-City Poor," *The Wall Street Journal*, May 29, 2015, https://www.wsj.com/articles/the-new-nationwide-crime-wave-1432938425.

23. Justin Nix and Justin T. Picket, "Third-Person Perceptions, Hostile Media Effects, and Policing: Developing a Theoretical Framework for Assessing the Ferguson Effect," *Journal of Criminal Justice* 51 (2017): 24–33. doi: 10.1016/j.jcrimjus.2017.05.016.

24. David C. Pyrooz et al., "Was There a Ferguson Effect on Crime Rates in Large US Cities? *Journal of Criminal Justice* 46 (2016): 1–8. doi: 10.1016/j.jcrimjus.2016.01.001.

25. William Pierce, "Chicago Police Department Coaches Officers on How to Avoid the Same Social Media Surveillance They Themselves Employ," *MuckRock Project on Social Media Surveillance*, April 11, 2018.

26. Todd Drake, "How Cops Can Protect Themselves from Doxxing," *PoliceOne*, October 19, 2016, Accessed from https://www.policeone.com/Officer-Safety/articles/233207006-How-cops-can-protect-themselves-from-doxxing/.

Chapter Sixteen

Risk, Technology, Surveillance, and the Future of Policing

This chapter examines the future of policing. Police have evolved from the political era of the late 1800s to early 1900s, when political agendas were enforced; to the reform era lasting from approximately 1930 to the 1980s, of professionalism and corruption eradication; to the community era in the 1990s and to a large part today, where departments emphasize proactive community engagement and problem-solving. Bookending these eras of police were the days of the night watchman, when community norms were enforced over rule of law, and the post-9/11 homeland security era, during which some criminologists suggest, police have prioritized more militaristic and tactical strategies.

Each era of policing is highlighted by underlying fundamental changes to the core functions and mandates of police. These changes in policing often parallel watershed moments in society that are sometimes sparked by police action, such as urban riots, and other times shock the collective conscience and produce sea-changes, such as the September 11, 2001, terrorist attacks.

Some of the underlying changes in the past few decades to police were caused by modernity and advances in technology associated with the **information age**. The information age is demarcated by changes in computer technology, digital information, and new media. The new changes to police core mandates can be considered arguably more fundamental than previous changes. This is not to suggest that police do not focus primarily on crime control, making arrests, and enforcing the law, but the means in which this is done has changed.

This chapter focuses on several central themes such as:

• The *information age* and its effects on the core functions of policing

227

- Policing risk, managing danger, and knowledge workers
- Surveillance society
- Information and risk-based strategies (Broken Windows, [1,2] COMPSTAT, and Platescan).
- Future technologies (drones, cameras, etc.)

GROWING DEMANDS FOR SERVICE MET WITH EFFICIENCY

As demands for service have increased dramatically in the past few decades, police have been quietly evolving to deal with the changes. The population of the United States and its major metropolitan areas has grown rapidly since the 1950s, doubling from approximately 150 million in 1950 to over 300 million in 2010. The population, especially in metropolitan areas, is projected to continue to grow rapidly, in line with rapid growth in the overall world population. The expansion of police, however, has not kept up with this pace while demand for services continues to increase.

More people living in denser areas means more conflicts, as discussed before by Durkheim, in which different cultural norms clash. The breakdown of information social controls where residents are unable or unwilling to settle disputes, results in greater reliance on formal forms of social control and to more calls to the police for services. These disputes can range from something as simple as ongoing disputes between neighbors to handling traffic incidents and more criminal incidents, such as burglaries and thefts.

For local police, increases in population density and calls for service means officers must do more with the same resources. This is evident from the rapid increase in the police/citizen ratio, especially in large urban areas. The LAPD, for instance, is particularly impacted by this ratio, which currently has a citizen to police ratio of 426:1. The NYPD, by comparison, has a lower ratio of 228:1. According to the FBI, large cities such as New York, Philadelphia, and Baltimore, had approximately forty officers per 10,000 citizens in 2016. The reality for today's officers is that they are far outnumbered by residents who require policing services, with that trend continuing into the foreseeable future.

Police departments have adopted crime control strategies and technologies to make each officer more efficient, to compensate for the increasingly large ratio of citizens to police personnel. Historically, for example, police adaptation of two-way radios coupled with police cruisers allowed fewer officers to cover large areas, relative to walking beats during the days of the night watchman. 9-1-1 emergency call systems have meant faster response times to calls for service that satisfy citizens' needs, which minimizes the relevancy of having more officers. In addition, the use of helicopters has dramatically increased the capacity of police to rapidly respond to calls of service.

The use of crime control technologies and strategies, however, has not necessarily translated to direct reduction in crime. According to police researcher George Kelling, technologies that have expanded the capacity of policing, such as preventative patrol, rapid call response, team policing, and investigations technologies has failed to achieve crime reduction goals set in the 1970s.[3] In fact, these technologies have served to exacerbate strained police/citizen relations, as discussed throughout this book. Nevertheless, police, out of necessity, have adopted crime control technologies at a rapid pace to compensate for limitations in personnel and budgetary resources.

The information age of digital information, networked computer technology, and new forms of media, has not only accelerated police adoption of crime control technologies but shifted the paradigm of policing. Police have realized the power of information and developed tools to collect, manage, and process that data. However, this process of information gathering and processing has fundamentally altered the role of officers who are now required to interpret and use that information. The new police officer is required to possess the technical skills and knowledge to navigate this new role, yet face hazards and concerns that threaten to further strain police-community relations.

THE INFORMATION AGE

The information age is a concept coined by sociologist Manuel Castells in the 1960s and 1970s, and revised in the 1990s, in his seminal three-volume trilogy of books called *The Information Age: Economy, Society, and Culture*.[4,5,6] Castells' work describes the transformation of society driven by networked information. He describes three elements that produce a new order in what he calls "network society:"

1. The information technology revolution
2. The economic crisis of capitalism and communism related to Marx
3. The proliferation of social movements, such as the feminist movement

The network society is the synthesis of these three processes. The network society is the result of a transformative process that encompasses social and economic life. Interlinked networks which include networks of production, distribution, financial circulation, power, information, communication, images, and experience, when taken together, is the basis of globalization and **informationalism**.

The power of interlinked social networks can be empowering or disempowering depending on access to the networks. Groups that may be excluded from these new social networks find themselves at a large disadvantage politically, economically, and socially. This exclusion is called the "**digital divide**," a dichotomy between groups that have access, and therefore power, to networked information and communications.[7] Groups that have access to and can manipulate information can gain power in the information age.

The police are one of these groups that have made efforts to redefine themselves based on information. The ability to access, manipulate, and use information has become the great equalizer that police have used to compensate for insatiable demands for service, while facing budgetary constraints that limit growth. This use of information has significant ramifications for officers who are tasked directly with information collection, manipulation, and application.

POLICING RISK AND OFFICERS AS "KNOWLEDGE WORKERS"

Police have become an institution that deal with risk in the information age. To minimize the dangers that the police organization confronts daily, officers must make calculated risks based on as much information as possible. This requires the organization to collect as much information as possible. The more information the organization possesses, the more they can minimize danger.

The function of information accumulation is not unique, but rather similar to other institutions that manage this risk. For example, insurance companies assess prices and clients based on the level of risk, and act accordingly. Similarly, financial institutions make loans based on an assessment of risk, using credit scores based on as much information as possible. Police today are no different. Akin to military units preparing for battle by scouting the enemy and battlefield, police departments and agencies have become risk-management institutions that primarily function to collect information and assess degrees of danger.

The risk that police must manage is based on real and perceived notions of danger that is inherent in police patrol work. Patrol work was considered a very labor- and capital-intensive part of the occupation. Whereas police traditionally only required the traditional firearm, baton, handcuffs, and whistle, and other basic equipment, modern police officers are equipped with an array of crime-fighting technologies, ranging from radio-equipped cars to networked computers.

Criminologist Benoît Dupont described three major changes that have occurred in policing technology: (1) widespread mechanization of police transportation, (2) telephone and radio networks, and (3) computer aided dispatch, where operators do not even need the caller to give an address.[8] These technologies have produced maximum efficiency of police services and more importantly, used them in a manner that minimizes the dangers of the job through better risk management.

The most important aspect of managing risk to minimizing the dangers of the job is information gathering. Sociologists Kevin Ericson and Richard Haggerty discussed the transformation of police.[9] The researchers defined risk as any "external danger," which includes natural disasters, technological catastrophes, or threatening behavior by any person or persons. They examined the social institutions that manage these risk communication systems—or processes and logics (rules, formats, and technologies) for managing these dangers. Police are an institution that claims expertise pertaining to a given risk and the need for knowledge about that risk shapes police behavior. In other words, police have shifted their function primarily to gain knowledge about the risks and dangers that are relevant to their work.

Ericson and Haggerty assert that police have become primarily "**knowledge workers**" whose primary purpose is to gather raw data, process information, and interpret that information. Police have the need to "risk profile" any event they may encounter. Specifically, the more knowledge a police agency has of any given situation or subject, the better it can allocate resources to deal with it. Police also produce and distribute information for various institutions that may use this knowledge to better manage their own risks. Accordingly, as Ericson and Haggerty put it, "As new risk management needs arise, institutions develop new ways of categorizing, classifying, thinking, and acting that demand police participation."

Consequently, police have become obsessed with information gathering. Police are engaged in a perpetual quest to produce certainty in a world that is uncertain and potentially dangerous. As a result, police have incorporated more information technologies, such as networked computers in police vehicles that give officers information at their fingertips, before an encounter with any persons. The standard operating procedure for virtually every patrol officer today when pulling over a car is to take time to pull up information on the vehicle to warn the officer of any potential danger. For example, if the officer finds outstanding felony warrants on the registered owner after running the license plate of a vehicle he or she just stopped, the officer processes that information and minimizes potential danger by calling for backup before approaching the vehicle very cautiously.

After each encounter, whether it was eventful or not, more raw data is entered into the system for future use. According to Ericson and Haggerty, this ability to store and retrieve information has empowered officers, who are "equipped with sophisticated surveillance technology and having access to knowledge about the suspect may reduce their own uncertainty." The authors explain the new role of policing in what they call **surveillance society**:

The emphasis on surveillance redirects the law, the police, and risk institutions to continually invent new ways of accessing and disturbing knowledge. The main task of police is to 'front load' the system with relevant knowledge that can later be sorted and distributed to interested institutional audiences.

One can clearly see the role that information technology has on police. When one is stopped in a routine traffic stop, the police immediately access their MDTs with the vehicle license plate information. This in turn produces a screen with information that the officer can view, process, and act on accordingly. The information on the screen is used as a risk assessment of the individual by the knowledge worker (police officer). This stranger, in which prior to using the MDT police had no knowledge of, put police in a power deficit. With this information, however, police can approach the vehicle with at least some knowledge, thus reducing danger by managing risk, and moreover, asserting power and dominance. Once the encounter is completed, new information is recorded into the system for future reference by other officers and agencies. This perpetual recording of data creates a more complete database of risk knowledge.

When taken collectively at the societal level, this constant and unending accumulation has larger social and privacy implications. Some scholars have dubbed this phenomenon surveillance society, with implications of a slippery slope that can lead toward an Orwellian dystopian hegemonic surveillance society described in the classic novel *1984*.[10]

SURVEILLANCE SOCIETY

The most important function in policing the information age is gathering information. This information is recorded through officer encounters and interactions with the public as well as previous incidents that require police action. Supplementing this data gathering method is the use of surveillance. As a practical matter, it further increases police efficiency in the face of a growing population and demands for service. Like the adoption of police cars with two-way radios, police coverage of areas can be almost ubiquitous without the need for a physical presence.

The city of London, England, for example, is famous for its use of closed-circuit television (CCTV) video surveillance in one of the most surveilled countries on the planet. The city employs its Police Public Space Surveillance Camera System that feeds into police control rooms where they are monitored by police officers and department staff, in virtually all public spaces in the city. These cameras are supplemented by the countless privately operated surveillance cameras in the country. In 2015, the city of London was given the power to access these private CCTV cameras from consenting shops and businesses.

While the city and police department tout the system's effectiveness in deterring crime and apprehending suspects, it has often been criticized. First, the ubiquity of being under constant surveillance has been described as creating a "Big Brother" effect, referencing Orwell's *1984* novel slogan, "Big Brother is watching you," in Oceania, the fictional continent or state that encompasses the Americas under dictatorship rule.[11] In his novel, Orwell paints a picture of a **panoptic society**, a reference to Jeremy Bentham's panopticon prison design where individuals placed in solitary confinement are subjected to the uncertainty of constant surveillance, which results in self-surveillance. Under such surveillance conditions, absolute power is exercised over society in very subtle and "invisible" ways. Citizens obey rules and are unaware of the conditions of their own imprisonment. Ultimately, personal freedoms and rights are eroded by censorship, and actions are taken in the name of vague ideas, such as public safety and national security.

Second, the effectiveness of CCTV has come into question. The London Metropolitan Police disclosed that each year less than one crime is solved per every 1,000 CCTV cameras, after an internal report was released under freedom of information law request.[12] This is problematic given the over one million cameras deployed in London, according to the same 2009 report. Despite police claims of CCTV cameras being instrumental in solving crimes, the report's release drew sharp public criticism for high operational costs and for creating a surveillance state without actually making citizens any safer. Criminologist Peter Fussey argued that there is little evidence to show any real reduction in crime and terrorism, but the constant monitoring of its citizens comes at a high social cost of personal freedom and privacy.[13]

The proliferation and reliance on CCTVs creates a slippery slope for further erosion of privacy. More recently, the phenomenon of combining crowdsourcing with CCTV, which allows for public access to streams and footage to assist in crime-fighting, has furthered broad social concerns of privacy.[14] Not surprisingly, surveillance has drawn plenty of public attention in recent years in the United States.

In 2013, former NSA contractor Edward Snowden drew international attention to US surveillance and information gathering when he leaked top-secret National Security Agency documents that revealed the surveillance capabilities of the United States. US citizens and foreign governments were shocked at the extent to which the United States had been gathering information via wire taps, interception of electronic communications, and the ability to access all Internet history and other private information. The NSA's global surveillance program showed the NSA mass-harvesting millions of email messages, cell phone locations and conversations, and even online video games.

One program that was brought to light by Snowden is **PRISM**, an electronic data mining program launched in 2007. PRISM collects mass data and mines these Internet data for suspicious activities related to terrorism. Electronic communications, both unencrypted and encrypted, could be collected and analyzed by the NSA, including communications using popular web services by companies such as Google, Apple, Microsoft, and Yahoo. Furthermore, the NSA has been working with British and other international counterparts to achieve an expanded surveillance capacity.

Policing strategies in the past few decades have become increasingly invasive under the justification of national security, terrorism, and public safety. These justifications and patterned responses drive a cycle: police organizations use more resources for surveillance and other crime control technologies—if nothing happens, it justifies its effectiveness and more resources, but if something happens, it also justifies more resources. Some may refer to this is *Pyrrhic Defeat Theory*, which describes a situation where the criminal justice system only fights crime to the degree that it does not get out of hand, which highlights the difficulties while never actually reducing or eliminating crime.[15] This losing battle ultimately justifies continued use of resources and unending collection of data.

The collection of information is often prioritized by police. Since the 1990s, large police departments have gauged their performance based on crime statistics. Specifically, the use of data management tools referred to as CompStat (*COMP*uter *STAT*istics or *COMP*arative *STAT*istics) has drawn criticism that police over-rely on inaccurate measures of crime.

COMPSTAT

The CompStat database system uses geographic information systems (GIS) technology to map crime and "**hot spots**" where police management teams meet regularly to analyze and discuss the data, which is then used to strategically deploy officers and resources to address the area of concern. GIS technology is essentially the modern-day equivalent of push-pin crime mapping, in which police used colored pins on a physical map to show patterns of crime. However, with GIS software, trends and patterns of crimes can be augmented with detailed graphs and statistics, allowing police to act as knowledge workers.

According to the BJS, four core components of CompStat include:[16]

1. Timely and accurate information or intelligence
2. Rapid deployment of resources
3. Effective tactics
4. Relentless follow-up

Accordingly, it is described as a "strategic problem solving" ideology that efficiently manages and deploys resources. Its effectiveness was put to the test in the early 1990s in New York City, during the tenure of NYPD transit police chief William Bratton under Mayor Rudy Giuliani. Chief Bratton reoriented the police to focus on crime prevention using CompStat by assigning precinct commanders to employ strategies in reducing crime through working with their communities. According to the US DOJ Bureau of Justice Assistance, these commanders implementing three fundamental changes:

1. *Information sharing* between divisions
2. Commanders were given more discretion and authority in *decision making*
3. A change in the *organizational culture* which allowed for creativity, flexibility, and equipment to manage risk

With virtually all policing technologies, CompStat is not without critics. Economist Steven Levitt explains that the crime drop in the 1990s was not impacted using CompStat and similar programs.[17] Among the different factors, he points to are the integration of the New York transit police with the NYPD; hiring of more and better qualified officers; clearing a backlog of 50,000 unserved warrants; 500,000 new jobs created during the economic boom; and a shift from the crack cocaine epidemic to a much less violent marijuana market.

Perhaps one of the biggest criticisms of CompStat is the over-reliance on crime statistics as a measure of performance. Under the CompStat model, police supervisors and managers meet regularly to present data in their areas of operation. These supervisors are held accountable for being knowledgeable about and affecting crime rates in their assigned areas. These meetings focus too much on statistics, without critical thinking and open dialogues for discussion. Instead, commanders are under immense pressure to perform, which can ultimately shift the focus on manipulating statistics through changes in policing activities, such as overlooking certain crimes while channeling resources to others.

The reliance on CompStat was dramatized in the critically acclaimed HBO television series, *The Wire*, to show the systematic dysfunction of police. In the series, Baltimore Police commanders were pressured by their superiors to reduce murder rates and other metrics of crime by a certain percentage or face severe consequences. Commanders would then pressure lower supervisors and officers to "juke" the statistics by ignoring varieties of crimes, including serious felonies, to artificially generate positive progress to the public, such as reducing crime in certain areas. This scenario was played out in real life by NYPD officer Adrian Schoolcraft, who in 2008 blew the whistle on the department for having arrest quotas, underreporting, and other statistical manipulations ordered by supervisors.

AUTOMATED LICENSE PLATE RECOGNITION SYSTEMS

Automated license plate recognition (ALPR) systems, commonly referred to by the ALPR California company, PlateScan, is another controversial technology that police have deployed in the information age. These automatic license plate recognition systems mounted on patrol vehicles are increasingly deployed by police departments to assist officers in actively looking for violations, such as stolen vehicles and warrants. These systems scan multiple license plates simultaneously, scanning and storing photographed information and instantly matching them with plates associated with hot vehicles stored on multiple databases. Prior to this technology, officers had to manually enter license plates into their MDTs, and prior to that, radio in to dispatchers. From an efficiency standpoint ALPR technology makes sense, it saves time, and is highly accurate in identifying wanted vehicles. Moreover, it further serves officers' roles as knowledge workers. However, like many policing technologies, it does not come without controversy.

The ACLU contends that these broad technologies violate privacy by tracking everyone in a vehicle, and constitute mass surveillance.[18] They argue that the systems are configured to store photos of drivers, time, and date of all vehicles encountered for a period. More recently, law enforcement agencies have begun buying access to large private databases. These private companies collect vehicle information from sources such as tow truck drivers and repossession agents or "repo men."

The efficiency of data collection is staggering. The largest database company, California-based Vigilant, touts 3,000 client agencies, with over 30,000 law enforcement subscribers to its LEARN database. The firm can collect 1,600 plates every hour from each vehicle and has discretely collected and permanently stored 80 million plates monthly, with an estimated 2.2 billion license plates from the company's inception in 2007, to 2016.[19]

The lack of oversight and laws governing these companies raises concern for civil rights groups and lawmakers, who point out potential abuse. For instance, public agencies usually have data retention policies that limit the amount of time information is stored, while many private companies, like Vigilant, store the information indefinitely. The ACLU argued that police should obtain a warrant to access private databases. License plate information is captured and geotagged, which can potentially be used to establish a detailed pattern of a person's behavior.

While Vigilant and similar companies argue that this information is merely a snapshot of a moment instead of continual tracking, such as GPS technologies. However, the Supreme Court has noted that GPS data collection "at a moment in time," as argued by Vigilant, with over 2 billion data points, is virtually equivalent and equally as intrusive. Privacy concerns were also raised with non-police matters. For instance, vehicles could be tagged in locations with expectations of privacy, such as parked in medical and law offices. Further research that examines the legal and social ramifications of this technology is needed.

CROWDSOURCING: CITIZENS AS POLICING AGENTS

Part of the future of policing may be a greater reliance on partnerships. These partnerships range from everyday citizens to corporations. According to the *Nodal Governance* theoretical framework, a new model of policing has emerged wherein each group is considered a security stakeholder with unique assets they can bring to the table.[20] Police act as only one, albeit very central, security actor in a non-hierarchical security network. By collaborating resources (security capital) and mentalities, policing can be more robust and efficient—something that is increasingly necessary in the information age. The key to success is police willingness to share responsibilities with non-police entities, something that is extremely difficult when one considers the "us versus them" cynicism that is prevalent in the police subculture.

One area that is gaining popularity is the use of citizens as policing agents. Some researchers contend that citizen groups on the Internet are taking it upon themselves to assist in justice matters. Some have looked at online groups that dealt with catching online child predators, finding that there are possible resources and collaborations between citizens and police.[21] However, cultural and structural impediments, such as legal liability, prevent full collaborations from occurring regularly.

The limited use of citizens by police has prompted the phenomenon of crowdsourced crime fighting by public communities. Internet crowdsourcing justice was first documented in 2006 in China.[22] A video of a woman stomping a kitten to death using her stiletto heels went viral and outraged Internet users. When police were unwilling to act, online communities quickly analyzed the video, identified the woman living in a small province, and got her fired from her nursing job, in addition to harshly shaming her. This mobilization of resources became known in China as the "human-flesh search engine," or *renrou sousuo yinqing*.

Today, the emerging field of crowdsourcing criminology has begun looking at the growing popularity crowdsourced crime-fighting and the implications for the present and future of policing, including the functional relationship between police and online groups. Whether police agencies accept or reject direct help from the public, it will continue to organically form from various online communities.

The potential for crowdsourcing is tremendous. During the Boston Marathon bombing in 2013, for example, social media and other online communities such as Reddit spontaneously formed topical groups that shared and scoured photos and surveillance videos to find clues to help police.[23] The large body of diverse users with unique esoteric knowledge of virtually every subject matter was able to identify baseball caps, pressure cooker models, and other factors that they shared with law enforcement.

Crowdsourcing police work is not without controversy and hazards to police. While Reddit users were able to come together to share knowledge and resources, such as serving as a hub of communications, and many users even offered free transportation and pizzas to stranded Bostonians, they ultimately made a huge mistake by identifying the wrong person. Operating without legal bounds and incomplete information, the Reddit community misidentified Sunil Tripathi, a missing twenty-two-year-old, and seventeen-year-old Salah Barhoun. Consequently, the families of both men were harassed and threatened by Internet users. The site later officially apologized when the real Boston bombers, Dzhokhar and Tamerlan Tsarnaev, were identified by police, but not without both men being featured on the front page of the *New York Post* as wanted "bag men," in reference to them carrying backpacks.

Police tend to avoid direct assistance from Internet sleuths for legal and practical reasons. The common thread among the men falsely identified by Internet users was that they were of similar racial backgrounds. The British magazine *New Statesman* described the crowdsourcing activity as a "racist Where's Wally."[24] Furthermore, police do not typically share or reciprocate active investigative information back to members of the public. Finally, legal considerations of essentially deputizing members of the public, who have not been trained in evidentiary guidelines to participate in active investigations, can put departments and officers at risk for litigation.

Without the public's direct help with investigations, it is up to police officers as knowledge workers to decipher the endless streams of information and use it daily. This requires the new breed of officer to not only be street savvy, but well educated. However, how much does education impact an officer's ability?

EDUCATION AND POLICE:

Going back to the beginnings of police reform and August Vollmer's original vision of the police officer as the highly educated, autonomous crime fighter is still a goal that is largely unmet. This goal was underscored as police sought the level of prestige and pay of scientists, physicians, and other professionals during the reform era. Today, the officer as a knowledge worker in the information age increasingly requires certain levels of education. A 2013 FBI study revealed that nearly half (48 percent) of police officers surveyed possessed a bachelor's degree, a statistic higher than the national average of approximately 30 percent.[25] The trend among most police departments is pushing toward this vision, with some departments requiring bachelor's degree.

However, despite the desire for a highly educated workforce, a seemingly uncontroversial issue, many have begun questioning whether a college education makes a better cop. FBI researchers contend that the trends of higher tuition costs, lower direct payoff for education, and income stagnation for police officers have made a college degree a "luxury" that officers, especially in smaller towns and rural areas, cannot afford.[26] Moreover, respondents who held bachelor's degrees mostly stated that their college education positively affected their work performance, but they were unable to specify how and why. Perhaps one of the biggest criticisms of the college educated officer is the boredom of the job, which often leads to costly higher attrition rates.

Most officers who seek a bachelor's degree do it to be more competitive with promotion opportunities. The FBI study found that half of the respondents sought a degree for further career advancement, with 21 percent stating personal achievement. The reality remains that an officer going up for promotion has nearly a 50 percent chance in most places of being in competition with someone with a degree. Despite these practical and personal reasons for education, there is evidence that college-educated officers are qualitatively different than non-degree officers.

Researchers have noted that officer education directly affects arrest and use of force. Criminologists Jason Rydberg and William Terrill examined three factors related to police discretion: arrest, search, and use of force in relation to education.[27] The researchers noted that while arrest and search were not affected by the officer's level of education, college educated officers tended to use less force and were overall more effective communicators and used to being problem-solvers and debaters of issues.

An article published in the popular police site and forum PoliceOne, touted a laundry list of benefits of higher education:[28]

- Better skilled in independent decision-making and problem-solving
- Fewer on-the-job injuries and assaults
- More proficient in technology
- Less likely to be involved in unethical behavior
- Less likely to use force as the first response
- Less use of sick time (work ethic and seeing the big picture)
- Greater acceptance of minorities (diversity and cultural awareness)

- Decrease in dogmatism, authoritarianism, rigidity and conservatism
- Improved communication skills (oral and written)
- Better adapted to retirement and second-career opportunities

The article further cited a study by Rebecca Paynich showing college-educated officers were more likely to:[29]

- Better understand policing and the criminal justice system
- Better comprehend civil rights issues from multiple perspectives
- Adapt better to organizational change
- Have fewer administrative and personnel problems

Moreover, college-educated police tend to receive fewer citizen complaints, higher promotions, and better minority recruitment.

SUMMARY

Police have once again evolved from community cops to knowledge workers whose primary function is to reduce risk by collecting, storing, and processing information gathered on the job. While this has increased the efficiency of police in the face of greater demands for service while serving increasingly larger populations, it has societal ramifications. There is pressure to place society at greater levels of scrutiny and surveillance, something that has drawn considerable attention and controversy in light of the NSA-Snowden whistleblowing incident in 2013. This has of course sparked debate on the limits of government and law enforcement, who many fear has created an Orwellian dystopian society described in *1984*.

In the new era of police as knowledge workers that collect, decipher, and apply endless streams of information, new challenges arise. Police departments find themselves balancing data collection with privacy concerns, especially with incorporating new networking technologies, such as ALPR. In addition, they must contend with growing public demands for service that when unmet, can fuel online vigilante activities in the form of crowdsourcing.

These added responsibilities often require a new type of officer who is tech-savvy and perhaps more educated than previous generations. This brings up questions about whether it is necessary to have a college education in an environment where it may not make fiscal and practical sense. However, researchers and many police organizations themselves, have found more reasons why education is beneficial, perhaps coming full circle to completing August Vollmer's original vision of the autonomous, well-educated, scientific crime-fighter who is a skilled communicator and jack-of-all-trades.

NOTES

1. George L. Kelling and James Q. Wilson, "Broken Windows: The Police and Neighborhood Safety," *The Atlantic*, March 1, 1982, http://www.theatlantic.com/magazine/archive/1982/03/broken-windows/304465/.

2. Hope Corman and Naci Mocan, "Carrots, Sticks, and Broken Windows," *The National Bureau of Economic Research*, July 2002, http://www.nber.org/papers/w9061.

3. George L. Kelling, "Police Field Services and Crime: The Presumed Effects of Capacity," *Crime and Delinquency* 24, no. 2 (1978): 173–184. doi: 10.1177/001112877802400203.

4. Manuel Castells, *The Rise of the Network Society, the Information Age: Economy, Society and Culture*, vol. I. (Oxford: Blackwell, 1996).

5. Manuel Castells, *The Power of Identity, the Information Age: Economy, Society, and Culture*, vol. II (Oxford: Wiley-Blackwell, 2010).

6. Manuel Castells, *End of Millennium, the Information Age: Economy, Society and Culture*, vol. III (Oxford: Blackwell, 1998).

7. Pippa Norris, *Digital Divide: Civic Engagement, Information Poverty and the Internet World-Wide* (Cambridge: Cambridge University Press, 2001).

8. Benoit Dupont, "Policing in the Information Age: Technological Errors of the Past in Perspective," in *Policing the Lucky Country* (Sydney: The Federation Press, 2001).

9. Richard V. Ericson and Kevin D. Haggerty, *Policing the Risk Society* (Toronto: University of Toronto Press, 1997).

10. George Orwell, *1984* (New York: Harcourt, 1949).

11. Orwell, *1984*.

12. Christopher Hope, "1,000 CCTV Cameras to Solve Just One Crime, Met Police Admits," *The Telegraph*, August 25, 2009, https://www.telegraph.co.uk/news/uknews/crime/6082530/1000-CCTV-cameras-to-solve-just-one-crime-Met-Police-admits.html.

13. Pete Fussey, "Beyond Liberty, Beyond Security: The Politics of Public Surveillance," *British Politics* 3 (2008): 120–135. doi: 10.1057/palgrave.bp.4200082.

14. Daniel Trottier, "Crowdsourcing CCTV Surveillance on the Internet," *Information, Communication and Society* 17, no 5 (2012): 609–626. doi: 10.1080/1369118X.2013.808359.

15. Jeffrey Reiman and Paul Leighton, *The Rich Get Richer and the Poor Get Prison: Ideology, Class, and Criminal Justice*, 11th ed. (Upper Saddle River: Pearson, 2016).

16. "CompStat: Its Origins, Evolution, and Future in Law Enforcement Agencies," Bureau of Justice Assistance. Police Executive Research Forum, 2013, https://www.bja.gov/publications/perf-compstat.pdf.

17. Steven D. Levitt, "Understanding why Crime Fell in the 1990s: Four Factors that Explain the Decline and Six that Do Not," *Journal of Economic Perspectives* 18, no. 1 (2004): 163–190.

18. Tami Abdollah, "Police Buying Access to Huge, Private License-Plate Scan Databases," *Associated Press*, October 2, 2015, https://www.pressherald.com/2015/10/07/police-buying-access-to-huge-private-license-plate-scan-databases/.

19. Conor Friedersdorf, "An Unprecedented Threat to Privacy," *The Atlantic*, January 27, 2016, https://www.theatlantic.com/politics/archive/2016/01/vigilant-solutions-surveillance/427047/.

20. Scott Burris, Peter Drahos, and Clifford Shearing, "Nodal Governance," *Australian Journal of Legal Philosophy* 30 (2005): 30–58.

21. Laura Huey, Johnny Nhan, and Ryan Broll, "'Uppity Civilians' and 'Cyber-Vigilantes': The Role of the General Public in Policing Cyber-Crime," *Criminology and Criminal Justice* 13, no. 1 (2013): 81–97. doi: 10.1177/1748895812448086.

22. Tom Downey, "China's Cyberposse," *The New York Times*, March 3, 2010, https://www.nytimes.com/2010/03/07/magazine/07Human-t.html.

23. Johnny Nhan, Laura Huey, and Ryan Broll, "Digilantism: An Analysis of Crowdsourcing and the Boston Marathon Bombings," *British Journal of Criminology* 57, no. 2 (2015): 341–361. doi:10.1093/bjc/azv118.

24. Alex Hern, "4Chan Plays Racist Where's Wally to Find the Boston Bomber," *New Statesman*, April 18, 2013, https://www.newstatesman.com/world-affairs/2013/04/4chan-plays-racist-wheres-wally-find-boston-bomber.

25. Susan Hilal and James Densley, "Higher Education and Local Law Enforcement," *FBI Law Enforcement Bulletin,* 2013, https://leb.fbi.gov/articles/featured-articles/higher-education-and-local-law-enforcement.

26. "Crime in the United States Police Employee Data," Federal Bureau of Investigation, 2016, https://ucr.fbi.gov/crime-in-the-u.s/2016/crime-in-the-u.s.-2016/topic-pages/police-employees.

27. Jason Rydberg and William Terrill, "The Effect of Higher Education on Police Behavior," *Police Quarterly* 13, no. 1 (2010): 92–120. doi: 10.1177/1098611109357325.

28. Rick Michelson, "Why Cops Should Pursue Higher Education," *PoliceOne*, March 8, 2016, https://www.policeone.com/police-jobs-and-careers/articles/153751006-Why-cops-should-pursue-higher-education/.

29. Rebecca L. Paynich, "The Impact of a College-Educated Police Force: A Review of the Literature," February 2009, https://www.masschiefs.org/files-downloads/hot-topics/96-the-impact-of-higher-education-in-law-enforcement-feb-2009-and-summarypdf/file.

Glossary

Actus reus: Latin legal term meaning the guilty act.

Age of Enlightenment: A period of time during the seventeenth and eighteenth century in Europe that was considered a social and cultural renaissance that stressed modern concepts, such as free thought, free will, and individualism that serve as a foundation for many of the core principles of our criminal justice and legal system.

Anomie: Term coined by French sociologist Emile Durkheim to describe a state of "normlessness" that often occurred during times of social turmoil when informal social controls break down.

Auburn system: Incarceration philosophy based on principles of austerity and manual prison labor with rehabilitation achieved through learned discipline.

Automated license plate recognition: Automatic license plate recognition systems mounted on patrol vehicles increasingly deployed by police departments to assist officers in actively looking for violations, such as stolen vehicles and warrants.

Badge bunnies: A pejorative term for women who are looking to date cops and can be seen hanging out around police stations hoping to score an officer.

Blue brotherhood: Term often used to describe the strong family-like bond and trust among police officers.

Blue flame syndrome: A term used to describe enthusiastic rookies who get teased by their veteran peers for excessive bravado and standing out while off-duty by broadcasting their police identity instead of blending in.

Blue wall of silence: Term used to describe a purported unwritten code or norm where officers do no report a fellow officer's mistakes, misconduct, or criminal activity.

"Boots": Informal term used to describe rookie police officers.

Broken windows theory: Concept developed by George Kelling and James Q. Wilson in the 1980s based on the metaphor of broken windows as signs for abandonment, neglect, and the lack of guardianship. If left unfixed, a broken window signals to potential criminals that an area is not under surveillance and therefore would be an acceptable place to commit crime, such as dealing drugs.

Bureaucracy: Administrative systems that organize human activity and maintain order using a rules-based hierarchical structure that distributes power among its members.

Brass: Informal term for management or supervisory officers, often starting at the lieutenant level and above.

Burnout: A psychological term used to describe the results of prolonged exposure to stress, which is a breakdown of positive coping mechanisms that results in cynicism, depression, and other negative manifestations.

Clearance rate: Crime statistic measured in by the FBI's Uniform Crime Report that is the ratio of crimes that have been "cleared," (arrests have been made and legal paperwork forwarded for prosecution) to the total number of crimes reported.

Collective efficacy: The ability of a community, such as a neighborhood, to defend itself against, or resist crime and disorder.

Command presence: A verbal and nonverbal conveyance of authority, as a deterrent for violence.

Community policing: A paradigm and approach to policing that focuses on rebuilding police-community relations through a proactive, problem-solving approach that focuses on the causes of crime and disorder.

CompStat: *COMP*uter *STAT*istics or *COMP*arative *STAT*istics data tracking program used by police management on crime data and geographic location.

Corporate veil: Illegal activities that are masked behind the complex compartmentalized relationships and diffused responsibilities of the organization.

Criminal justice funnel: Informal term used to describe the discrepancy between large number of criminal acts committed and relatively few people incarcerated.

Crowdsourcing: The collective mobilization of a large group for a common goal.

CSI effect: Exaggerated abilities by crime scene investigators and forensic scientists to solve crimes accurately and quickly, as a referenced in the hit television series *CSI: Crime Scene Investigation* that routinely solves cases neatly and definitively through physical evidence, and all within a short amount of time.

Cultural transmission: The continuance of norms, customs, and values through storytelling and other forms of communication from previous generations to the next.

Daubert standard: Legal standard since 1993 for the admission of scientific evidence in a courtroom that must be considered by a judge to be derived from the scientific method based on empirical testing, falsifiable, and peer reviewed in a publication.

Deinstitutionalization: The process of replacing large monolithic psychiatric institutions with smaller, tailored community mental health centers to take their place.

Detached concern: The extreme mental oscillation between professionalism and compassion, that contributes to officer burnout.

Digital divide: A dichotomy between groups that have access, and therefore power, to networked information and communications.

Direct supervision: Incarceration philosophy based on detention officers proactively engaging with inmates and building rapport to detect tensions and prevent major issues that may lead to violence.

Dirty Harry problem: Moral dilemma that occurs when morally good ends are achieved with morally dirty means as depicted in the Hollywood *Dirty Harry*, where Clint Eastwood's character, Officer Harry Callahan, tortures a suspect and is justified under exigent circumstances.

Discriminatory omission: Withholding or not providing adequate police services based on racial or other forms of discrimination.

Double oppression: Gender discrimination compounded by racial discrimination faced by women of color.

Doxing/doxxing: The unauthorized public disclosure of personal information, such as home address.

"Driving while Black": Informal term used to describe the experience of African Americans while driving where they are more likely to be targeted by police and harassed for small infractions.

Egoistic suicide: Suicide based on the idea that a person no longer feels that they are part of society.

Emotional intelligence: The ability to understand, interpret, and manage self-emotions and the emotions of others.

Ethnographical research: A form of qualitative research based on empirical data from interviews, observations, and other non-numerically quantified or calculated data that looks in-depth at groups and cultures in their own social environments.

External control: The ability of a third party or society to get a person or group of people who have violated social norms, rules, or laws, to re-conform to these expectations of behavior.

False negative: In a polygraph examination, it is failing to detect untruthful individuals.

False positive: In a polygraph examination, it is the result that wrongly identifies something being truthful as lying.

Federalism: The dual system of government defined by the Constitution that grants power to both the federal government and state governments.

Ferguson effect: Phenomenon when crime rates rise from public agitation of the culmination of negative stories of police misconduct, derived from the police shooting of Michael Brown in Ferguson, Misouri.

Field training: A training period immediately after the academy when a new officer is assigned a field training officers (FTO) whose primary role is to further educate the new officer while evaluating officer performance and competency in a real-world setting.

Field training officers: Police training officers that supervise, evaluate, and train probationary rookie officers in a real-world setting.

Formal control: Efforts to get a person or group of people who have violated social norms, rules, or laws, to reconform to these expectations of behavior by state actors, such as police.

Formal social control: Use of official state-sanctioned authority, such as police, to maintain order and enforce rules in a given society.

Free zones: Legal incentives for crime created when minimum thresholds do not reach the level of prosecution that result in criminals free to operate with impunity.

Full enforcement of the law: Nondiscretionary arrest of all crimes.

"G-Men": Informal term used to describe FBI director J. Edgar Hoover's agents who were known as "government men."

Group cynicism: Part of the police subculture where shared dangers and experiences create mistrust towards individuals and groups who are not law enforcement, as characterized by an "us versus them" mentality.

Guardian mentality: Mindset that prioritizes service as part of community policing over strictly crime fighting that was emphasized under the more traditional FTO-based San Jose model of field training.

Heterogeneity: Diverse

Hot spots: Concentrated areas of crime.

Implicit bias: Automatic assumptions by persons or groups who are not bigoted that often subconsciously manifest in biased actions without prejudicial intent.

Index crimes: Eight categories of crime measured by the FBI that include willful homicide, forcible rape, robbery, burglary, aggravated assault, larceny over $50, motor vehicle theft, and arson, used in the annual Uniform Crime Report.

Informal control: Efforts to get a person or group of people who have violated social norms, rules, or laws, to reconform to these expectations of behavior by non-state actors.

Informal social control: Use of non-official state authority, such as family, friends, and organizations, to maintain order and enforce rules in a given society.

Information age: New era of society based on changes in computer technology, digital information, and new media.

Informationalism: Technological paradigm that succeeds industrialization focused on human progress through technological determinism.

Insane asylum: Term used to describe early nineteenth century psychiatric hospitals that were closed by the 1970s when operating methods became harshly criticized.

Institutional racism: A subtle form of racism that is not reflected in official policies and procedures but exists in the culmination of police actions that produce disparities.

Internal control: The ability of a person to control themselves through a process of internalizing society's norms.

Internet protocol "IP" address: Unique code that links a physical place to cyberspace, akin to a telephone number with area code.

Knowledge workers: Police in the information age whose primary function is to gather raw data, process information, and interpret that information.

Litmus test: Elimination test where passage means continuance of training and failure means removal from candidacy based on both decision-making and physical performance in the police academy.

Management cop culture: A culture among high ranking management and supervisory officers based on loyalty to their circle and political associations rather than to line officers.

Mens rea: Latin legal term meaning the guilty mind, or intent.

Minnesota Multiphasic Personality Inventory (MMPI): Psychological test administered to most police applicants, that uses different clinical subscales to measure and assess psychopathology and personality.

Moral panic: The process of creating widespread unreasonable fear of an issue or group by certain groups, media, or individuals.

Night watchmen: Early form of police who were informal, untrained peacekeepers who were later criticized for being inept and corrupt.

Order maintenance: A primary function of police that includes activities that do not involve criminal matters, such as traffic duties.

Panacea: A universal solution or "cure-all" for problems or difficulties, adopted from a term used in medicine with diseases.

Panoptic society: A reference to Jeremy Bentham's panopticon prison design where individuals placed in solitary confinement are subjected to the uncertainty of constant surveillance which results in self-surveillance.

Panoptic surveillance: A form of social control based on self-surveillance adopted from French philosopher Michele Foucault and applied by Enlightenment thinker Jeremy Bentham's panoptic prison design.

Paramilitary bureaucratic command: Hierarchical system of organizational governance based on rules that are external to any one individual often used in militaries.

Penn system: Incarceration philosophy based on the principles of William Penn that stresses solitary confinement and corrections through penitence.

Police misconduct: Police acts of deviance and law breaking.

Police subculture: Set of normative values unique to police that influence group thought and behavior.

Political era of policing: The municipal police system that replaced the night watchman style police system in the late 1700s and lasted to the early part of the twentieth century that was criticized for police being an enforcement arm of the political group in power.

Polygraph examination: A controversial procedure often referred to as a "lie detector test," that uses a device to measure physiological reactions or responses, such as blood pressure and respiration, with a series of questions administered by a polygraph examiner.

Post-traumatic stress disorder (PTSD): Defined by the national institute of mental health as a disorder that develops for those who have experienced a shocking, scary, or dangerous event that results in symptoms such as flashbacks and disabling feelings of fear and anxiety.

PRISM: A clandestine large-scale NSA surveillance and electronic data mining program that collects mass data and mines these Internet data for suspicious activities related to terrorism that was discovered by whistleblower Edward Snowden.

Procedural justice: The examination of the nature of interactions between police and the criminal justice system with the public and how that interaction shapes public perceptions and ultimately, police-citizen relations.

Professional courtesy: An informal term used to describe etiquettes extended between members of the same profession, such as not issuing traffic citations to fellow officers in the world of policing.

Professionalization: The process of transforming a group that is perceived as being incompetent, into prestigious, respectful, and deserving of high pay, such as by physicians and attorneys.

Pyrrhic defeat theory: Principle of a victory that cost so much in troops and treasure that it amounts to a defeat in the overall sense.

Quality of life policing: Policing strategy based on broken windows theory where officers target smaller forms of deviance, such as panhandling, to prevent signaling an escalation to more serious crimes.

Racial profiling: The use of race as a determining factor by police, whether to engage in law enforcement activity.

Reactive patrols: Police responding to calls for service without taking efforts to communicate with citizens on non-crime related matters, to build rapport.

Reno field training/PTO model: Policing field training model developed in Reno, California, that stresses independent problem-based learning that encourages critical thinking in complex situations in the community context for probationary officers who are evaluated on problem-solving ability rather than predefined competencies.

Replacement effect: The continuous cycle of new offenders replacing ones that have been incarcerated resulting in a net effect of zero effect on crime.

Rule of law: Also known as the supremacy of the law, rule of law is a fundamental legal principle in the United States and Western democracies that states the power of government resides in predefined laws and processes and not arbitrarily with any given individuals or groups.

San Jose field training/FTO model: Model of field training developed in San Jose, California, where new probationary officers are evaluated and rated by field training officers on predefined competencies.

Shift work: Work shifts based around atypical schedules derived from providing continual service twenty-four hours per day, seven days per week.

Shooter bias: The higher likelihood of officers to shoot Black suspects more often than White suspects.

Sixth sense: Acuteness for detecting things out of the ordinary, such as behavior and circumstances deemed suspicious developed through experience as a patrol officer.

Sludge running: A type of white-collar or corporate crime committed by toxic waste disposal companies that do not properly dispose of toxic waste but instead open a spigot on a waste disposal truck to let toxic waste drain while driving through different neighborhoods.

Social contract: The tacit agreement of relational arrangement between individuals and society where individuals are granted certain services and protections in exchange for limitations on liberty.

Social control: Efforts to ensure conformity to norms in society.

Sovereign citizens: Individuals who believe the US government is illegitimate and therefore reject police legal authority and openly challenge an officer and therefore give police officers a tough time, ultimately risking forms of street justice.

Storytelling: A form of cultural transmission through the telling of stories that emphasize qualities valued by police, such as toughness.

Street cop culture: A culture based on loyalty among line officers to each other and only each other.

Street justice: A means to force respect towards the officer using unjustified and often illegal use of force.

Stress training: A type of training that is based on creating a high-stress environment for recruits designed to mimic the highly stressful environment police officers face daily on the job.

Strict scrutiny: The most stringent Constitutional litmus test that state (government) entities must pass in order to suspend fundamental rights or classify groups in a suspicious manner (suspect classification). The state must have a compelling government interest, craft the law or policy in a narrowly tailored way which uses the least restrictive means.

Subculture: a set of normative values and beliefs held by a subset of the population that shapes the group's worldview and subsequent behavior based on those values and beliefs.

Supremacy of the law: Also known as the rule of law, supremacy of the law is a fundamental legal principle in the United States and Western democracies that states the power of government resides in predefined laws and processes and not arbitrarily any given individuals or groups.

Surveillance society: Surveillance and information gathering society that police operate in as knowledge workers.

Suspect classification: Legal term that means that any time the state (government) wants to classify people according to race for differential treatment it is considered a very "suspect" without a strong justification to do so.

Symbolic assailants: Persons and groups deemed by police to be suspects and possibly dangerous based on the officer's culmination of stereotypes, which include race.

Symbolic interactionism: Sociological theoretical perspective that views everyday social interactions between individuals as based on the viewpoint of oneself, based on the assumed and interpreted perceptions of the self by others, often referred to as the "looking-glass self."

System capacity theory: The ability or overall capacity of the criminal justice system to mete out justice that is dependent upon the smallest limiting factor

Temperance movement: Social movement against the consumption of alcohol beverages based on the ill effects on personal and family life as well as religious morals.

Thin blue line: Aphorism that police see themselves as the moral force standing between good and evil, order and chaos.

Third degree: Informal term or euphemism used to describe harsh and often violent interrogation tactics or torture.

Tokenism: The symbolic effort of presenting a historically underrepresented group to give the appearance of progress without addressing discriminatory conditions.

"Us versus them" mentality: A worldview often held by police officers based on the antagonistic relationship between the public and police.

Warrior mentality: The mental toughness that officers need to maintain in an intensely dangerous and hostile working environment, akin to a battlefield, no matter what the difficulties are.

Weapons effect: Studied phenomenon in which the presence of a gun results in more aggressive behavior during confrontations and conflicts.

White Anglo Saxon Protestants: Powerful group whose morals and political activities were heavily influenced by Victorian-era values.

White-collar crime: Type of crime coined by renowned sociologist Edwin Sutherland to mean "crime committed by a person of respectability and high social status in the course of his occupation."

Worldview: A sociological term to describe a perspective held by different groups and individuals.

Zero-tolerance policing: Policing style based on little to no discretion for all crimes, large and small.

Index

About the Author

Johnny Nhan is associate professor and graduate director of criminal justice at Texas Christian University (TCU). He has written on a variety of policing topics, focusing mainly on the intersection of law enforcement and technology. His book, *Policing Cyberspace: A Structural and Cultural Analysis*, was published in 2010. He was the lead developer in creating the Leadership, Executive and Administrative Development (LEAD) graduate certificate program at TCU that unites top police supervisors with academia to find solutions to timely issues facing law enforcement today.